WOMEN WORKERS
IN TURKEY

To my parents

WOMEN WORKERS IN TURKEY

Global Industrial Production in Istanbul

SANIYE DEDEOGLU

Tauris Academic Studies
LONDON • NEW YORK

Published in 2008 by Tauris Academic Studies,
an imprint of I.B.Tauris & Co Ltd
6 Salem Road, London W2 4BU
175 Fifth Avenue, New York NY 10010
www.ibtauris.com

ISBN: 978 1 84511 478 7

A full CIP record for this book is available from the British Library
A full CIP record is available from the Library of Congress

Library of Congress Catalog Card Number: available

CONTENTS

TABLES

ACKNOWLEDGEMENTS

This book would not have been possible without the intellectual, practical and emotional support of family, friends and colleagues. Many people made important comments on drafts of chapters that eventually became part of this book. Among those, Deniz Kandiyoti deserves my foremost gratitude who generously shared with me her time and knowledge. Ruth Pearson and Jane Wills provided valuable comments that improved the research further.

My very special thanks are for my parents who provided me with a very strong 'fall-back' position at all times. Financial problems and emotional times were all eliminated due to their undying support for what I wanted to do with my life and their enduring love for me. A warm thank you is due to two friends in Istanbul: Sultan Atılgan and Nurten Ateş. Sultan Atılgan shared with me every step of my work and this process would have been harder without her. Nurten Ateş supported me with all the documents and books that I needed to read for my work or sometimes for my heart.

Solmaz Tavşanoğlu made plenty of time in her busy life to read the final version of the chapters. Traute Meyer, Wendy Bottero, Graham Crow and Viv Mackay were great supporters. Bruce Hunt's offer of English correction was a great relief. My utmost appreciation goes to all these people.

A very special thanks goes to my partner, Gökhan Atılgan, for his support and encouragement.

Finally, to the women in Istanbul who generously opened up their homes and hearts to me, no words of thanks are enough. I only hope that I have managed to remain somewhat true to their own perspectives and stories, and that these perspectives will find their way into broader debates about low-income working-class women and strategies for advancing women's interests in Turkey.

FOREWORD

This book explores and explains an apparent puzzle in the literature on gender, globalisation and development. One of the best documented trends in global manufacturing has been the expansion of the female workforce since the shift to export-oriented industrialisation from the late 1970s onwards. Both statistical and qualitative studies, especially in the rapidly industrialising countries of Latin America and Southeast Asia, point to a marked increase in women's labour force participation.

In Turkey, however, despite the surge in export-orientation following the economic liberalisation policies of the 1980s we witness seemingly stagnant or slightly declining levels of recorded female labour force participation. This is despite the fact that the garment industry, a major employer of women worldwide, played a central role in Turkey's export drive. How may we explain this discrepancy? In what ways do the particular forms of deployment of female labour in Turkey's garment industry contribute to women's near invisibility as a workforce? How do global demand factors that shape the garment industry in Turkey interact and intersect with local supply factors that embed women workers in their families and communities? These are the key questions tackled in this text with meticulous attention to the links between the macro and micro-level determinants of women's employment in the garment industry in Istanbul.

Building upon the insights of the global commodity chains approach, this study reveals crucial links between the structure of workplaces, the types of labour they employ and the intended market niches of their products. Factory and atelier-based production geared to upmarket domestic consumption or export goods for large retailers in European (or western) markets make different demands than the cheaper goods destined for the transitional markets of the former Soviet Union that operate primarily through informal trade networks. Different levels of skill, capital and quality control requirements are reflected in the types of workforce deployed. The lower down we get in the value chain, the deeper the process of informalisation of female labour, tapping into an abundant, if hidden, reserve of home-based piece workers and unpaid women who consider 'helping' with their family enterprises as a natural extension of their domestic and marital obligations. The differentiated nature of labour regimes in the garment sector- spanning factory work, informal atelier and home-based piecework – builds upon the availability of different categories of women workers whose contributions are disguised by the predominantly informal nature of export-led industrial production.

While global pressures that stimulate informalisation tell us one part of the story, an equally significant consideration, sensitively analysed in the text, concerns the role of gender ideologies that define women's work as an intrinsic component of their contributions to their families as wives, mothers and daughters. To the extent that women's work remains confined within the circles of family, kinship and neighbourhood-based networks, through their participation in family-based atelier production, their employment in the garment industry serves to affirm and reinforce the centrality of their domestic roles. Any tensions that may arise around women's breadwinning roles are defused by invoking their primary commitment to domesticity. Provider roles are justified in terms of family needs and work is subject to the consent and permission of family elders. Working women's efforts to subscribe to and act in accordance with these premises brings returns: it acts as a means to retain 'patriarchal security' and enhance their status as self-sacrificing family members. Feminist approaches to globalisation compel us to treat gender regimes and relations as social forces in their own right. This text shows us convincingly that getting beyond official statistics and understanding the complex interactions between markets and labour regimes demands a serious engagement with gender.

Deniz Kandiyoti
School of Oriental and African Studies

1

INTRODUCTION

This book examines how global industrial production and the channels of global trade have adapted their labour demands to and made use of local female labour supplies and the culture of work that is continuously geared towards making women's work invisible. It explores the relationship between industrial production and the employment of women in the global era from the perspective of the most invisible participants in that production. The material presented here explores the strategies and responses that have evolved in response to contemporary changes in global industrial production and its effects on women's labour supply, and how the production for global markets that has penetrated into the local labour markets of Istanbul, Turkey, is contributing to patterns of community-based survival strategies.

Sharing the basic premise of Beneria and Roldan, developed in *The Crossroads of Class and Gender* (1987), that the demand for women's labour represents a response to competition in international markets that pushes companies to resort to flexible home-based subcontracting arrangements, my argument is that global industrial production strategies rely on increasingly diversified forms of women's labour performing for different markets such as domestic markets, Western markets, and informal international trade. The concerted efforts of international capital to find cheaper sources of labour supply also utilise women's home-based work by integrating it into global industrial production without changing women's roles within the family as mothers and wives.

In the current phase of capitalist development, global industrial production and trade are examined within a web of relationships between producers located in different countries. The global commodity chain approach analyses how industrial production is organised around the market-driven needs of large retailers. 'Buyer-driven chains' are formed by large retailers or branded marketers which arrange for the manufacture of their products through global sourcing linkages (Gereffi 1994:99). The workforce in developing countries, which has been an adjunct of global economic restructuring, meets the labour requirements of this production. Global economic restructuring has generated a large supply of jobs and casual labour markets that facilitates the employment of disadvantaged workers, such as women and immigrant workers, all over the world. In most places, associated with the increasing flexibility and casualisation of labour markets, the number of women workers has been recorded to be increasing (Standing 1999; Pearson 1998; Elson 1996). It is also observed that the demand for female labour is highly differentiated, generating employment in advanced factories, in sweatshops and at home.

This research presents original findings in a number of ways. The dynamic nature of the relationship between global production and the variety of local work patterns created by this production and trade has been neglected in the current literature of globalisation and work, which has been generally preoccupied with constructing one single image of industrial production and employment rather than with the ways in which a tendency towards increasingly homogenised production through global firms, vertically integrated firms and global production networks demands an extremely diversified labour force. The empirical sections document the complexities of the labour market and women's employment in the garment industry of Istanbul, which is a highly global industry producing for world markets. Different segments of garment production together create a demand for different patterns of women's work, ranging from factory employment to atelier work and home-based work. These patterns are strongly related to how the industry integrates with global markets and reveals the prevalent organisation of production today in one of the key industries of Turkey. The book therefore offers a contribution to the literature on women, gender and global markets, drawing on anthropological and sociological perspectives in order to address questions of critical importance to the social sciences.

Research for the book was conducted among the women workers of Istanbul's garment industry, which has been recorded as the export champion of Turkish outward development strategy since the early 1980s. A fifteen-month period of fieldwork carried out in Istanbul and a close investigation of the garment industry, topped up with participant observation and in-depth interviews, included women workers, garment sweatshop owners, their families, factory managers, and those engaged in informal work and other forms of invisible work in the garment industry. At a descriptive level the book reveals the lives of women engaged in the insecure, invisible, and low/unpaid end of the labour market and the production relations of the global industry in Turkey, and its place in global markets.

1.1 Globalisation, Industrial Production and Women's Work

The informalisation of women's work all over the world has come hand in hand with a feminisation of employment that has been a partial result of the increasing casualisation of labour markets as a result of global economic restructuring. A similar trend of increasing use of women's informal work has been observed in many areas of urban Turkey by feminists and other scholars. Garment production in Istanbul has been one of the major sectors creating a high demand for women's informal work at various levels. The most important forms of demand for women's work have been atelier work and home-based piecework drawing women into garment production. Therefore, the first objective of this research is to explore the nature of women's employment in the garment industry of Istanbul, where no official increase has been recorded in women's labour market activities. Although women's labour is largely unacknowledged in Turkish society and unrecorded in the official statistics, and it appears that women's involvement in labour market activities is decreasing, constituting Turkey as an exceptional case against other developing countries such as Latin America and Southeast Asian countries where the rates of female employment have been increasing with the implementation of export-oriented policies, a challenge to official statistics in Turkey is needed to make women's work more visible. A similar situation is found in Mitter's study on London's garment industry, where a sizable portion of garment work was shifted to home-based producers, mostly women, as a result of labour market restructuring and firm downsizing, resulting in the exclusion of these women's work from official statistics (Mitter 1986).

The second objective of this research is to examine the demand factors that condition women's work in Istanbul's garment industry. The structure of the industry and the forms of garment production's integration into world markets affect the ways in which women enter into garment production. The dominance of small-scale family-run garment ateliers in the industry provides the grounds for attracting women from the same family circle into production, often informally and usually unpaid, while keeping their domestic identities as mothers, wives and daughters intact. The engagement of women in family-based garment production under the shadow of their domestic identities, without any public recognition of their work, casts doubts on the separation between women's public and private sphere activities. The entanglement between women's domestic and public activities provides a useful case study to show how difficult it is to separate the one from the other.

A very useful distinction made by Elson (1999) between women's labour force participation, which includes all types of employment status (employee, self-employed, and unpaid family labour), and labour market participation, which excludes unpaid family labour, shows that women's garment work in Turkey remains unrecognised and under-recorded due to the fact that it is considered as labour market participation. Elson (1999) points to the measurable gaps that exist between women's labour force and labour market participation. Labour force participation including all types of employment status or 'productive activities' is counted as a part of national production. On the other hand, the unpaid, unmarketed caring activities of women, the 'reproductive economy', are also crucial for the functioning of society as a whole and contribute to the reproduction of 'productive' labour, but are excluded from national accounts. Elson suggests that a large gender gap between labour force and labour market participation exists in every society (1999:614).

Istanbul's garment industry produces for different markets. These markets differ in terms of their place in global commodity chains, the domestic market and informal international trade, creating a diversified demand for women's labour at each level. Pearson (1998) emphasises the different forms of industrial production, which demand different patterns of female employment. A historical account of women's industrial work indicating the changing roles and places of women's work shows the variety of forms of women's engagement in industrial production. My aim in this research is to show that the various forms of work, factory, informal atelier and home-based piecework, exist in a single sector combining the different demands of women's work. Analysing formal factory, small-scale atelier and home-based garment production together enables us to identify different categories of women workers, whose work is disguised mostly by the informal nature of export-led industrial production. The recognition that manufacturing production consists not only of formal large-scale production but also extends into more diversified forms, combining small-scale atelier, subcontracted and home-based production (Beneria and Roldan 1987; Cinar 1994; White 1994), reveals the utilisation of different categories of female labour, varying in skill and wage composition. The subcontracting relations utilised in Istanbul's garment industry that effectively connect firms, households and communities to one another also increase the need for flexibilisation of the workforce and for the use of informal workers, mostly women. My objective is, therefore, to analyse how different types and scales of industrial production, such as factory, atelier and home-based production in the garment sector, utilise different categories of female labour in Turkey, in ways that conceal the extent of women's actual labour force participation.

The location of the Turkish garment industry provides a useful case study of garment production regimes, offering a geographically specific example of supply chains and a contribution to debates about economic globalisation. The global connection that the Turkish garment sector has established through different market niches, such as the domestic market, transitional markets in the former Soviet Union, Eastern Europe, and European markets, offers a contribution to the further development of the literature of value chains at the same time as divorcing it from its Eurocentric focus by endorsing industrial production and trade channels at a real global level. The global commodity chains approach (Gereffi 1994) analyses the garment industry organised around the market-driven needs of large retailers. 'Buyer-driven chains' are formed by large retailers or branded marketers that arrange for the manufacturing of their products through global sourcing linkages (Gereffi 1994:99). However, not all garment production in Istanbul is done for large retailers and European (or western) markets. Therefore, the diversity of markets and consumption niches that govern garment production and its labour requirements is highlighted.

The focus of enquiry of this research is on the garment industry and women's employment, and it seeks to explore the structure of the industry, women's role in it and the social construction of women's work in Turkey. Thus, my third objective is to provide an understanding of the supply factors conditioning women's entry into garment production in Istanbul. The factors affecting the supply of women's labour to the industry include household structure, gender ideology and relations, migration and community in urban areas, and the need for economic survival at the level of the household. These factors interact in specific ways to mediate women's work in Istanbul, to shape the nature of women's employment, and to determine the degree of employment opportunities accessible for women, causing women to be a cheap labour source for garment production. It will also be shown how the prevailing culture of Turkish society and its gender relations are mediated and renegotiated in order to make women's entrance into production possible. The operation of family-run ateliers and the location of garment production in low-income neighbourhoods are important factors affecting the extent of women's work.

The employment opportunities offered in the informal economy are a good focus for an illumination of the relationship between industrial production and women's work and its interaction with gender relations. Women's work in garment ateliers and home-based piecework has been shaped by the priority given to their traditional roles as mothers, wives and daughters. Traditional roles and ideologies are enforced through the conditions under which women's work is conceptualised as temporary and men's work as the main source of household income. The double burden of wage work and domestic labour, together with prevailing ideologies of gender and womanhood, continues to portray women as supplementary workers even when they are becoming increasingly important economic contributors to the household economy. Therefore, a radical alteration in women's domestic and public roles is not experienced when women's work is heavily controlled by family members in the same workplace. For all these reasons, it is possible to argue that as long as women's work is confined within the circles of family, kinship and neighbourhood-based networks, employment is practised as an extension of those domestic roles and as a temporary state rather than a radical departure from the confines of the patriarchal system. Rather, women's employment in the garment industry enforces their domestic roles as mothers, wives and daughters, due to the dominance of family-based atelier production.

Women's trade-offs between 'patriarchal security' and paid employment and the conflicting images of working women and the 'woman of her home' (evinin kadını) are eased through a set of mediating factors adopted by the community and the families of women workers. The justification for taking paid work is almost always connected with the aim of providing for their families, and before women can take up paid employment the consent (izin) of the male or senior female authority must be secured at all times. Despite the crises created over women's identity through paid work, women themselves very often make an extra effort to show that priority is always given to their domestic identities. Even their public demands and negotiations are voiced by the utilisation of those roles and remain within their confines. Seemingly, women's internalisation of traditional gender roles and identities allows them to move into the public arena and take up paid work without losing social protection and security. In this regard, women exchange their labour in the informal economy as a symbol of the manifestation of their community membership and identity in urban Turkey.

Family and community relations not only mediate women's labour into the informally operated family-run ateliers but also are used effectively to allow women's entrance into the labour market. Recruitment strategies utilised in different segments of the garment sector are sealed by the dominance of family and kinship relations, allowing the reflection of socially constructed male dominance that filters through into women's workplace experience. This research will help to show that labour markets are 'bearers of gender', in the sense that they are instantiations of the gender relations in the society in which the labour market is embedded. Social relations as bearers of gender, although not gender-ascriptive, reflect existing problems of gender domination and subordination at institutional levels, such as household, community, the market and the state (Elson 1999:612). The embeddedness of the labour market in Turkey results in the invisibility of women's work without any public recognition of the work that is done, even in the case where the contribution women make has a great deal of importance for their families, communities, their country and world production.

The overall aim of this research is to render women's work more visible in Turkey by highlighting the role of women in the garment industry. Women's public invisibility and their exclusion from official statistics are the result of the intersection between the nature of demand in the garment industry and traditional gender roles affecting women's labour supply for Istanbul's garment industry. By looking at the intersection of these two sets of factors, demand and supply, I use my data to illuminate the nature of women's work and women's entrance into global production networks. There is a further intention to contribute to debates about economic globalisation, the feminisation and informalisation of employment, and the interrelations of such developments with gender relations.

1.2 Studying Women's Industrial Work

Given these concerns a qualitative and biographical approach would be the most appropriate. In exploring the dynamics of the relationship between global industrial production and the implications for local female labour supply and the culture of work in Turkey, the focus was on the categories that women employ in their everyday lives and on the community networks that sustain women's social links. Chamberlayne and Rustin, advocating the use of a biographical approach, note that a biographical method, through contextualising statistical data and demonstrating what they mean for individual lives, contains implications for social policy, and furthermore that such an approach can highlight the network of existing relations between the individual and others (1996:21).

The point is that people live their lives within the material and cultural boundaries of their time span, and so life histories are exceptionally effective historical sources because through the totality of lived experience they reveal relations between individuals and social forces, which are rarely apparent in other sources (Lumis 1987:107–8).

In-depth, open-ended, non-structured interviews and oral narratives were the methods utilised to give voice to the women whose experiences of industrial work are at the centre of this study. Using these methods is the most suitable way of describing and analysing women's experiences from their own perspectives and making sense of their place in the world. These methods also capture interactions and interconnections between people and events, as they provide flexibility for explanation and allow space to the narrator to express himself or herself by reducing the control and direction of interviewer over interviewee (Borland 1991; Gluck and Patai 1991). In addition, open-ended and in-depth interviews, according to Anderson and Jack, represent a shift from asking the right questions to focusing on process and 'the dynamic unfolding nature of the subject's viewpoint' (1991:23).

My interest in exploring the connections between global industrial production and local female labour supply and the structure of the local informal networks affecting women's access to labour markets meant that developing a more situated understanding of the interactions between gender relations and culture of work involved locating myself within the communities where the urban poor lived in Istanbul. Wolf has pointed out that researchers need to locate themselves and their personal objectives and experiences within the context of their research (Wolf 1996). The representation of Third World women as poor and powerless in contrast to educated, better-off middle-class Western women has often been criticised (Ong 1988, Mohanty 1988, Marchand and Parpart 1994). These critics also drew attention to the inequalities and power relations between the researcher and the researched. Given increasing self-awareness by feminist researchers of their limitations, many are focusing on the reflective mode or simply depicting women's voices rather than representing their own (Wolf 1996). In producing a more situated knowledge on women's industrial work and to reflect those women's voices it was felt that my social background as an insider would prove to be a valuable asset in conducting this research. My position goes beyond being an insider, since I was doing research on people with whom I share a similar background and class position. I am from a working-class family and my mother used to be a textile factory worker. Moreover, I live in the outskirts of Istanbul in a neighbourhood that was similar to the locations where my informants lived. During the fieldwork I continued to live in the place I grew up, which was a good location to observe low-income working-class families and their day-to-day experiences. This was vital in accounting for factors particular to the locality and to broader structural factors in understanding how women's work has been shaped by gender relations as well as social relations.

Gaining access to a sample involved utilising personal connections and was guided according to the nature of the information sought. This approach is a snowball or chain-referral method, in which friends and associates in Istanbul introduced me to people to interview. Snowball sampling is especially appropriate where populations are hidden and no sampling frame is available, and randomly samples the population, which was a very suitable method to collect information on women's garment work in Istanbul, which is highly informal and invisible (Faugier and Sargeant 1997). For this purpose I conducted interviews with 50 women working in different segments of the garment industry in Istanbul over 15 months in 1999 and 2000. Having a few key informants working in different parts of garment production—large-scale factories, garment ateliers and home-based work—later branched out into meeting with other respondents. Gaining access to connections and networks improved my relationships with women and their families, and thus I traced my way to their households and to the locations of various social networks and livelihood activities. I also interviewed a limited number of men. These were mainly workshop owners and the male managers of large-scale factories.

My sample was a purposefully composed one, which was not aimed at ensuring the statistical representation of women. It was rather intended to select categories of individuals using lifecycle and employment criteria. 'Theoretical sampling' involves sampling on the basis of concepts that are relevant to the study (Glaser and Strauss 1968:47). As a consequence it tends to promote a sample that is homogeneous in its attributes, rather than providing linkages to groups whose social characteristics are different (Lee 1993). Moreover, a homogeneous population was itself advantageous in exploring the nature of women's industrial work and the relationship between global industrial production and local labour supply, how individuals and households use employment opportunities, the kinds of informal opportunities that informal networks provide, and the processes of having access to those opportunities. To overcome problems of bias and gain a more comprehensive view of life and labour in Istanbul's low-income communities, interviews were also conducted with other residents living in my neighbourhood and women who did not engage in garment work.

The fieldwork also involved sketching out the structure of the garment industry in Istanbul, on which no reliable data is available due to the large number of unrecorded and informally operating firms and the extensive usage of subcontracting links. In these circumstances, where interviews were the only way of identifying the subcontracting relations, employment patterns and foreign trade practices of the industry, I interviewed large-scale factory managers, atelier owners and officials from the Turkish Commerce Union (TCU). Additionally, a data set collected by TCU including 4000 firms operating in Istanbul was classified in terms of size, location and product type, revealing some basic features of Istanbul's garment firms.

Besides visiting workshops and factories, I attended women's social gatherings on different occasions such as marriage ceremonies, religious meetings, and afternoon meetings (kadın günleri) devoted to chatting and rotating savings associations. These meeting were particularly useful for observing women's relations with each other away from the patriarchal domination of men at the workplace or in the household. I listened intently to gossip as a form of communication that transmits information about customs, change and ideas, as well as the opinions of women. Gossip is a powerful tool not only to ensure women's conformity to social customs and ideas but also to release information on issues that otherwise would be impossible to reach.

Throughout all my interviews with women, I tried to be as open and honest as possible and also tried to limit the inequality between researcher and researched discussed above. In-depth interviews and long intimate chats helped to generate a more relaxed atmosphere in which women could more easily share information with me. The conversations about women's life and work history sometimes made some of my informants very emotional when talking about their life stories. The best way to eliminate the distance between my informants and myself was to visit them periodically and to make them feel that I cared about our relationships.

From time to time I shared information about my parents and myself so I was able to develop intimacy and familiarity with women, and told them how my mother had had a long history of work in a textile factory. Even though my social class was useful in the elimination of hierarchical positions between my informants and myself it was not possible to achieve the aim of complete equality. Not only social class position, but also my parents' regional origin and religious sect were sometimes investigated by my informants so as to develop a sense of familiarity or distance. In most cases, I was open to sharing the origin and religious sect of my parents and myself, but I was always reluctant to share my political and religious beliefs with them. For instance, I concealed some of my beliefs, particularly when talking about issues related to sexuality and religion. It was hard to be straightforward with personal information and beliefs, because it might have damaged the relationships with the women I interviewed. My attitudes on these issues may not have been tolerated, and I feared being rejected as an unrespectable person. For example, Ayten, a subcontracting worker and a practising Muslim, once told me that earning money for a good Muslim woman was sin and that she asked for God's forgiveness each time. In this case, I did not try to challenge or reject her ideas and beliefs but rather told her that my thinking on religion was different.

Moreover, I recorded Turkish proverbs pertaining to gender and family relations that reflect the families' perception of immigration and their survival strategies. I recorded both those that emerged spontaneously in the course of an interview or conversation, and also the proverbs that provide an accurate description of reality. Women often used these idioms and proverbs to articulate their views and to express their work and daily life. As tools for filtering how women conceptualise their social situations and their own reality these idioms are a resourceful way to 'map out a field of meaning based on local categories, and give people a language to talk about differences, as well as providing local definitions and understanding of concepts like values, status, power, equity, injustice and domination' (El-Kholy 1998:125). Conducting the research entailed collecting a mass of data, only a small proportion of which is presented in the book. This process inevitably entails omission of a large quantity of data that may represent a significant aspect of the respondents' lives, highlighting the central tensions between the complexity of social life, and the textual strategies and techniques available for representing it (Hammersley and Atkinson 1995). The explanatory framework will also depend upon the researcher's interpretation of the ways in which individuals' perceptions, experiences, and behaviour intersect with cultural, social, and economic forces. It shows that women's roles and female employment can only be understood in the context of a complex web of social relations in which social dynamics and industrial structure influence the shape that female employment takes. Moreover, it should provide insights into the types of survival strategies that low and/or lower middle income families adopt when they move to Istanbul, and to what extent female labour is deployed to make certain kinds of investments such as house building or children's education, which are in a sense the main coping strategies of low-income immigrant families in Istanbul.

The selection of examples was guided by the research objectives, which seek to explore low-income women's employment in the garment industry in Istanbul. The book does not offer an exhaustive account of women's lives, but focuses on the economic and social strategies that are deployed, and the 'cultures of solidarity' in response to the problem of their survival in the city

(Fantasia 1988:14). Giddens argues that an individual's sense of 'ontological security' is the confidence that people have in the continuity of their self-identity, and in the constancy of their social environments (Giddens 1990). The data presented explores the way in which women attempt to maintain their lives and also try to better them through their work and paid employment.

The structure and content of the book reflect the fact that it is analysing the supply and demand factors conditioning women's industrial work in Turkey, and the lives and situations of women working in the garment industry. The theory chapter is an analysis of emerging trends in global industrial production and trade in the context of wider debates concerning the increasing impact of global corporate firms, described as 'global buyers', on local production and trade. The chapter outlines the major theoretical and empirical perspectives and how these broad accounts explain both the emergence of new trends in industrial production in developing countries and the existence of regional trade networks that affect export production in developing countries. It also includes a historical account of women's industrial work, indicating the changing roles and places of women's work and demonstrating the variety of forms of women's engagement in industrial production, such as factory, informal atelier and home-based piecework. The contention of this chapter is to show that these forms exist in a single sector combining the different types of women's employment.

Chapter 3 is an outline of the macro-economics and social changes taking place in the last quarter century in Turkey and their implication for women's industrial work. It shows how informal work and home-based piecework are the emerging forms of employment, and why women's work in urban Turkey remains invisible and fails to receive any public recognition. *Chapter 4* marks the beginning of the ethnographic section of the book. The chapter addresses the local impact of the globalisation of garment production in Turkey and the patterns of production and trade discussed in *Chapter 2*, through sketching the particularities of garment firms operating in Istanbul. This contextualises the ways in which the structure of the industry and its connections with global commodity chains and other markets influence production and subcontracting as well as women's employment.

The next three chapters of the book deal with empirical material related to the factors affecting women's labour supply in the garment industry. *Chapter 5* explores the lives and motivations of a sample of women working in Istanbul's garment industry. The chapter opens with a discussion of the debate over the determining factors of women's labour supply that provide the backdrop to the lives of those women workers. The ethnographic sections conducted with a sample of women workers explore the demographic characteristics and household structures of women who are engaged in three different work patterns, factory work, garment atelier work and home-based piecework, in an attempt to find out whether the differences and similarities in the women's backgrounds and family lives had any bearing on their different incorporations into the garment industry and the patterns of work they engaged in.

Chapter 6 deals with a particularly controversial area of women's studies and explores the role of the gender relations and cultural constructs of work that affect women's paid work in Turkish society. In Turkish society, where social organisation is heavily based on the family unit, family and marriage are important sources of identity and security as well as economic support for women. Women mitigate 'patriarchal risk' through marriage and through complying with traditional gender roles and relations. Publicly voicing themselves through the roles of motherhood and wifehood, women can only gain status and decision-making power to the extent that they assume those roles. *Chapter 7* consolidates and develops the themes that labour markets are the bearers of the relations and institutions of the societies in which they are embedded. This is most explicit in the recruitment practices of the garment industry in Turkey, in which identities and hierarchies are constantly renegotiated and reconfigured. Recruitment processes not only carry existing hierarchies into the workplace but also generate new forms of seniority, surveillance and authority between workers. The ethnography examines how gender ideologies, cultural practices, and local discourses on women's work translate into wider processes of cultural justifications for the release of women's labour, and also examines how these processes are acted out and sustained in people's everyday lives and the way that they are reshaping social relations and the notion of gender in low-income communities in Istanbul.

The final chapter summarises the arguments and themes developed in the main body of the book. Some general conclusions are drawn from the research, concerning the potential of current developments in global industrial production and labour markets to assist in improving women's visibility in Turkey. The implications surrounding the changing nature of labour markets, global production and women's work in developing countries are discussed to analyse the condition of women living in those areas. The chapter argues for a relational and perceptual understanding of the effects of global industrial production and trade on local communities that encompasses the lifestyles and cultural practices of the communities in which the production takes place. From this perspective, women's invisibility is experienced as a result of gender roles that delegate to women the major roles of motherhood and wifehood, while the same gender roles are manipulated through a number of strategies that release women's labour for global production. The chapter closes by highlighting some important methodological issues that the research raised, and points towards a new direction in women's studies research.

2

GLOBAL INDUSTRIAL PRODUCTION AND FEMALE EMPLOYMENT

The underlying theme of economic globalisation is globalising tendencies in the discourses and practice of corporate actors and in global financial and trade flows, which have been accompanied by new methods of organising production and labour, along with an accelerating mobility of capital, labour, goods and information. Although globalising entities have been the locus of the literature of economics globalisation, feminist analyses have emerged from a variety of socio-political locations, drawing on a grounded approach that examines context-specific relationships between 'globalised' capital and 'localised' labour.

An explicitly feminist treatment of gender and globalisation, Marchand and Runyan (2000) in *Gender and Global Restructuring*, proposes that gender analysis is well suited for developing understandings of globalisation that go beyond the narrowly defined economistic characteristics of the mainstream economic globalisation literature (2000:2). In the recognition of gender as a significant boundary marker and identity producer, Marchand and Runyan emphasise that gender is a focal point of and for global restructuring (2000:18).

Extensive feminist work on gender and global processes shows that globalised forms of production are embedded in particular national and local cultures and how these cultures shape the connections between production processes and the organisation of reproductive labour. Wolf (1992) highlights the contradictions and complexities of industrial capitalist proletarianisation through the lives and voices of Javanese 'factory daughters', while Mohanty (1997) illustrates how the global processes of capitalism use local ideologies and gendered identities for their own ends. Marie Mies studies the home-working lacemakers in Narsapur to show how capitalism mobilised the ideology of women as housewives to define lacemakers as non-workers and label their lacemaking for corporations as a leisure activity (Mies 1982).

This study is also an attempt to show how the global garment industry in Istanbul has adopted and negotiated the offerings of women's local labour supply and the culture of work that shapes women's entrance into paid work as formal or informal workers. The garment industry of Istanbul has been the leading sector of Turkey's global industrial production, in which integration into global markets has been achieved through low labour costs, informalisation and diversification of garment production. The role of women's work in achieving the global competitiveness of the garment industry has been vital; however, it has remained unrecognised in Turkey.

To examine the intersection of the economics of demand and the culture of supply that conditions women's entrance into garment production, this chapter, drawing on various sources of literature, outlines the literature on women's industrial employment in the Third World and on the debates surrounding gender, patriarchy and the household that inform the degree of women's labour force participation. Putting all these diverse literatures together shows that the nature of women's industrial work is a result of a dialectical relationship shaped by the supply and demand factors conditioning female employment. In the rest of the chapter, the demand factors for women's labour are examined through global industrial production and international trade and the different forms of women's work that have emerged as a result of changing production and trade relations. Later, gender, patriarchy and household factors conditioning women's labour supply are analysed to explore their impact on women's industrial work and the various patterns of that work.

2.1 The Demand for Women's Labour: Global Industrial Production

Since the early 1970s, global industrial production has moved at a pace that corresponds with the integration of economies globally and an increase in the exchange of goods. Facilitated by a number of changes, including the removal of trade barriers and the opening of local markets to foreign investment and technological innovations, the globalisation of industrial production is one of the main drivers behind globalisation, which requires the cooperation of firms or transnational corporations, states and financial institutions such as banks, speculators, and investors (Hirst and Thompson 1999).

As Bell showed in *The Coming of Post-Industrial Society* (1973) globalisation and the growth of the world economy have created a decline in the number of blue-collar industrial workers and the growth of flexible and deregulated labour markets characterised by part-time, short-term jobs and self-employment, so-called non-standard forms of employment in low-paid and labour-intensive sectors such as hotels, catering and retail (see also Harvey 1989). The increasing mobility of capital and goods, achieved through changes in the mode of production processes and labour management, has seen the industrialisation of the Third World and the de-industrialisation of core countries, which have turned to specialising in services (Lash and Urry 1987).

The integration of Third World countries into the global economy has occurred through the growth in industrial production and trade. A movement towards export-oriented production strategies imposed through structural adjustment policies under the directives of the IMF and the World Bank, together with the rapid internationalisation of production and trade activities governed by transnational corporations, has provided the basis for the global economic integration of developing countries. As a consequence of these changes, Third World countries now constitute an important portion of global industrial production and are an important source of the supply of garment products (Jenkins 1992; Dicken 1998).

2.1.1 Global Economic Restructuring and Industrial Production
The global reorganisation of industrial production has been examined through two different analytical perspectives, one of which is the new international division of labour, and the other global commodity chains. Although these different approaches explain different aspects of the current world economy, each of them is considered to be a separate system in the sense that what drives and governs it is identifiable and distinctive. In the mid-1970s, the new international division of labour (NIDL) analysed the geographical relocation of the industrial production in which the unskilled and labour-intensive sub-processes of production were relocated in the cheap labour-reserved countries of the Third World (Frobel *et al.* 1980).

The NIDL refers to a spatial division of labour at the international scale, which includes social division of labour, divisions of labour between production and exchange, and spatial divisions of labour at scales other than the international (Sayer and Walker 1992). Starting in the 1960s, this was encouraged through the creation of export processing zones which offered incentives to foreign corporations in terms of tax holidays, cheap labour rates and lack of unionisation of labour, particularly in South East and East Asia. (Frobel *et al.* 1980; Safa 1981). These regions succeeded in significantly expanding their share of world production and the export of manufactured goods, allowing them to penetrate into the key markets of the advanced industrial countries (Jenkins 1992; Dicken 1998).

Export processing zones were used to attract foreign investment and large-scale manufacturing, whereas the term global commodity chains (GCC) describes the chains of activities that bring a product from its conception to the final consumer. The globalised production process takes place across different parts of the world, bringing together the activities of multinational corporations and their production relationships with local producers that link firms, households and communities (Gereffi *et al.* 1994). Through global commodity chains, the production done in large-scale factories, sweatshops and homes could be part of global production and trade.

It is important to note that the analytical distinction between global commodity chains and export processing zone becomes blurred in real life. The adoption of flexible production techniques and the increasing informalisation of industrial production made the global connection of industrial production possible. The shift from a Fordist mode of production (mass production) to a post-Fordist mode of production (flexible specialisation) has changed the ways in which manufacturing production is organised not only at the level of the plant but also globally (Piore and Sabel 1984; Amin 1994; Standing 1999a). Technological advances enabled companies to adopt flexibility in their production, especially in the car industry, where it became possible to produce a number of different models on the same assembly line (Jenkins 1992; Elson 1996). Thus, flexible specialisation is defined as the manufacture of a wide range of customised products using flexible, general-purpose machinery and skilled, adaptable workers (Piore and Sabel 1984; Hirst and Zeitlin 1991).

According to Atkinson and Meager, flexible firms decentralise their organisations and use measures such as dividing their workforce into 'core', with secure jobs, and a 'periphery', which can be dismissed and re-employed (Atkinson and Meager 1986). In addition to this, Elson (1996:76) shows how the term flexibility refers to different dimensions of the economic system: flexibility in the organisational structure of firms, whereby large firms subcontract to other firms and separate their workforce into a 'core' and a more temporary 'periphery'; labour market flexibility, referring to changes in regulations; and contracts, which facilitate employers' ability to hire and fire labour flexibly in patterns of production through rendering the division of labour less rigid, a process often labelled flexible specialisation.

International outsourcing and subcontracting networks have been part of the flexible organisation of global industrial production. These networks, based on the production-based linkages between different-scale firms (Piore and Sabel 1984), made possible the connection of production between modern mass assembly lines and sweatshop and home-based production. The flexible organisation of global production has blurred the dividing line between formal and informal economies by generating both the informalisation of the activities previously performed in the formal sector and increased business connections between these two sectors (Portes and Castells 1989).

The informalisation of production processes has led to the integration of informally operating small-scale firms into global production through subcontracting and outsourcing. The employment of unprotected wage labour and disguised wage-workers in small enterprises has become the main source of cheap labour supply for global production (Portes and Schauffler 1993). Although the informal economy may mean different things in different settings, there have been a number of attempts to define the informal economy (Rakowski 1994; ILO 2002) and distinguish it from the formal sector (Sassen 1997). Portes and Sassen-Koob (1987) define informal work as 'all those work situations characterised by the absence of (1) a clear separation between capital and labour; (2) a contractual relationship between both; and (3) a labour force that is paid low wages and whose conditions of work and pay are not legally regulated' (1987:31). Similarly, Bromley and Gerry question the adequacy of the dichotomy between formal wage employment and informal self-employment. They suggest that there is a continuum from stable wage work to true self-employment, passing through four categories of casual work: short-term work, disguised wage-work, dependent work and finally true self-employment (1979).

Here the emphasis is on the working poor, many of whom are producing goods and services, but whose activities are not formally recognised, recorded, protected and regulated (ILO 2002). According to Portes and Castells, the informal economy is a 'process of income generating activities characterised by one central feature: it is unregulated by the institutions of society, in a legal and social environment in which similar activities are regulated' (1989:12). Therefore, as highly related to the formal sector the informal economy has a role in the persistence of small-scale production and the proliferation of cheap labour supply (Beneria 2003).

It is important to note that various production strategies are adopted by multinational corporations in different developing countries, and there are various ways in which national economies enter into global production. For instance, in Malaysia transnational production is carried out mainly in export-processing zones with mass-assembly plants, whereas in Hong Kong most export production is undertaken by subcontracting family firms operating under sweatshop conditions (Ong 1991). New employment opportunities for women are generated in each segment of these diffused production processes, where employment in export-processing zones, subcontracted work and home-based work are some of the forms women take up. Before going into explanations of these different forms I shall turn my attention to why the approach of global commodity chains is a useful tool in the analysis of global industrial production and the global trade channels that shape this production.

2.1.2 Global Commodity Chains and Garment Production in Turkey
The term global commodity chains is used to describe the chain of activities and value added produced at the various stages of production and trade. The process takes place across different parts of the world and connects different forms of industrial production, underpinning different actors' economic performance at various geographical scales (Gereffi 1994; Cook and Crang 1996; Hughes 2000). Thus, 'the GCC approach explains the distribution of wealth within a chain as an outcome of the relative intensity of competition within different nodes' (Gereffi *et al.* 1994:4).

Hopkins and Wallerstein define a commodity chain as 'a network of labour and production processes whose end result is a finished commodity' (1986:159). Gereffi *et al.* (1994) have argued that global commodity chains are 'sets of inter-organisational networks clustered around one commodity or product, linking households, enterprises, and states to one another with the world economy. These networks are situationally specific, socially constructed, and locally integrated, underscoring the social embeddedness of economic organisation' (Gereffi *et al.* 1994:2). This approach has been used to study global networks at the sectoral level in order to observe the linkages between economic activities, their locational spread, and the roles and power relationships that exist among the various actors in an industry, such as the global automobile and garment industries[1].

Gereffi (1994) has proposed two typical distinctions between producer-driven and buyer-driven chains[2], which, he argues, have dominated global commodity chains since the mid-1970s. Buyer-driven commodity chains are those in which 'large retailers, brand-named merchandisers, and trading companies play the pivotal role in setting up decentralised production networks in a variety of exporting countries' (Gereffi 1994:97). This pattern of trade-led industrialisation has become common in labour-intensive, customer goods industries such as garments, footwear, toys, house-wares, consumer electronics, and a variety of handicrafts. In addition, the global commodity chains perspective has the potential to analyse the development significance of both international production and distribution systems of transnational corporations and the subcontracting networks constructed by independent firms in particular industries, as part of a coherent whole (Czaban and Henderson 1998:586)

My aim here is to locate Istanbul's garment industry and explore its structure through production and trade patterns by using its linkages with global markets and its place in global value chains. As the most global sector of the Turkish economy, Istanbul's garment industry produces for different types of international and domestic markets. The markets for which Turkish garments are produced determine the place of the industry in the global value chain. That is why its place in the global garment chain does not correspond to a single fixity but is rather multiple and changing. There are three distinct markets for which Istanbul's garment industry produces, namely European or Western, domestic markets, and the markets of the Former Soviet Union. The production techniques differentiated along the lines of the different consumption markets also affect the way in which women contribute to garment production in Turkey.

In Istanbul's garment sector, large-scale factories produce high quality products for exports and domestic consumption. Garment ateliers mainly produce for international markets, and their products are sometimes destined for the European market, and sometimes for the markets of Former Soviet Union countries. The latter are organised through an informal trade channel between Istanbul and these countries. The production of the garment sector organised around different market niches creates a differentiated demand for labour and requires the utilisation of differentiated subcontracting links between firms.

The GCC approach, developed to explain the production networks between different countries, focuses on commodity production, which is usually for the markets of advanced countries. Therefore, it neglects the diversity of markets and consumption niches that govern international trade and garment production in Turkey. However, the GCC approach enables us to analyse the interconnectedness of all these differentiated aspects of production and consumption markets at the global level. Even garment production for domestic consumption is not free from the global competition of other companies producing for similar tastes and buyers.

The peculiarity of the garment industry in Istanbul is its central role in the informal international trade that takes place between Turkey and the Former Soviet Union countries, creating an extra-global commodity circuit. Unrecorded trade and movement of people across national borders, which has increased in importance with globalisation, have generated new lines of production in those national economies. There are now alternative markets in which international commodity trade is taking place at an informal but global level.

Although the evidence on unrecorded international trade is rather scant, informal trade activities are not a new phenomenon. This is mostly apparent in Africa, the Caribbean, Eastern Europe and the former Soviet Union (FSU) (Cheru 1989; MacGaffet 1991; Epstein 1993; Nuggent 1996; Sik and Wallace 1999; Yükseker 2003). For example, in Zaire landless and unemployed rural people, urban dwellers whose salaries are not enough for survival, and corrupt government and customs officers are among the actors in this type of trade (Mukohya 1991). In Africa, people made use of the different tax and customs systems to initiate cross-border trade and smuggling. Scholars have pointed out that the flourishing of informal international trade is a result of the debt crisis and the bankruptcy of nation states (Cheru 1989; MacGaffey 1991). For instance, in Barbados there is a woman's suitcase trade with other Caribbean islands, as well as trade between Miami and Venezuela catering for the clothing needs of fashion-conscious female office workers at multinational data processing firms. Workers fly to neighbouring countries to buy cloth and garments with their savings and in doing so they participate in the globalisation of tastes in consumer goods and fashions (Freeman 1998). For Turkey, my focus will be on shuttle trade (*bavul ticareti*) between Turkey and the republics of the FSU together with the implications of this trade for garment production and labour processes.

This research is an analysis of the garment industry in Istanbul, which is governed by different market niches, to provide a geographically specific approach to the study of supply chains, with a special reference to local production and labour trends, without taking the analysis away from the global scale. It also identifies formal and informal segments of the Turkish garment industry, based on the characteristics of the markets for which they produce. Stressing the market destination of commodities shows that Turkish garment production can be situated in global commodity flows in three different ways. One line of garment production is to reach European and North American markets; a second is to remain for domestic consumption; and the third is a more regionally located market of cross-border and transnational trade[3].

2.2 The Role of Women's Work in Global Industrial Production
The increased mobility of capital has distinct effects on the formation of labour markets and the regulation of a global labour force. The increased mobility of capital has generated on the one hand homogenisation of economic space

through the standardisation of consumer goods and production techniques, and on the other hand the reproduction of structurally differentiated labour markets and labour supply. The production of different ranges of commodities from apparel to electronics for the world market has been spatially and socially reorganised.

> [The] dispersion makes possible access to peripheralised labour markets, whether abroad or at home, without undermining that peripheral condition. Such labour markets remain peripheralised even when the jobs are in leading industries producing for the world market, for example, electronics production in the Third World export processing zones. (Sassen 2001:32)

Global economic restructuring has generated a large supply of jobs and casual labour markets, which facilitates the employment of disadvantaged workers, such as women and immigrant workers all over the word. The differentiation and dispersion of labour markets have immensely helped to create more employment opportunities for women. In most places, associated with the increasing flexibility and casualisation of labour markets, the number of women workers has been recorded to be increasing (Standing 1999; Pearson 1998; Elson 1996). It is also observable that the demand for female labour is highly differentiated, generating employment in advanced factories, sweatshops and homes. It is now clear that as 'industrialisation proceeds and diversifies in different 'theatres of accumulation' the process of deconstruction and change in the gendering of the industrial labour force is in a constant state of flux' (Pearson 1998:177).

Women's work in the garment industry of Istanbul is highly diversified and ranges from factory employment to atelier and home-based work. These patterns are strongly related to how the industry integrates with global markets and reveals the prevalent organisation of production in one of the key industries of Turkey. The aim of the rest of this chapter is to analyse women's changing work practices in a global context, where a tendency towards increasingly homogenised production through global firms, vertically integrated firms and global production networks demands an extremely diversified labour force.

2.2.1 Female Employment in World Factories

Female employment in large-scale factories is usually associated with production in export processing zones and foreign firms located in developing countries. Investment by large corporations in export-oriented production activities has increased women's wage employment in labour-intensive sectors such as textiles, garments, and electronics industries (cf. Elson and Pearson 1981; Wolf 1992; Ong 1987). The increasing visibility of women working in world factories led to the identification of export-oriented industrialisation as 'female-led industrialisation' (Joekes 1987). Now, there are many sources stressing the 'feminisation of the labour force' and of employment at the world level (ILO 1996; Standing 1999).

Many scholars have focused on issues such as the impact of the new factories on labour force composition, the nature of the labour market, the gender division of labour, class consciousness, and relations within family structures. Transnational corporations have taken advantage of and reinforced women's structurally subordinated position within the labour market and the family by adopting discriminatory hiring practices, paying women lower wages and placing them in repetitive, monotonous tasks with no job security or advancement opportunities. As a consequence of their low-ranking positions in the factory, many of the tasks performed by women are not covered by health and safety regulations. Nor are women provided with insurance and retirement benefits (Grossman 1979; Elson and Pearson 1981; Salaff 1981; Nash and Fernandez-Kelly 1983). According to Elson, women enter the market place with gendered disadvantages in which ascriptive gender relations affect women's position in a labour market that is also the bearer of gender (Elson 1999).

This literature identifies the lower wage rates associated with female employment as being the key to the high and growing proportion of women in export-oriented manufacturing industry. Other explanations for the rise in female employment are attributed to perceptions of women's docility, subservience and manual dexterity (Elson and Pearson 1981). Within this context, there has been a considerable documentation of the fact that rises in female employment have been largely concentrated among young single women (Salaff 1981; Fernandez-Kelly 1983; Heyzer 1986; Lim 1990; Wolf 1992).

Many case studies show that employers value the reliability, stability and flexibility of female workers relative to male workers, which translate into lower unit costs for female workers than for male workers (Elson and Person 1981; Nash and Fernandez-Kelly 1983; Lim 1983; Joekes 1985; Humphery 1985). Moreover, their findings generally point to a central question of whether the employment of women is an experience of liberation or of exploitation. While some analysts conclude that Third World women are exploited by global factories due to low wages that are even sometimes below the subsistence level of the worker's daily costs (Chapkis and Enloe

1983), others argue that women are better off with factory employment (Lim 1983).

Factory work for women in Istanbul's garment industry, shaped under similar structures to those outlined above, offers privileged employment opportunities for low-income women. Factory workers have social security coverage, pension rights, annual bonuses and a stable employment prospect, provided by the formal organisational structure of factories where large-scale garment factories owned mostly by national capital producing for upper middle class domestic market consumption. The privileged position of factory work is of course relative, as the other forms of employment in the garment industry are mostly precarious and subcontracted work with no secure employment prospects. In Istanbul, women who have higher educational levels, have settled in the city longer than atelier and home-based workers, and have a relatively better-off family structure are employed in factories. The observed differences in women's personal backgrounds and the pattern of garment work they engage in point to the segmentation and differentiation of labour markets that assign women with more personal and family resources to relatively better-off jobs than casual and marginal ones. Women's factory work is not the only form of industrial work, and the relationship between industrialisation and female employment is very diverse. The forms of women's work change from one social and economic context to another[4]. Therefore, the focus on women's factory employment, which comprises a small portion of women workers, has been criticised for neglecting the larger number of women engaged in informal forms of production. A growing number of women work in small sweatshops or in their homes under subcontracting arrangements that are involved in a wide range of industrial activities in the informal sector (Pearson 1992:235).

2.2.2 Women's Informal Work
Globally organised industrial production by, as Mitter (1994) calls them, 'hollow corporations', has resulted in the informalisation of production, as precarious employment and the weakening of labour standards have become the hallmarks of labour markets all over the globe (Standing 1999a). In many countries, workers in the informal sector are comprised mostly of women who experience permeable and overlapping boundaries between their informal work and their household work. Women's involvement in the informal economy has increased as economic restructuring reduces job opportunities in the formal sector as well as increasing the need for additional family income (Delahanty 1999; Beneria 2003). Thus, discussions on female employment have been broadened by the inclusion of women's informal

and unpaid family work (Beneria and Roldan 1987; Mitter 1994; White 1994; Beneria 2001). Women's engagement in different forms of informal production ranging from contract-based or part-time work to unpaid family work, including home-based industrial work, highlights the latest trend in female employment. Thus:

> Women have emerged as very desirable employees in these circumstances because their relationship to the labour market has traditionally displayed the characteristics of flexibility so much wanted in the current conjuncture (Jenson, Hagen and Reddy 1988:10)[5]

Standing (1989; 1999) has connected flexibility and informalisation in the process of production with the feminisation of the labour force. In the context of developing countries, Standing (1989) claims that this flexibility, by 'making it easier to alter job boundaries and the technical division of labour' (p. 1078), has generated the 'feminisation of many jobs and activities dominated by men' (p. 1080). The feminisation of jobs has gone hand in hand with the casualisation of existing jobs and a dramatic increase in informal sector employment, which has taken many different forms in different geographic locations. In some locations, more and more women are involved in home-based production, whereas in other locations, atelier work is the most popular form of women's informal work. Elson (1999) warns against the trend of 'masculinisation' rather than feminisation, through which more and more jobs have become open to market forces and women's traditional activities have become commercialised and transformed into what was previously defined as a male domain (1999:613).

The number of women engaged in informal activities varies from region to region; however, women comprise a significant portion of workers in informal economies. A recent ILO study reveals that women's share of women in non-agricultural informal employment is higher than men's (ILO 2002:19). Charmes's estimates, based on national statistics during the period 1970 to 1990, show that women's share of self-employed informal work has increased all over the world, including in the developed regions. The share of women in non-agricultural self-employment is 38 per cent in Africa, 28 per cent in Latin America, 27 per cent in Asia, with an overall 24 per cent worldwide (Charmes 2000). Some writers claim that women's informal work has increased over the last 10 to 15 years as the result of poor levels of economic output and negative rates of growth, particularly in Latin America and Africa (Rodgers 1989; Moser and Sollis 1991).

The lack of labour market mobility, low skills, and childcare and domestic activities forces women from poor households to enter into informal activities to generate income. The survival strategies developed by the poorest households and their growing reliance on precarious forms of income production have also affected other sectors of the economy (de la Rocha 2000). Women's informal activities to support household survival strategies, including short-term wage labour, home-based work, street vending, self-employment and even temporary migration to find employment opportunities, are strongly linked with large-scale production located in urban areas and labour markets.

Gender-based hierarchies and a division of labour are the main characteristics of women's informal work. Patriarchal relations have kept women within the confines of particular activities in the informal economy, hindering women's financial and social gains through their paid work (Mies 1982; Redclift and Mingione 1985; Beneria and Roldan 1987). Women's informal work demonstrates the significance of gender relations and ideologies signalling the specific place and role of women in different societies. For example, Nelson delineates the different work experiences of female and male migrants in the informal sector squatter areas of Nairobi, and emphasises the significance of applying gender analysis to the study of informal work. As Nelson observes, 'women sell in the informal marketplace skills they normally practise in the home' (Nelson 1988:200). The range of informal jobs available for female migrants is gender-specific and reflects local gender ideology. A. M. Scott (1995) shows that in Lima, Peru, poor women's informal work is usually concentrated in domestic services and small-scale enterprises in which women earn less than men.

Women's informal work in Turkey is rarely visible in official statistics, but its existence and different forms are recorded by many studies (Ecevit 1991; Eraydın and Erendil 1996; White 1994; Cinar 1994; Eyüpoğlu et al. 1998; Özar 2000; Özbay 1998; İlkkaracan 2000). This study on Istanbul's garment industry explores how women's informal work takes place in small-scale workshops and in homes. Informal activities in the garment industry exist at different levels, sometimes in the form of evasion of rules and regulations, the utilisation of informally operating ateliers, and the informal employment of workers. These activities also generate different social hierarchies between different groups of people depending on ethnicity, class and gender. The most striking case of informalisation crystallises in family-run ateliers that use family labour and women, usually under very poor working conditions and on an informal basis. Women enmeshed with patriarchal relations take up such jobs without any retention or promotion, with little remuneration, and sometimes with long hours of unpaid work.

These women drawn into employment as family workers are not even seen as workers, but rather as helpers. In Istanbul's garment industry, the payment women receive as reward for their informal work is usually conceptualised as the social charity of business owners to poor women living in their own family and/or community.

2.2.3 Home-based Workers

The commodity chains approach has contributed to an understanding of the connections between global buyers and informal work in developing countries, and also offers a way of conceptualising how labour market informalisation affects women (Gereffi and Korzeniewicz 1994). Along the same lines, Carr, Chen and Tate (2000) have pointed out that technological change has facilitated 'lean retailing', which demands the 'quick and timely supply of goods associated with the just in time inventory system' (126). Thus, this system results in an increase in homework in the garment sector, particularly in countries close to the main markets of Europe and North America. This process has connected women's traditional informal work with the globalisation of industrial production.

The increasing use of home-based work is associated with intensified global competition in industrial production and with the drive of local exporters and producers to minimise costs and thus accumulate more capital. Home-based work is linked to the international production system through a chain of dependent relations between multinational companies, their buyers and local exporters, and between exporters and contractors and workers. Beneria and Roldan (1987) pointed out the growing concentration of women in the informal sector by focusing on the political and economic implications of these trends for women's home-based industrial work that was promoted through urban employment policies in Mexico City. The diverse range of home-based work activities, including garment production and textile work, undertaken by women was conditioned by class, gender and the dynamics of social relations in the workplace and household.

No clear data exist showing the number of women who work as home-based workers. Charmes's study only estimates the percentage of women in total home-based workers in developing countries, in which women comprise more that 80 per cent of all home-based workers (Charmes 2000). Although variations between countries exist, home-based work is a widespread option for making a living for low-income women in developing countries. Due to their limited mobility and the narrower range of options available in the labour market, especially married women make up the majority of the home-based workforce (Beneria 2003). Women do not leave the industrial labour force when they get married, but continue their income-generating activities at home by combining their domestic duties with home-based work (Beneria and Roldan 1987; White 1994).

Home-based work puts women in a vulnerable situation, as very limited bargaining power to improve their working conditions is held by such women. Subcontracting also makes it very difficult to hold a single employer responsible for protecting workers' rights due to the many layers of production chains (Beneria 2001; Beneria and Roldan 1987). Thus, women's earnings are lower than in the formal sector with no consistency of work contracts, difficult working conditions and long hours of work.

The case of women's home-based work in Istanbul's garment industry illustrates that the organisation of women's piecework and atelier production is based on gender and social relations as well as kinship relations, in which women's work is embedded. This in turn causes both men and women to devalue women's home-based work. These relations and ideologies also provide a mechanism whereby women produce cheaply for international and national markets. Thus, women's labour, both paid and unpaid, is conflated with their social and gender identity and membership of social groups such as the family. Women's informal work in home-based piecework or in garment ateliers tends to reproduce the patriarchal character of social relations without any public recognition of the work.

The first half of this chapter attempted to examine women's changing work practices as a result of the changing demands of global industrial production, which has moved from factory employment to subcontracted home-based work. The most dramatic development is the increasing importance of women's informal work in global industrial production. Istanbul's garment industry provides an opportunity to explore how different market and consumption niches create differentiated demands for women's labour. The extent of the labour demand in the garment industry, mainly organised around informal labour, including factory work, atelier work and home-based work, will be explored in the following chapters. Women's informal work in the garment industry is also highly invisible, something that is shaped not only by labour demand factors but also by the supply factors that facilitate women's labour market entry.

2.3 Factors Conditioning Women's Labour Supply

Factors standing at the crossroads of gender and the form of industrial production condition women's labour supply and demand and shape female employment. Prevailing gender ideologies not only determine the insertion of women into paid work but also affect the opportunities available to women in the labour market. In Istanbul's garment industry, gender ideology and relations facilitating women as a cheap labour source also make their work invisible to the public eye. Gender and the cultural settings that shape the specific forms of gender relations are therefore important in conditioning women's work and in determining new emerging forms of intersection between the supply and demand factors of women's labour. Therefore, a clarification is needed of how the terms gender and patriarchy are used in this research and how this research contributes to a further understanding of the gender ideologies that affect women's industrial work.

2.3.1 Gender and Patriarchy

In feminist analysis, gender is a very ambiguous concept and has undergone various phases of conceptualisation. These variations in the definition of gender lead to the production of ambiguities, inconsistencies and contradictions in feminist practice and the presentation of women's interests. The concept of gender has been used differently by different scholars. Gender was initially conceptualised as distinct from sex in order to present differences between men and women that are not biological. Thus, gender was a concept used to identify cultural and social differences related to biological differences (Nicholson 1994). Gendered categories and attributes such as behaviours, roles, personality traits, and attitudes embodied in the notions of masculinity and femininity are argued to be socially and culturally constructed categories. As socially constructed categories, they are not fixed but can change and transform over time and space.

Socially constructed gender differences are a reflection of the unequal relations that reproduce the social and cultural differences between men and women, through which the female/male distinction reproduces inequality in access to, and control over, resources at every institutional level (Moser 1993; Agarwal 1994; Hart 1995; Kandiyoti 1998). Scholars arguing for the heterogeneity of social categories such as men and women point to multiple, contested and contradictory meanings associated with male/female identities and distinctions. Moreover, these relationships and differences within the categories of male and female also take different shapes within each specific socio-economic and historical context (Moore 1994).

The conceptualisation of gender as a relational category in analysing women's access to and control over available resources in relation to men is a useful tool, as it reflects the categories used by members of local communities themselves. This is more desirable than importing Western conceptual frameworks that are dismissive of local articulations and understandings (Kandiyoti 1998). This approach also allows a consideration of how patterns of subordination are reproduced at the level of household, economy and society. As Hart puts it:

> Gender, in the sense of the social construction of biological difference, is not only a system of discrimination, but a key analytical concept for clarifying *how* socially constructed inequality is made to appear 'natural', the ongoing processes that reinforce or undermine particular gender definitions, and the conditions under which these meanings are called into question (Hart 1995:58 [Italics are original.]).

Gender is also crucial in understanding not only what the relationships are within and beyond the household but also how these relations are defined, reinforced, renegotiated and challenged (Kandiyoti 1998; Agarwal 1994; Hart 1995). Therefore, a gender approach helps us to see 'how multiple understanding of 'male' and 'female' are socially constructed and embodied in every day practices both within and beyond the household' (Hart 1995:41). Therefore, one could argue that gender operates in at least three distinct yet interconnected ways: (1) ideologically, especially in terms of gendered representations and valorisations of social processes and practices; (2) at the level of social relations; and (3) physically, through the social construction of male and female bodies (Marchand and Runyan 2000).

Institutionalised forms of inequality in which women overall occupy a relatively disadvantaged position relative to men is supported by the existence of a wide range of indicators of 'gender gaps' in many societies. As Oldersma and Davis (1991) argue: 'despite the variety of forms that gender inequality takes and has taken in the past, it remains something that can be perceived in various otherwise highly dissimilar settings and cultures.' (1991:1). In Turkey, these asymmetries have received relatively little attention in political and scholarly agendas even though national statistics reveal consistent gender gaps throughout women's and men's life cycles. These are reflected in higher rates of female illiteracy and fewer years of education; lower wages for women both in the informal and formal economic sectors; and a different range of restrictions on women's access to material and social resources (World Bank 1993; TÜSİAD 2000). A better understanding of the political, cultural and economic implications of systems of gender relations and identification of the ways in which these have implications for women's work would contribute to changing such systems.

To identify at least some of the forms of inequality that women experience in their daily lives and to articulate these inequalities from women's own perspectives is one of the aims of this research. It is also argued that gender as a relational category determines the degree of women's involvement in garment production and that women's position in the family helps to draw them into production. Women's different roles such as wives, daughters and mothers shape their contribution to industrial production as well as the social and personal gains made through women's work in the garment industry. Therefore, considerable attention is paid to family and community and women's roles and responsibilities in the family and community, revealing the fact that gender relations and roles not only determine women's place in society but also facilitate women's access to industrial work.

2.3.2 Bargaining with Patriarchy

Gender inequalities in social structures and cultural practices manifest themselves in the patriarchal forms of male dominance. The term patriarchy is a contested concept and broadly refers to a complex of male dominance over women. Lerner defines patriarchy as the 'manifestation and institutionalisation of male dominance over women and children in the family and the extension of male dominance over women in society in general' (1986:239). It is elaborated in the attempts of feminist scholars to develop a conceptual basis for the study of gender inequality.

The concept has been criticised for being ahistorical and acontextual and for falling short in accounting for cultural and class differences (see Acker 1989; Walby 1990; Waters 1989; Duncan 1994). Walby defends the concept against these charges from various scholars, pointing to its potential to embody differences, and defining patriarchy as 'a system of social structures and practices in which men dominate, oppress and exploit women' (Walby 1989:20). Specifically, Walby identifies six structures of patriarchy, namely paid employment, household production, the state, cultural institutions such as religion, education and the media, sexuality and male violence, which together form the system of patriarchy. Her recent focus on the historical changes in patriarchal structures and practices has shown that it has not declined in today's modern societies, but rather has changed forms: it has moved from private patriarchy (domestic gender regime) to public patriarchy (public gender regime) (Walby 1997). Focusing solely on the structures of patriarchy has the potential to lead to neglect of the dynamism of patriarchal relations in which women engage in negotiations and bargaining whereby both women and men are actively involved in making a 'gender contract' (Hirdmann cited in Duncan, 1994). The concept of patriarchy in this critical re-evaluation has come a long way, and it has the potential to reveal the persistent and systematic character of women's domination by men. According to Acker (1989), its 'critical-political sharpness' makes it a useful and valuable theoretical tool in the social sciences.

Given the problems of treating patriarchy as a singular phenomenon or indeed as a system in its own right, it is treated here as a systemic property with implications for all institutional domains: household, the community, markets and the state. One of the features of market-based societies has been the institutional separation of the 'private' domain of family and kinship from the other more 'public' domain of the market and state. Ascriptive gender helps to define the gendered positions within the family domain. Thus, to be a husband, wife, mother, father or uncle is to be either a man or a woman. 'Familial relationships are however a primary mechanism through which social meaning are invested in, and social controls exercised over women's bodies, labour, sexuality, reproductive capacities and life choices' (Kabeer 1994:58). Gender inequalities and male dominance in the 'private' domain manifest themselves in the 'public' domain of the market and state. In this research, an attempt will be made to examine male dominance in the household, the community and the market as factors that condition women's employment in Turkey.

[Therefore] instead of posing a universal structure of patriarchy, a social-relations approach suggests that apparent commonalities in gender subordination across the world are constructed through historically specific class and gender relations, and consequently have different implications for what men and women can and cannot do'. (Kabeer 1994:58).

Attempts to challenge the existing male dominance institutionalised in household, community, market and state are theoretically examined in relation to women's roles and bargaining positions in households and communities. The rules and practices through which familial relations are constructed, and the scope that they give to women to challenge, negotiate and transform them, are variable, taking different forms over time and in different settings (Kabeer 1994).

Duncan (1994) further developed the concept by studying patriarchy in the context of Scandinavian welfare states, hence incorporating some geographical variations into the concept. My focus will be on the region broadly described by Kandiyoti as the 'belt of classic patriarchy' (1988), where the dominance of men overpowers not only women but also young men, and where family honour is closely linked to the control of women's virtue (Yuval-Davis 1997). 'Classical patriarchy' rules in South and East Asia as well as in the Muslim Middle East (Acker 1989) and in 'a region where patriarchal structures remain most resilient' (Moghadam 1996:15)

In Turkey, patriarchy as a system of male dominance is mostly manifested in the domains of kinship and family relations as well as in the cultural practices of Turkish society. The paternalist gender system based on male authority gives senior men power over women's labour and reproductive capacity. Rather than confining itself to a more specific set of activities, male authority is diffused and infused to all aspects of a woman's and subordinate's life. Individuals mutually bonded through protection and responsibility are the subject of the power of a senior man's authority. In this system, men, as fathers and husbands, bear responsibility for the security, honour, and reputation of their families, and women should be legally, economically, and morally dependent on men. Women's code of behaviour, whose identity is constructed on their dependence and submissiveness, may bring their family honour, or otherwise shame. Kandiyoti (1988) describes women's relation to this system of male domination as 'bargaining with patriarchy'. Women receive 'protection and security in exchange for submissiveness and propriety' (1988:280).

Socio-economic changes in Turkish society, coupled with urbanisation, migration and the commodification of agriculture, have generated 'new areas of uncertainty and a renegotiation of relationships based on gender and age' (Kandiyoti 1995:307). The result of the social changes has been that men's unquestioned authority has become less secure and less taken for granted. Women's diverse responses to male authority have taken the forms of accommodating and subverting. My aim here is to show that the transformations of the social conditions in which the authoritarian and protective patriarchy is embedded do not always mean a general change in the relationships between men and women or a radical reform of what it means to be a man-husband or a woman-wife. The reproduction of familiar traditional practices continues in new social contexts. Whatever the forms that women's responses to changing patriarchy take, whether accommodating its traditional protection or subverting it, they need to be contextualised within the framework of classical patriarchy, which women themselves internalise.

My argument is that women's employment in the garment industry, especially in the prevailing form of women's informal work, provides conditions under which patriarchal gender roles are maintained through the exercise of traditional control over women's work and their work-related conduct. The conceptualisation of women's work as temporary and men's work as the main source of household income does not bring about a radical alteration in women's domestic and public roles. Rather, women's employment in the garment industry further highlights their domestic roles as mothers, wives and daughters, due to the dominance of family-based atelier production. Although a woman's work in the garment industry brings her into contact with people outside the family and kin, it does so in a context that is potentially controlled by family members in the same workplace. The male or senior female authority over women's work manifests itself in the concept of permission or consent (izin) before they can take up paid employment. For all these reasons, it is possible to argue that as long as women's work is confined within the circles of family, kinship and neighbourhood-based networks, employment will be practised as an extension of those domestic roles and as a temporary state, rather than as a radical departure from the confines of the patriarchal system.

My research also finds that the gender system is not perceived as oppressing women by generating gendered disadvantages through male power and authority. Rather, it is seen as a string of cultural practices that are equally exercised and internalised by both men and women without questioning their gender-based inequalities, which also bring access to social membership, certain social roles, and social responsibilities, as well as rights and material resources. As Kabeer argues, 'The incentive for members to cooperate is not simply individual need but also powerful normative pressures backed up by the threat of social sanctions, which make the 'choice' of the household membership a social, rather than a purely individual one' (1994:67).

2.3.3 Family and Social Networks

An examination of the supply of women's labour conditioned by family, social networks and community provides a better understanding of the specific relationships taking place between the process of globalisation and local communities that further shape women's access to local jobs. The household also occupies a pivotal position between the individual and the wider economy; it mediates the release of different members into the labour force and at the same time reshapes itself in response to the changing activities of individual members. It thus exerts an important influence generally on the supply of labour and especially on women's participation in the labour market. The household is of great importance in influencing the release of women into the labour force, through its role in transmitting wider cultural and ideological values, and as a decision-making unit (Anker and Hein 1986). The household is not only crucial to determining employment decisions but also determines the intra-household allocation of resources and decision-making through its organisation and inner structure. These processes determine who gets what and who does what in the household and in the labour market (Agarwal 1994; Kabeer 1994). The effects of these processes on the lives of women range from levels of nutrition to education and life expectancy.

Thus, the household should be considered not only as having a vital influence on the release of women into the labour market but also as determining the conditions under which women enter the labour market. For example, female household heads may have a far greater need to participate in the labour force than women with a resident male partner in paid work. Life cycle characteristics and domestic workloads condition the type of work women choose to perform, whether it is factory work or home-based work. In short, the household will affect the aggregate supply of labour, the age and sex composition of the labour force, the patterns of participation by age and sex, and the supply price and thus wage levels for various categories of workers (Stichter 1990).

Feminist writers prioritise the household as a site of women's likely oppression; Moore suggests that 'both the composition and the organisation of households have direct impacts on women's lives and in particular in their ability to gain access to resources, labour and to income' (1988:55). Moreover, Barrett (1986:211) argues that the family is 'the central site of the oppression of women' and mentions that gender ideology is formed principally within the family through women's dependence on a male wage and is reflected at other levels of society such as the workplace and the state. Some writers, however, argue that to some extent marriage and family life have been deployed by women as one of the major strategies to reflect their own interest in their lives (Hoodfar 1997). Hoodfar shows that in Egypt, marriage negotiations, done through the involvement and consent of the parents within the acceptance of Islamic ideology, traditionalism and conservatism, are secured to accommodate women's preferences and to put them in a relatively stronger position vis-à-vis their husbands (Hoodfar 1997).

The literature on female employment in the Third World is full of interesting examples that show the interrelations between work and household relations. Salaff (1981) notes that in Hong Kong working class parents viewed daughters as a 'poor long-term investment' and working daughters saw themselves paying back their natal families for giving them life and nurture before they left home. However, Southeast Asian cases also indicate that industrial employment generates a break in the customary practices that confine unmarried girls to the home. The influx of factory jobs meant that for the first time village girls had the chance to go away to work, to handle their own money, to save for higher education, and to choose their own husbands (Wolf 1997). Therefore, access to wages did gain young Asian women some personal forms of freedom, weakening customary family claims to varying degrees. In the Chinese case, wage employment has allowed daughters to demonstrate how 'filial' they can be, and that thus they can be considered 'worthier' than before.

The study of Beneria and Roldan (1987) in Mexico points out that the pre- and post-marriage work histories of husbands and wives (provided that the women's engagement was in informal activities such as industrial home work, personal services or autonomous sectors) facilitate different and generally higher-paid labour opportunities for the husbands. 'The historical conformation of Mexico City's proletariat is therefore a product not only of migratory waves from the hinterlands, but also of gender and generational 'waves' of female proletarianisation and sub-proletarianisation of wives, heads of household, and daughters who facilitate the proletarianisation of spouses, sons, or fathers' (1987:103). The demonstrations of the studies regarding the interrelations between family dynamics and women's labour strategies have pointed to the divergent impact of family structure on female employment ranging from the pattern of work that women engage in to the implications of waged work for the liberation of women. However, it should not be assumed that the family is the only institution that shapes the pattern of women's employment, nor that it is the only source of gender inequality. Other institutions such as the state, religion, education and the media are also bearers of gender inequalities, and these inequalities are reflected as male dominance over the institutional frameworks of a society at state, community, market and household levels (Agarwal 1994).

In addition to family dynamics, another area of investigation is kinship. People do not necessarily define themselves as individuals with separate rights independent of a large group, but rather see themselves as part of a larger community or family. Women are also enmeshed in a complex web not only of exploitative relations, but also of relations of solidarity and reciprocity, based on kinship. Thus, kinship, family and other forms of social web relations become important components of female employment. White shows that women's paid employment often takes place in the informal economy in which kinship relations play a key role in mediating labour relations (White 1994). In this context, work relationships often adopt kinship idioms and values such as solidarity, mutual indebtedness and reciprocity. She also provides insights into how these relations are manipulated to facilitate migrant women becoming involved with marginalised and low-paying labour. The relations based on kinship and families are mainly pointed out as oppressive and exploitative; however, it is necessary to acknowledge the changing and dynamic characteristics of these relations.

Chant's study on Mexican women shows that female labour force participation has been associated with a reconfiguration of the household structure in the case of economic recession (Chant 1995). Therefore, households deliberately adjust their survival strategies through the adoption of additional household members to free up women for economic activity. For example, in Chant's study, most households invite their female kin and family members to come and live with them in order to manage the household chores and childcare. The multiple implications of family and kinship relations for female employment and more widely for capitalist production relations are also questioned by Fernandez-Kelly in the case of Mexican border industries. Her study shows that relationships based on the systems of reciprocal obligations and social values such as trust, solidarity and co-operation are of crucial importance in the survival of working-class families. These relations at the level of the household and the neighbourhood facilitate the daily maintenance of workers. For these workers, whose wages continue to be lower than the cost of living, such exchanges are fundamental for subsistence. They extend purchasing power beyond the natural limits of wages. As Fernandez-Kelly (1983:175–6) puts it,

> The articulation of informal transactions into the broader national (and international) economy has importance for capitalists and for workers. From the point of view of the latter, they operate as a part of a strategy to maximise resources. From the vantage point of capitalists informal economic transactions among workers contribute to maintain wages at low levels.

Conclusion

The aim of this chapter has been to provide theoretical accounts of the ways in which the intersection of women's industrial labour demand and supply can be captured through the existing literature, highlighting the global restructuring of industrial production and women's involvement in these transformations. The supply of women's labour is conditioned by gender relations, family and community relations. These relations also shape the role and place of women in a society, creating the element of the 'culture of supply' of women's labour. Without an examination of those supply factors, an analysis of women's employment only as an outcome of demand conditions offered by firms is incomplete. Supply factors influence under what conditions and when women can enter labour markets, as well as what kind of employment opportunities can be accessible to women. These supply factors releasing women's labour for paid work also condition how far women can challenge and reform existing social and gender relations as a result of their employment, linking this with culture, kinship and family organisations on the one hand, and with the institutionalised power structures of society such as workplaces, etc., on the other hand. Although to a limited and subordinated degree, there are always reformations and negotiations between men and women, and also within communities, that redefine existing roles and relations.

The economics of demand for female labour are mostly conditioned by industrial production. Global trade networks govern the latest trends in industrial production and lead to the connection of different geographically and socially specific local relations in both industrial production and labour markets at the global level. Women have continued to be the insignificant and marginalised component of the global industrial labour force. Debates on informalisation and subcontracting as facilitating women's engagement in industrial production at various levels have provided a new perspective on female employment. Thus, the aim of this research is to provide a geographically specific approach to those debates about global industrial production and networks by looking at industrial production and the labour relations of the garment industry in Istanbul as a specific case study.

In Turkey, women's industrial work in small-scale garment ateliers and at home constructs an important aspect of garment production and is highly influenced by the ways in which the Turkish garment industry is integrated into global markets through production and trade networks. The specific focus of the research is on how the garment industry produces for different markets, how women are involved in the different labour processes, and how these two interact with one another. This focus is supported by a perspective reflecting women's own perspectives and views about their work, which promises not only to further our understanding of gendered forms of work, but also to be of potential value for developing policies and strategies for social change.

3

THE MACRO CONTEXT
Socio-economic Change, Labour Markets and Female Employment in Turkey

The years since the 1980s have been years of structural adjustment and change in Turkey. This is not only because Turkey implemented structural adjustment programmes as recommended by the IMF and World Bank, but also because Turkey has been going through major socio-economic transformations induced mainly by urban migration and the liberalisation of economic policies. The integration of the Turkish economy into global markets and domestic social changes have together affected women's economic roles and labour market participation.

The relationship between liberal economic polices and female employment has been widely discussed in the literature, as the experience of export-oriented industrialisation in developing countries went hand in hand with increasing female employment, especially in labour-intensive industries (Pearson 1992; Standing 1999; Beneria 2003). Latin American and Southeast Asian countries have been the prime examples of the feminisation of employment trends. However, Turkey seems to be an exceptional case where the implementation of export-oriented policies has not resulted in the feminisation of industrial employment. Against the observed pattern of increasing female labour force participation in other developing countries, female employment in Turkey has remained stagnant over the last 20 years.

The stagnant female employment rate is the story that the official statistics tell us about women's work. However, what is observed in the realm of women's informal work tells another story. Urban and feminist studies have pointed out the variety of income-producing activities undertaken by women and the increasing role of women's income generation in the survival of migrant families; subsequently, women have become a potential labour source for the informal economy. The contrast between women's officially recorded participation rates and their informal activities brings out the need for scrutinising official data collection methods and techniques.

This chapter provides an overview of the main socio-economic transformations and their implications for labour markets, female employment and informal work in Turkey, with the aim of understanding the context-specific form of the feminisation of employment and why women's work in urban Turkey remains invisible and fails to receive any public recognition.

3.1 Turkey's Socio-economic Transformations

Turkey's never-ending but reluctant struggle to be a member of the European Union (EU) has pushed the country to radically reform its governmental and legislative structure in recent years. The regulations and policy changes taking place at institutional, legislative and governmental levels will eventually affect the organisation of Turkish society. Although Turkey's outlook regarding EU membership seems bleak and unpromising, widely shared aspirations for democratic governance and economic stability are underpinned by the hope of accession.

Turkey is a large developing nation undergoing rapid social transformation. Tekeli (1990:3) described it as a society 'on the brink of a social mutation'. The Republic of Turkey was established in 1923. Kemalist ideology and reforms had their intellectual roots in European liberalism and modernisation, and were established on the core principle of a secular national state. Most interpretations of Turkish modernisation acknowledge the fundamental and active role of the state both in economic and social development, and in the production of regulatory discourses and policies on modernity, especially concerning gender relations and private life (Kandiyoti 1997).

Until the 1950s Turkey was a single-party state, and this party was the Republican People's Party (CHP). The foundation of an opposition party, the Democrat Party, and its accession to power after the 1950s with rural votes, marked the beginning of a new period in Turkey. National planning was introduced in the early 1960s to develop a national industry with the help of an import substitution growth strategy, which lasted until the late 1970s. The economic crisis of the late 1970s was thus ended with the implementation of export-oriented industrialisation, which was shortly after enforced by a military coup on 12 September 1980. Military government between 1980 and 1983 made it easier to curb the power of trade unions, freezing wages and limiting the rights of labour. This meant a shift in economic activity towards outward orientation, by increasing the role of the private sector and market forces. Today, it is widely accepted among scholars that the 1980s adjustment reform programme would not have been possible under civilian conditions and without the authoritarian involvement of the military (Yeldan 1995).

From the early 1980s until today, successive governments of the Turkish Republic have committed themselves to liberalisation policies and the outward orientation of the economy under the strict control of the IMF and the World Bank. The main and immediate result of these policies has been the increasing rates of exports in labour-intensive industries such as garments, leather and footwear (Yeldan 1995; Boratav *et al.* 1996). Financial liberalisations and the devaluation of the exchange rate of the Turkish lira were the main policy instruments of economic liberalisation in Turkey. Although Turkey was a success story for the IMF in the implementation of structural adjustment policies (SAPs) (Celasun and Rodrik 1990), the potential rate of growth of the Turkish economy moved to a lower plateau during the 1980s and the early 1990s. The potential GDP growth rate of 4.1 per cent per annum recorded during the adjustment period is poor when compared with the growth rates of earlier decades (Boratav *et al.* 1996). Despite rising export incomes, the sustainability of Turkey's adjustment programme was compromised by low rates of investment and savings (Boratav *et al.* 2000). The weakness of the programme has manifested itself in high inflation rates and continuous economic crisis, which first struck in 1994, again in 1998, and most recently in 2001. The common outcomes of the crises have always been cuts in public spending, the deterioration of wage incomes against inflation and the devaluation of the exchange rate of the Turkish lira.

An analysis of changes taking place in the areas of urbanisation, poverty and informalisation shows how these socio-economic transformations are reflected in ordinary people's lives and in the socio-political settings of Turkish society. They have had serious implications for Turkey's political and social landscape[1]. Brief accounts of urbanisation, poverty and informalisation are provided below, since my research findings will be referring more specifically to these indicators.

3.1.1 Urbanisation, Poverty and Informalisation
Urbanisation and urban migration have marked Turkey's social development process since the early 1950s. The population share of rural areas has been declining while the share of urban areas has risen from 25 per cent in 1945 to 65 per cent in 2000. Since the early 1980s, the total urban population has risen from 20 million to 44 million (TURKSTAT 2005).

In the more rapidly expanding urban centres such as İstanbul, Ankara,

İzmir, Adana and Bursa, the population increase outstripped these cities' capacity to sustain an infrastructure for newcomers, forcing migrants to build their own houses and to create their own employment opportunities. Thus, the number of squatter settlements (*gecekondus*) mushroomed rapidly from 100,000 housing units in 1950 to 1.25 million in 1983 (Keleş and Danielson 1985). Every large urban centre in Turkey has faced the problems of provision of housing, education, health and the establishment of new infrastructure as well as employment creation for migrants seeking work.

The neo-liberal policies of the post-1980s negatively affected the living standards of low-income migrant families (Yentürk 1997; TÜSİAD 1999). For example, the liberalisation policies resulted in severe cuts in public services and in public spending on education, health, social security and social services. These have had direct influences on the budgets of low-income families, who mainly live in squatter settlement areas of big cities. The share of education and health in the government's social spending has dropped from 23.6 per cent in 1992, to 14.3 per cent in 1997 and 11 per cent in 1998. This has been achieved by shifting the burden of social reproduction to the private sphere, increasing women's role as carers, and shortening the years of schooling for children (TÜSİAD 1999; Boratav *et al.* 2000). Moreover, a high rate of child employment is one of the long-term consequences of public cuts and deteriorating income distribution in Turkey (Tunalı 1997).

Liberalisation policies are also associated with deteriorating income distribution and social polarisation. The World Bank's report on *Turkey's Economic Reforms, Living Standards and Social Welfare* describes inequality in income distribution as follows:

> Turkey is a country with large and entrenched inequalities. Income differentials across regions and social groups are wide and persistent. Turkish provinces are diverging in an absolute sense—or in other words, rich are getting richer, while poor areas are getting poorer. Unlike other OECD countries, in Turkey today there is very little redistribution of incomes through taxation or social spending. (World Bank 2000:17)

Assessment of income inequality reveals that the gap between rich and poor in Turkey is wider than in other middle-income countries. The income of the rich is more than seven times higher than the income of the poor, compared to an average for the Luxemburg Income Survey database of about 3.5 times (World Bank 2000:18). Income polarisation in Turkey resembles some highly polarised economies such as Peru and Russia, and it exceeds the levels of inequality observed in Central European and Mediterranean countries (*ibid.*). With regard to the poverty and vulnerability of social groups in Turkey, the State Planning Organisation's Eighth Development Plan has pointed out that in the past twenty years, social mobility among migrants has become more limited, and *gecekondus* (squatter settlements) have become more marginalised. Poverty rates in the *gecekondus* are much higher than in city centres and the prospects of escaping poverty for their inhabitants are limited, as some 70 per cent of all the urban poor live in the *gecekondus*. In addition, female-headed households and children in these urban settlements are singled out as most vulnerable to poverty (SPO 2001).

Liberalisation, coupled with the massive rates of urbanisation, has led to the intensification of informalisation in Turkey. This has involved not only the informalisation of the labour force and economic relations, but has also extended to the realm of governance and the everyday life of citizens in Turkey. Housing, public transport and international trade are some of the main areas in which informalisation has taken place. In addition, informalisation has meant the mobilisation of social networks based on kinship, place of origin and patron–client relations. These relations are also activated to gain access to resources and opportunities. In urban Turkey, informalisation has helped to make business 'off the record' and also created an ethic or a social morality in which survival has to be secured by any means. This ethic of social survival is based on the ideology of easy and fast moneymaking using any means possible, which reflects the social environment of Turkey after 1980[2].

The withdrawal of the state from active social and legislative regulations has not only increased but has also opened up state resources for informalisation. Boratav *et al.* (1996) analyse rent seeking and corruption in economic decision-making and policy implementation, which has created advantages for some individuals as the economic regime has moved further into liberalisation. These authors claim that there has not been any period in the history of republican Turkey when corruption and economic scandals so heavily dominated the public scene. Rent seeking and corruption have moved from being transitional phenomena to being an intrinsic feature of the society. Informalisation during the liberalisation period determined the forms of capital accumulation and state transfers (Boratav *et al.* 1996). Informalisation in Turkey, however, branches out into many aspects of life through different channels. It is more precise to conceptualise informalisation as a way in which Turkish society as a whole organises itself, rather than an exclusive feature of the economy.

As discussed earlier, the liberalisation of economic policies has resulted in the outward orientation of the economy. Urbanisation, poverty and informalisation coupled with socio-economic changes and increasing exports of labour-intensive products have far-reaching implications for labour markets and female employment in Turkey.

3.2 Labour Markets and Female Employment in the Post-1980s

Turkey has been successful in sustaining positive GDP growth rates throughout most of the recent period, but it has been less successful at generating employment. Between 1980 and 2004 Turkey's working-age population grew by 23 million people, yet during that time only 6 million jobs were created. As a result the employment rate is just 44 per cent, among the lowest levels in the world. Most countries have employment rates above 50 per cent, and in the EU-15 the average is 65 per cent (World Bank 2006).

The main characteristic of the Turkish labour market is the disparity between high growth rates of population and low levels of employment generation. The labour force has low levels of educational attainment and low skill composition. The share of agriculture in total employment is still high. Low labour productivity in agriculture, as well as in the informal sector in urban areas, the small share of wage earners in the workforce, and massive shifts in the sectoral distribution of the labour force through rural–urban migration are among the major structural characteristics. A further salient feature is the large share of the public sector in total urban employment. The high level of child labour in agriculture and the informal sector, together with the existence of seasonal migration in agriculture on a significant scale, are further factors to be considered in understanding the functioning of the labour market (TURKSTAT 2005).

Another key feature of the Turkish labour market is an extremely low level of female participation in urban areas. Female labour force participation has been falling in Turkey since the 1960s, stagnating at around 20 per cent over the past 15 years (World Bank 2006). This shows a sharp contrast when compared with the countries of South East Asia and Latin America where women accounted for almost half of total labour force participation (Beneria 2003). This low percentage for women holds in all age categories, but is most striking in the prime age group (25–54 years), where only about 3 in 10 Turkish women are active, compared to nearly 7 in 10 in other OECD countries. These female participation rates reflect differences between Turkey and most other OECD countries in terms of the division of labour by gender and marriage patterns (TURKSTAT 2005).

Movement out of the labour force is a striking characteristic of Turkey's labour market. The declining rates of labour participation have been documented by numerous Turkish academics, most recently by Bulutay (1995) and Tunalı (1997). Thus, only a small portion of women is in the workforce, while the majority remains inactive. The inactivity rate is around 75 per cent for women over 15 years old, and the largest share of inactive group is housewives, accounting for 68 per cent of the total inactive female population in 2005 (TURKSTAT 2005). The category of housewives outnumbers all other categories of students, retired, discouraged workers, and illness. The large number of housewives is a phenomenon of Turkish labour markets. Although no research exists addressing whether these women are engaged in any kind of income-generating activities, it is plausible to argue that a sizable portion is under-counted in labour market statistics, and that they serve as reserve labour for the informal economy in urban Turkey.

An increase in the recorded female labour force does not seem to be occurring in the Turkish labour market as experienced in some other developing countries (Standing 1989). Cagatay and Berik (1991) reported that there was no strong indication of the feminisation of the manufacturing labour force in Turkey. According to their findings, the demand for female labour increased faster in the private sector than in the public sector after the 1980s. In addition, there is a 'de-feminisation' in public sector manufacturing and a 'feminisation' in the private sector with the transformation to export-led growth. However, women are more likely to be found in labour-intensive small-scale firms rather than large-scale and public firms (Cagatay and Berik 1994). Therefore, the most female-intensive industries are those that are most labour intensive, such as the apparel, textile, food, and tobacco industries.

My proposal is to dispute the view of women's paid activities presented by the official statistics by arguing that women's labour has been an important element of industrial production in Turkey but has largely remained informal and invisible. Due to its character of self-assessment, HLFS should have captured an accurate increasing trend of women's work in small-scale, home-based and informal sector work. However, because of gender and measurement biases involved in the data collection process, urban women's work remains largely invisible in Turkey.

3.3 Measurement Problems and Gender Biases

The narrow coverage and low reliability of official data are issues that limit a coherent analysis of the labour market in Turkey. In an economy as complex as Turkey's, with a large agricultural sector and informal economy, the data collection methods in measuring the dynamism of the labour force bear some inaccuracy problems in reflecting the actual situation of the labour market. Household Labour Force Surveys (HLFS) conducted by the Turkish Statistics Institute (TURKSTAT) comprise the most comprehensive data set, which captures to a certain extent informal employment, self-employment and small-scale activities. It is relatively more accurate than data obtained from the social security registry and enterprise-based information. In textiles, for example, an enterprise-based survey yields a total employment figure of nearly 500,000 workers in 1994. For the same year, HLFS shows comparable employment in textiles of over one million workers (World Bank 2000). This is a dramatic underestimation of 50 per cent of the textile workforce.

Moreover, considerable statistical and conceptual problems in official data and the poor quality of data on agricultural and informal sectors are very widespread. The degree of under-reporting of the workforce is also evident in ethnographic studies in Turkey. For example, Berik (1987) pointed to a substantial discrepancy between the number of carpet weavers as reported by the 1980 census of population (40,000) in comparison to the estimated number based on carpet production and number of looms (500,000). Another researcher shows that the reported number of shoemakers, according to Istanbul's municipal authorities, involved 12 workplaces when, in fact, there are estimated to be 705 (Müftüoğlu 2000). Therefore, these examples show how difficult it is to make generalisations and measure the growth prospects of the labour force in Turkey.

Another economic activity that is difficult to measure in Turkey is home-based work. The labour force surveys indicate that home-based self-employment for women in Turkey increased by 94.4 per cent, from 71,400 to 138,800, between 1988 and 1992 (TURKSTAT 2005). Yet Çınar (1994) estimates that the number of home-based workers was 88,000 in 1988 in Istanbul alone. This number is actually more than the official figure for all of Turkey. On the other hand, Karslı (1992) estimates that 14,000 women home-based workers were working for three knitting firms in just one municipality of Ankara in the early 1990s. This number corresponds to 9 per cent of the unpaid family workers in the total population of Ankara.

Çağatay and Berik (1994) suggest that female participation in the workforce is underestimated in population statistics due to the gender biases and problems associated with measurement techniques during data collection. The primary respondent in these surveys is 'the head of the household'. In the questions, the head of the household is actually formalised with a 'gender neutralised' term but usually refers to the eldest male in the house. Therefore, the questions related to women's work are either asked directly to the male 'household-head', or in the best scenario, when the male household-head is absent, the questions are answered by women. Unsurprisingly, Özar (1996) also observes that heads of households might under-report women's informal market activities[3]. For most women their main occupation is described as housewives only, as their informal activities are not approved or are unrecognised by male members of the house.

HLF surveys conducted with the head of households cover only 23,000 households in Turkey. It is likely that these interviews are conducted in coffee-houses where local men spend most of their free time and socialise with their male friends. Interviewers are also mostly men. Being a male interviewer makes it more difficult to interview women as Turkish households rarely accept a stranger if not accompanied and introduced by an acquaintance. Women's seclusion and exclusion from the public sphere reduces the chances of women voicing themselves and taking part in the interview process.

Even if women become involved in data collection processes their informal, home-based work and handicraft activities are highly likely to remain unreported or under-reported. This is partially due to their perception of home-based work and partially due to their intention of keeping their work secret from their husbands and fathers. Especially, married women's income earned through home-working and traditional handicraft activities is usually hidden and kept in safe places unless an urgent need to use it arises.

In addition to all these data collection biases, the statistical category classifying most of the urban inactive female population as 'housewife' is open to scrutiny. Asking different and more specific questions of these women could make it possible to uncover some of the informal income-generating activities that some of these women might be engaged in. Thus, if the definition of work is extended to include forms other than wage work (Özbay 1990), the female participation rate could have been higher in urban areas. Overcoming women's invisibility is only possible by developing different concepts that can capture women's different economic activities. Using different definitional concepts and their application with a more gender-sensitive approach during data collection would result in a better measurement of women's work. Anker et al. (1988) found in India that appropriate survey techniques and questionnaire design can lead to more accurate and complete measurements of women's labour force activity. The reporting of female participation in home-related activities, such as animal husbandry, sewing, etc., was significantly higher when questions were very specific, and the participation rate was lower when the questions were of a general non-specific nature such as main activity, secondary activity and work (Anker *et al.* 1988:143).

The nature of production in labour-intensive industries helps to hide some portions of women's work. In spite of a growth in exports, especially in garments and textiles, no increase is recorded either in female labour participation or in women's share of the textile and garment labour force, due to the complex nature of labour-intensive production in Turkey, which involves both family-based atelier production and home-based work. Additionally, informal work and the experience of informal sector workers are more complicated than the frozen categories of a questionnaire and the cold appearance of numbers suggest. In my opinion, the most reliable information for labour-intensive, 'unskilled' and informal working activities can be handled through research specifically conducted on that topic, using ethnographic methods and case studies, instead of country-based surveys. This is the reason I opted to use ethnographic data in the analysis of women workers in Istanbul's garment industry.

As a result of problems related to the measurement process and gender biases in data collection, official statistics in Turkey reflect only a partial picture of women's paid activities, which rather reflects the employment figures of educated women and neglects low-income women's work. Therefore, analysing only official figures to draw a conclusion as to whether or not the feminisation of employment is occurring in Turkey is not sufficient. A similar situation was evident in Mitter's study of the London garment industry, where the experience of labour-shedding and declining investment during the 1970s and early 1980s resulted in the relegation of garment production to the home-working sector and small firms (Mitter 1986). Focusing on women's fashion wear, Mitter calculated that a total of 13,000 jobs had been shifted out of factories to create an equivalent of 17,000 jobs for sweatshops and domestic outworkers between 1978 and 1983. This was absent from official records (Mitter 1986). Similarly, even though women's work in garment production seems to be excluded from official statistics in Turkey, a confident conclusion can be drawn that a disguised feminisation of the labour force is emerging among low-income women living in the suburbs of Istanbul, and that the role of women in export-related production is not only substantial but also diverse.

The increasing exports of labour-intensive products and the commodification of women's traditional handicraft activities have offered low-income migrant women different income-earning opportunities in urban areas. Revealing key issues in women's informal work by exploring its value in the economy and highlighting women's participation in the productive labour force helps to increase the visibility of women's informal sector work at national and international levels. Therefore, such research can serve policy advocacy, aiming both to improve the conditions of informal work and to influence national policies on the informal sector in general, or women's informal work in particular.

3.4 Women's Informal Work

No macro-level empirical relationship between global industrial production and women's informal work in Turkey has so far been established in the literature. Only Cinar (1994) and White (1994) made a connection between garment exports and home-based piecework in Istanbul, although with no reference to other forms of women's informal work in the garment industry. My research aims to fill this gap with a focus on women's atelier work in family-owned businesses, and also to highlight the relationship between women's informal work and export-oriented production in Istanbul's garment industry.

Yıldız Ecevit stated, without providing firm empirical evidence, that subcontracting to women became the norm of industrial production in Turkey after the early 1980s (Ecevit 2000). The strongest proof could be found in the increase of women's informal activities documented by numerous studies and a causal relation established between the export-led labour intensive production and women's informal work in urban Turkey. My argument here is that the significance of informal work can be attributed to the way in which Turkey has been integrated into the global production system. Turkey's international competitiveness based on the production and export of labour-intensive commodities has resulted in the expansion of the informal sector, which utilises female labour. If this integration had been managed by multinational companies, as in Mexico or in Southeast Asian countries, the formal female labour force participation would have been much higher. Instead, in Turkey, the industrialisation trajectory and international trade have been based on the utilisation of small-scale production and informal labour. This seems to be a result of the low level of foreign direct investment, whose share in GDP remained insignificant throughout the 1980s and 1990s[4] (Arın 2003). The result of this process for the women's work is its marginalisation, which can clearly be observed in the cases of increasing home-based piecework, unpaid labour in small-scale family businesses, and informal domestic service work. Women's income-generating activities are now even more crucial for the survival of migrant families than before, and more and more women have joined the ranks of being an abundant cheap labour supply for the ever-expanding labour-intensive garment industry.

Migrant *gecekondu* women living in poor households are the main source of labour for the informal economy in Turkey. In a recent study, Buğra and Keyder (2003) show that women and children are the main receivers of urban marginal jobs such as cleaning, garment work and piecework, whereas men face the situation of declining employment opportunities, increasing unemployment and deteriorating wage levels under the threat of eroding stable jobs. However, earlier studies investigating the nature of *gecekondu* women's employment show rather a temporary state of employment and engagement in income-generating activities.

In a qualitative study of the conditions and factors affecting migrant women's labour force participation (in *gecekondu* areas of Ankara, İstanbul, İzmir and Mersin), Lazreg (1999) finds that migrant women in urban *gecekondus* tend to marry younger, have more children and have less education than non-migrant dwellers of *gecekondus* and city centre dwellers. A large fraction declares themselves as 'not working', and among those who do work, the majority report doing so without social security and health insurance. According to Lazreg, migrant women's apparently low labour force participation is largely a definitional issue, reflecting the low value attributed culturally and economically to women's work. Women in the *gecekondus* do not consider what they do as work, even when their earnings are essential to the survival of the family (Lazreg 1999). In addition to Lazreg, White also reports that women do not consider their activities as work, since 'work' is conceptualised as being formal work done for a salary outside the house.

In Şenyapılı's study on *gecekondu* areas, she observed that 'since girls tend to marry young and family size is gradually reducing, *gecekondu* women are not compelled to work full-time. In general, they venture into the labour market temporarily, whenever economic bottlenecks arise' (1981: 209). In this light, *gecekondu* women are considered to be a mainly peripheral and temporary urban work force. Moreover, Şenyapılı points to the negative aspects of women's economic activities in *gecekondus*. Namely, 'work, in general, will never be a source of social unification, equalisation and satisfaction...she will be subjected to further exploitation due to the basically unorganised, marginal nature of the labour force' (1981:212). Therefore, according to Şenyapılı, economic activities are pursued only in cases of financial necessity, and are seen predominantly as marginal. A number of factors seem to account for this marginalisation. Much of women's work is irregular, is performed at home, and is sometimes not remunerated.

Cultural and gender attitudes cast men as the only breadwinners, and the traditional division of labour within the family reinforces the notion that women's earnings are less valuable than men's.

3.4.1 Different Patterns of Women's Informal Work

Although insufficient scholarly attention has been paid to the relationship between export-oriented production and women's informal work, a rich source of empirical research documenting key issues and different aspects of women's informal work exists. Four main types of informal work can be identified in the existing literature. The first group is women's industrial home-based work (Berik 1987; Lordoğlu 1990; Cinar 1994; White 1994; Hattatoğlu 2001). The second type is women's domestic service work, which has been studied by Ozyegin (2001) and Kalaycıoğlu and Rittersberger (1998). The third group is women's unpaid family work in the urban centres of Turkey, on which no study has been done mainly investigating women's unpaid family work, although White (1994) and Ayata (1990) mention women's role in generating income as unpaid family workers. The fourth type is women's traditional handicraft activities.

No precise number is available for how many women are engaged in informal activities, but it is estimated that the number has dramatically grown with the increasing influence of economic liberalisation and flexible working conditions (World Bank 2000). In her study of women home-workers for small-scale textile firms in Bursa and Istanbul, Cinar shows that 88,000 women were working from home for the ready-made apparel industry. This number corresponded to about 3 per cent of the total female population of Istanbul in 1989. She also estimated that one in every four migrant women in Istanbul takes in piecework. Moreover, a study carried by Ayata shows that piece-rate workers made up the largest section of the industrial labour force in urban Turkey (Ayata 1986).

Emine Cinar provides sociological accounts of why unskilled women do not work in the formal sector in Turkey. The following factors are indicated as reasons for not getting a job in the formal sector and instead engaging in home work. Lack of husbands' permission to work in formal sector jobs was the first reason to take up home-based work. Flexibility of work hours, which is especially important to mothers of young children, provides women with the ability to stay home and earn some money as well as protect their reputation in the neighbourhood as 'good' housewives and mothers. Although women had low potential for salary increases, working from home gave them a safe work environment in which there was no potential factor of harassment.

The work by White (1994) on women's piecework production indicates an alternative interpretation of work among the urban poor, suggesting that women's involvement in informal and low-paying jobs is not necessarily exploitative and marginal in character. She concentrates on the implications of gender and community relations for women's home-based work. She also highlights women's income-producing activities, along with the more traditional labour of housewifery and motherhood, as being an expression of their identity as 'good' and hard-working Muslim women. The ways in which women represent their identity through perpetuating gender roles and identities in order to gain security and membership in low-income neighbourhoods of Istanbul ultimately generate a cheap labour source for global capital.

The second group of women's informal work is in the service sector, where women serve as domestic helpers, usually cleaners. Domestic work is mostly constructed as 'humiliating' and 'cleaning the dirt of others'. Thus, it is the last resort for women to make money. Despite the negativity attached to this type of work, the demand for it is growing as urbanisation and the employment of educated women have risen. According to Ozyegin (2001) and Kalaycıoğlu and Rittersberger (1998), women overcome this negative attribution by generating kinship-like relationships with their mostly female employers. Within this conceptualisation, the work is done for sisters, mothers, or aunts, even though some financial gains are earned at the end of the day.

The third type of women's informal work is unpaid family work, which usually takes place in small-scale family enterprises in urban areas. This category of work has remained largely under-recognised, not only because of its informal character but also because of the way women conceptualise their family work. In Ayata's work in Buldan, which is a towel-weaving town, he researched the subcontracting relations and market orientation of the towel weavers. He found that towel weaving takes place in houses, and is considered a family business. Men mostly operated looms, as the family business passed from fathers to sons. The significance of female labour was not mentioned in Ayata's work. However, all the men in his sample said that in their absence, for example, when they were out buying raw materials and dying materials, their wives or daughters took over the weaving. The small-scale nature of production had increased the reliance on family labour that required full dedication and long hours, and led many weavers not to employ paid workers, but to keep their business limited to the availability of family labour. Ayata also indicated that women's labour was withdrawn from towel production when there was a paid worker in the house (Ayata

1990). In White's study, there is an emphasis on the role of unpaid women workers in small family-owned establishments as mediators of community relations and providers of access to a cheap supply of female labour in the local community (White 1994).

The last group of women's informal work is their domestic handicraft activities. Until recently, this work was not seen as an income-generating activity but as a *çeyiz* (trousseau) making activity of young girls before their marriage. As women have started to generate small networks in urban neighbourhoods to sell and buy their materials, this kind of activity has become known as an income-generating activity. In a special issue prepared by the Study Group of Women's Home-based Work in Turkey, discussions with women reveal the importance of traditional handicraft activities. Women can market such skills in cases of financial need (Iktisat Dergisi 2002:3–17). By definition, every woman in Turkey must know how to clean, cook, serve, embroider, knit, and crochet, and above all keep her hands busy. Thus, the products of women's domestic handicraft, such as sweaters, linen, lace-making, knitting, and socks are in demand, usually from other women to use them as trousseaus, or for their home or personal clothing. There will be a more detailed account of women's handicraft activities in Chapter 5, regarding trade networks generated to market these products to larger national and international markets.

3.4.2 Women's Garment Atelier Work

The importance of the garment industry for women's work has increased since its export orientation began in the early 1980s. Diverse opportunities for income-generating activities, ranging from factory work to atelier and home-based work, are available for women. One of the important forms of women's work that has become more observable in urban areas is atelier work. Although there is no literature about women's atelier work in Istanbul, Chapters 4, 5 and 7 will highlight different aspects of women's atelier work and review the relevant literature.

It is difficult to establish a clear-cut definition of industrial atelier production. Since the definition changes relative to time, region and sector, it is only possible to make a relative description. Unlike the traditional 'self-sufficient' artisanal workshops, industrial ateliers systematically use wage labour (Ayata 1986). In the garment atelier case, at least three or four wageworkers exist in every workshop. In this range, there is no great differentiation in terms of working conditions, division of labour and machine profiles. Unlike artisanal workshops, a certain level of division of labour exists in the industrial atelier. Whereas artisanal workshops realise the whole production process, industrial ateliers specialise in a particular stage. There is a separation of tasks between the industrial atelier and other levels of garment production. Another important characteristic of ateliers is their location. The garment ateliers in Istanbul are located in residential neighbourhood districts rather than industrial zones. As a result they have different characteristics from the workshops that are located in the industrial zones. These ateliers are ground or basement floors of residential flats and look like residences from the outside. Physical concealment is important in terms of ensuring clandestineness, informality and flexibility. The location is also significant in terms of maintaining a domestic identity. From this perspective, the border between home-based work and atelier is blurred.

The main differentiation between atelier and home-based work relies on the place of work and the position of the employer. The ILO defines home-based work as work carried out at a place of the worker's own choice, usually the worker's home, with very little direct supervision or regulation by the employer (ILO 1996).

The garment ateliers do not coincide with any of these categories. Unlike home-based workers, atelier workers do not have control over the means of production and the labour process in economic terms. In addition, there are differences with regard to worker profiles and the socialisation of the workspace. However, as suggested above, there are also many similarities in terms of working conditions and environment. Similarly to home-based work, the ateliers are part of the unregulated economy.

Like home-based work, women's labour in these ateliers is affected by gender ideologies. Production takes place on the doorstep of the community. Because of the ideological constraints of gender identity, female workers in both sorts of production do not have the opportunity to make contact with the market by themselves, and their labour power is controlled by the family, community, and employer, as well as by the workers themselves.

Atelier production and home-based work are also close to each other in terms of workers' life histories. It is common to come across a mother at home doing de-threading work obtained from a workshop in which the daughter is working. A worker might start work in a workshop while she is young, and become a home-based worker when she gets married or becomes pregnant. Women are bound by gender ideologies both as home-based workers and atelier workers. The former represents an actual domestic space and the latter is perceived as one.

Conclusion

Turkey has been undergoing significant social transformations in recent decades. These changes are not only related to economic and social realms, but also extend into Turkey's political and institutional structures. Urbanisation, informalisation and increasing poverty, as consequences of economic liberalisation, are observed as major transformations affecting people's lives. The turn towards economic liberalisation has boosted the exports of labour-intensive products; their champion has been the garment industry, which offers employment to a sizable portion of the low-income women living in *gecekondu* areas of Istanbul.

Despite a dynamic and growing informal economy and women's informal work within it, the figures of female employment based on official statistics, mainly HLFS and population censuses, show a declining trend of women's participation. This represents Turkey as an exception to the case established in the literature of the feminisation of employment in developing countries that adopt liberal and outward-oriented economic policies. An analysis of women's work through official figures could lead to the conclusion that Turkey is an exceptional case where the feminisation of employment is not occurring despite the implementation of liberal policies and the export success of labour-intensive industries.

However, my argument is that a degree of feminisation of employment is easily observable in urban areas where women's industrial work usually remains hidden, under-recorded as well as under-recognised. This invisibility is a result of different factors affecting women's public visibility and women's work in Turkey. Firstly, gender biases and measurement problems render women's work invisible. Secondly, the way women define their work and income-generating activities omits an important portion of women's work. The fine line between women's domestic duties and informal activities taking place mostly at home or in a family-run workshop leads women to see those activities as the extension of their domestic duties. Thirdly, women's involvement in labour market activities in Turkey mostly takes place in the informal economy. This in a sense mirrors and extends the ways in which women carry their pattern of agricultural work as unpaid family workers in urban areas, by being the 'invisible' segment of the manufacturing sector. These factors rendering women's work invisible show that official figures fail to capture the hidden and neglected aspects of women's economic activities in urban areas.

The rest of the book is designed to analyse the nature of women's work in the garment industry, and the factors conditioning women's entrance into garment production in Istanbul. It will also set the foundations of an analysis that low-income urban women are an essential factor that affects the way in which Turkey integrates with global markets, through a globally competitive garment industry, where women's labour is exploited not only in economic terms at the global level, but also on moral grounds at the local level by their own families and communities.

4

THE GARMENT INDUSTRY IN ISTANBUL AND DEMAND FOR FEMALE LABOUR

It is a common scene in squatter neighbourhoods in Istanbul to see a group of young men aged between thirteen and their early twenties playing football during their lunch break, in front of their *atölye* (garment atelier) located on the ground floor of a multi-floored apartment building. Women are absent from this scene. The women's invisibility is by no means an indication of their absence from the labour force in the garment industry. This invisibility of women from the public gaze is mirrored to some extent in official statistics, and women's involvement in garment production is usually underreported.

Internationally women account for more than two-thirds of the global labour force in the garment industry and one in fifty of the total female labour force in manufacturing does garment work (Joekes 1995:1). The centrality of women's labour in garment production finds no exception in Turkey, where women's extensive contribution to garment production is for the most part publicly invisible with no official recognition. This is partially the result of the specific demand conditions that the industry generates for women's labour market entrance.

The aim of this chapter is to analyse the demand factors that condition women's work in Istanbul's garment industry, which is highly structured by the characteristics of firms and the nature of subcontracted work. Therefore, the structure of the industry and its connections with global commodity chains and other markets, such as domestic markets and the informal international trade, are the factors that influence production and subcontracting as well as women's employment. The ways in which women's entrance into Istanbul's garment sector is mediated through atelier production and home-based work are the main indicators of how the industry establishes its international competitiveness and maintains its flexible (unregulated) production conditions.

4.1 The Garment Industry in Turkey

The textile and garment industry has played a significant role in the industrialisation and the market orientation of the Turkish economy. Turkey's share in world garment export has risen from 0.3 per cent in 1980 to 4 per cent today. According to WTO statistics, Turkey is currently the world's fourth biggest garment supplier. In 2004 the formal textile and garment sector represented 17.5 per cent of total industrial production and accounted for 11 per cent of total employment and 30 per cent of industrial employment. However, since the informal economy is widespread in the garment sector it may present a considerably higher share of the total workforce than estimated. About 65 per cent of Turkish textile and ready-made garments go to the European Union. There are 60 textile and 15 apparel companies among the top 500 companies in Turkey. These statistics reveal the significance of this industry for the Turkish economy and its place within the labour market (Fair Wear Foundation 2004).

Eraydın and Erendil (1999) note that after the 1980s the dynamism of industry is closely related to changes in the foreign trade regime, real depreciation of the Turkish lira, and the tax exemption of exporting firms. Yeldan describes it as a source of wealth transfer from labour to capital, with repeated devaluations throughout the 1990s and 2000s, which have kept labour costs down and help the industry to remain competitive internationally (Yeldan 2001). In general, industry's labour productivity has remained very low, which has not translated into capital investment, and the ratio of capital to labour in the garment industry has, according to Yentürk's calculations, shifted towards labour utilisation (Yentürk 1997). Between 1981 and 1996, the industry recorded 2.4 per cent annual increases in real output while increases in recorded employment remained at 0.8 per cent (Boratav *et al.* 2000). Note, however, that these figures for low labour productivity, low capital investment and recorded employment are dubious due to the high degree of informalisation in the industry.

One of the most important characteristics of the Turkish garment industry is that it operates from unregistered workplaces, where labour legislation and social security regulations are ignored. The total number of registered companies in the sector is estimated at about 44,000, more than 80 per cent of which are small- to medium-size companies. Data provided by the Denizli Textile and Clothing Exporters' Union (DETKIB) show that the formal industry accounted for 10 per cent of GNP and 11 per cent of formal employment whereas informal industry accounted for 20 per cent of GNP and 20 per cent of informal employment. Although no statistics are available for those informal companies, it is certain that informal firms and informality are the engine of the garment industry in Turkey (DETKIB 2001).

Data provided by the Teksif Trade Union show that only 500,000 workers out of two million were formally employed in 1999. Other research by the same union shows that only 4,000 workers out of 60,000 in the Merter district, which is the centre of garment production in Istanbul, are registered under the social security system. It is estimated that while official figures show the number of garment workers as half a million, the figure may be nearer to three million when informal economy workers are included in the estimate (Clean Clothes Campaign 2005:33).

Employment conditions at these individual, unregulated workplaces vary enormously. The workforce is hired when orders have been placed and fired when orders stop coming in. This means that workers have no continuity of employment or job security. The working day in informal workplaces is often between 14 and 16 hours, depending on the nature of a particular order. Workers may be forced to work six or even seven days a week. Women and children are often required to work at night, which is prohibited by law. Companies frequently do not pay the statutory social security contributions on behalf of their employees, or falsify records in order to pay less (Clean Clothes Campaign 2005:33).

The network of subcontractors is an integral part of Turkey's garment export sector, and helps to reduce fixed costs and provide cheaper labour resources. These networks are not only established between different firms, but also extend into home-based workers, whose labour proves to be vital. Access to female and child labour made possible through subcontracting enables the industry to reach untapped resources of cheap labour (Esim, Ergun and Hattatoglu 2000).

The study by Kaytaz (1994) investigated subcontracting between large- and small-scale firms in the industry, which enabled them to stay competitive and flexible vis-à-vis those that did not use subcontracting. In his study among Denizli's towel weavers, Ayata identified two different types of subcontracting relations: one between small family-owned and large-scale firms, and the second between large-scale firms themselves, through which firms have the possibility of being able to specialise in a certain part of the production process on a complementary rather than a competitive basis (Ayata 1990).

In the industry, firms usually subcontract the sewing and embroidery parts of production, while cutting, modelling, and quality control are kept within the firm. Large corporate firms are not part of a unified web of subcontracting relations, but act independently in their subcontracting agreements. An interesting finding shows that small- and medium-scale firms have on average 23 subcontractors, whereas large-scale firms work with only seven subcontractors (Eraydın and Erendil 1999). Control over the production and quality standards of products is in the hands of export-oriented firms that manage the backward and forward linkages in the supply chain (Kaytaz 1994:150).

In summary, the industry has been characterised by the increasing subdivision of the production process, a high number of informal and unregistered workplaces and workers, and seasonal and fashion-related fluctuations in demand (Ansal 1995; Eraydın and Erendil 1999). My approach in analysing the production and labour relations of the garment industry in Istanbul is to locate it within global commodity chains (GCCs), through which the industry's different patterns of production and labour requirements are shaped in relation to its place in global commodity networks and trade channels. In this regard, three distinct forms of firms exist in Istanbul, producing for domestic markets, European-market-oriented exports, and the informal international trade between Turkey and the former Soviet Union done through Laleli market in Istanbul. The distinctiveness of Istanbul's garment industry and its place in the global garment markets provide an opportunity for grounding debates about supply chains in geographical specificity, by looking at local trends in both industry and labour.

4.2 Istanbul's Garment Firms

Istanbul is the centre of industrial production and commerce as well as being the centre of international economic activities in Turkey (Aksoy 1996; Sönmez 1996). The garment industry has played an important role in the industrialisation and market orientation of the Istanbul's economy. Characterised by the domination of small-scale firms geographically clustered in a number of areas in Istanbul and by the production of light products such as T-shirts and sweatshirts by simple and basic machinery, Istanbul's garment firms accounted for more than 72 per cent of total garment exports[1] in 2002 (Fair Wear Foundation 2004). The data provided by the Association of Istanbul's Textile and Garment Exporters in 2001 covering 4,000 firms specialising woven and knitted garments, employing around 80,000 people, is the only source of information on Istanbul's garment firms[2].

Even though the industry's export performance has attracted foreign trade companies, and exporter associations (Eraydın 1993) small- and medium-size companies compose 80 per cent of all firms. Clustering in and around a couple of residential areas in Istanbul is the main characteristic of the geographical distribution of firms. The *gecekondu* neighbourhoods where migrant families live are the prime locations of small-scale garment ateliers because of easy access to the pool of abundant labour and cheap business premises. With more than 35 per cent of total firms, the constituency of Bakırköy, which hosts the highly populated neighbourhoods of Merter, Güngören, Şirinevler and Yenibosna, is the centre of garment production. Other districts such as Küçükçekmece, Bayrampaşa, Gaziosmanpaşa and Zeytinburnu are close neighbours of the core area, where the mostly small-scale ateliers working as subcontractors are located. Another main activity area is Şişli, where fancy garment shops serve the demand from domestic consumers, whereas Bakırköy and its periphery are more focused on export-oriented production.

Diverse and changing products are manufactured by firms, the majority of which make products such as T-shirts and sweatshirts, called 'light products', produced by simple and basic machinery (Eraydın and Erendil 1999). Once machines adequate for producing T-shirts are set up, the same firm can easily produce a wide range of products and switch between different products, determined by the degree of the firm's capacity and the flexibility of their machinery. The physical capacity of machine set-up can affect production, but subcontracting is a way of overcoming capacity limitations. Although some suppliers are large and well integrated, all make extensive use of subcontracting. Subcontracting of some parts of production such as weaving, dyeing, printing and embroidery to sewing, improves flexibility and helps firms to avoid the costs such as taxes and social security payments.

Faced with intensive international competition, Istanbul's garment firms tapped into the resources available in the informal sector, which are atelier production and female labour. In order to be as competitive as possible, manufacturers cut costs and increase their flexibility by decreasing the number of core or regular workforce and passing work on to smaller producers and home-based workers. For these reasons much of the expansion in women's employment has been in the informal sector, where regulation of working conditions is very limited (Atauz and Atauz 1992).

Globalisation and the growth of the industry through international trade channels have increased employment opportunities for women living in urban areas. Eraydın and Erendil (1999) examined the role of female labour in the industrial restructuring of Istanbul's clothing production, where they place an emphasis on the competitive conditions of the industry that are dependent on flexibility in labour supply and the flexible structure of production, achieved through high rates of labour turnover and the use of the temporary labour of women (1999:262). The extensive employment opportunities provided through the availability of atelier and home-based work attract numerous women into garment work, in which women make up 40 per cent of the total workforce. It is the only industry in Turkey with such a high number of women workers (Eraydın and Erendil 1999).

4.3 Garment Production and Subcontracting Relations in Istanbul

The expansion of global production networks in the garment industry over the past two decades is associated with the market-driven needs of large-scale retailers, and 'buyer-driven chains' organise the manufacturing of their products through global sourcing linkages (Gereffi 1994; Palpacuer and Parisotto 1998). As economies of scale are replaced by a 'unique combination of high-value research, design, sales, marketing and financial services' (Gereffi 1994:99), the garment industry is becoming more 'vertically disintegrated' through the intensification of subcontracting activities (Appelbaum and Christerson 1997). As a result, multinational firms subcontract to local firms, which subcontract to middlemen, who further subcontract to petty commodity producers and home workers (Delahanty 1999). The increased need for flexibilisation in the workforce and the use of informal workers in the industry has resulted in reduced fixed labour costs through a shift from direct to indirect forms of employment (Palpacuer 2002).

Subcontracting is a basic production relation between two firms and plays a significant role in garment production. Piore (1990) identified two main types of production units: sweatshop production and mass production. Sweatshop production involves minimum capital investment, and workers are paid by units of output such as piece-rate and deprived of a minimum wage and basic health and safety standards, whereas mass production involves capital investment and units of capital that are specialised for certain types of production, with workers being paid a minimum hourly wage and enjoying basic health and safety standards. In Piore's analysis, the importance and potential of flexible specialisation as a form of industrial organisation is centred on small and medium-sized enterprises that are clustered in and around industrial districts (Piore 1990).

In garment production, mass production is only one type of business strategy, and sweatshop and home-based production act as complementary stages of subcontracting chains in the whole production line (Appelbaum and

Christerson 1997). Therefore, rather than being two competing strategies of business and production, mass and sweatshop production complement each other, even though a great contrast exists between mass and sweatshop production in terms of market access, power and competitiveness, as smaller and more informal businesses have less access to resources and markets with less decision-making power over production relations.

The garment industry in Istanbul is a classic example of decentralised production networks where the administrative centres of TNCs and international brand names play a leading role in different segments of commodity chains. However, the distinctiveness of garment production in Istanbul is that production for TNCs and international brands has a partial effect on the industry's structure and production processes, but the domestic market and informal international trade mediated through the Laleli market in Istanbul also has a significant role in shaping the structure of industrialisation and labour requirements.

My fieldwork included 25 garment firms, five of which were large-scale garment factories with one firm acting as a national representative of international brand names. The remaining 19 were garment ateliers. Three corporate textile and garment factories produced for the domestic markets, while the two remaining large-scale factories were mass producers of standardised ready-made clothes for export. Eight of the ateliers specialised in producing for designers and brand-name products, whereas the remaining eight ateliers were the producers of standard garment products such as T-shirts and sweatshirts. The last group of three ateliers worked especially for Laleli market. The following is an in-depth analysis of these three distinct production units of Istanbul's garment industry.

4.3.1 Factory Production

Domestic market, mass export-oriented production and national branches of international brand names are the main types of factory production in Istanbul, which takes place in formally organised companies employing more than 100 workers. Although size is an inaccurate criterion for describing a company's scale, because some ateliers may also employ over 100 workers, the main features of a large-scale firm are being an independent producer able to establish forward and backward linkages with subcontractors, and showing managerial activities to organise production and marketing and the legitimate regulation of labour relations.

The first factory type is formal and large-scale corporate firms built during the import substitution period in which national industries were supported and protected through trade regimes and subsidy systems. The best-known names are *Vakko, Altınyıldız* and *Bossa*, producing for up-market domestic consumption. Having a prestigious brand name and targeting upper-class customers secured their viability after the abolition of protectionist policies. They managed to compete in quality and price with foreign brands, and enforced their brand-identity through advertisements. For example, *Altınyıldız* is a textile factory mainly producing fabrics for suits and jackets. Recently, the company generated a chain of shops with a brand name, called *NetWork*, which produces designer clothes, and the brand is presented as the equivalent of Armani in Turkey. In these factories, the organisation of production is an integrated one in which the factory undertakes all the stages of production from yarn to garment, and manages most of the production under the same roof. All forms of activities including recruitment are formally operated within the regulations and requirements of state legislation. Their subcontracting relations are, therefore, restricted to certain kinds of activities that must occasionally be performed outside the production complex.

The production line of the second category of garment factories such as *LCW* and *Delta Moda A.S.* is geared towards West European and North American markets and extensively subcontracts some parts of production to smaller ateliers. At the same time, these firms are massive producers and exporters of standardised products such as T-shirts and sweatshirts. Labour-intensive parts of production such as sewing and finishing are usually subcontracted to small ateliers, especially during times of high demand from European and US retail companies in order to overcome and supplement the limited production. Most garment ateliers in Istanbul work as subcontractors for these kinds of factories.

Table 1
Factory Production and Subcontracting Relations in Istanbul's Garment Firms

	Domestic Market Production	Mass Export-Oriented Production	National Representative of International Brand-names
Characteristics of Production	Up-market domestic consumption	Mass production of standardised commodities	Every stage of production subcontracted
	Limited use of subcontracting	Large number of employees Extensive use of subcontractor ateliers	Design and modelling dictated from foreign headquarters (Gereffi's Global Commodity Chains Model)
	Large-scale textile corporations	Export to Europe and USA	
	Mostly owned by national capital	Heavy control of production processes	
		Some parts of design and modelling kept in the company	
Subcontracting Relations	Subcontracting of specialised parts of production	Capacity-oriented subcontracting to ateliers Subcontracting of labour intensive parts of production.	Subcontracting of all stages of production

The third group is the national representatives of 'global buyers'. In clothing, many leading brand name companies are not involved in production themselves; instead they concentrate on design and marketing and subcontract production to their national representatives. Their strength as global buyers enables them to dominate the other stages of production through which labour, production, and distribution processes are connected together globally (Humphery and Schmitz 2000). Such global networks also link households and enterprises spread across several countries to one another within the world economy, and in Istanbul the focal force of such linkages is the garment atelier, whose role in the subcontracting chain is to support these large factories in meeting orders from European and American markets.

4.3.2 Garment Ateliers

The number of garment ateliers has recorded a phenomenal increase in Istanbul since the 1980s, most vividly observable in *gecekondu* neighbourhoods where abundant cheap migrant labour is available. For this labour source, ateliers are not only a rich source of employment but also open up an opportunity window for some to own their own businesses. As discussed in the following pages, family ownership is a noticeable feature of these ateliers, supported by family labour and initial capital pooled through familial solidarity networks.

Garment ateliers manufacture garments for export shaped by the demands of European and American fashion brand names. The most common type of ateliers specialise only in the sewing and trimming of the finished parts of standardised products such as T-shirts and sweatshirts, while some produce high quality brand-name products requiring highly skilled labour and expertise in a certain aspect of production, such as embroidery, lace making, needlework, or stitching. The third category of ateliers produces for Laleli market.

The ateliers working as subcontractors of highly specialised goods that require high labour skills, such as shirts, women's wear and men's suits, are usually owned by those who are former garment workers with long years of working experience. This is the only way to meet the quality and design specifications demanded by export firms. These specific ateliers are identified by having longer subcontracting relations with their principal firms and employing highly skilled labour whose training takes many years. Although the subcontracting relations between large-scale firms and ateliers are usually short-lived and volatile in Istanbul, this type of ateliers has been reported to work for the same clients for more than 11 years.

For ateliers undertaking the production of the labour-intensive stages of standardised garments, such as cutting, sewing, ironing, packaging and embroidery of finished garments, subcontracting patterns are mainly based on short-term agreements. Most of my informants reported that their working contracts with a specific firm do not last more than three years due to the intensity of competition from newcomers offering cheaper prices to principal firms for similar tasks.

An asymmetry between large and small-scale firms governs subcontracting relations where small firms do not have control over the production process or power over the decision-making process (Taylor and Thrift 1982; Beneria and Roldan 1987). The findings in Istanbul show that large-scale producers are independent agents of garment production, while ateliers are more dependent on orders coming from these large or international companies. Although the orders usually passed from big firms to ateliers, horizontal subcontracting relations between ateliers are practised if different specialisations and skills are needed. For example, garment ateliers producing designer or brand name products can subcontract to ateliers doing mainly ironing, packaging and finishing of garments, or to those ateliers acting as distributors of piecework.

In Eraydın and Erendil's work, the most common way of forming subcontracting relations for an atelier is to establish a reputation in the market. In the case of standardised products, principal firms are usually eager to make deals with new firms, which offer cheaper piece rates (1998:142). Weak connections between principal and subcontractor firms are the result of the very volatile and flexible nature of the garment business. Bad quality of work, timing and price factors are some of the reasons why principal firms change their subcontractors.

My research findings suggest that the ways in which small-scale garment ateliers contact principal firms vary in each case and change over time. Most ateliers began their business with a few sewing machines and a small initial

Table 2
Types of Garment Ateliers in Istanbul

Ateliers working for brand-name export	Ateliers working for standard exported garments	The Laleli Market
Specialised, quality-oriented products	Production of standardised and simple products (t-shirt, sweatshirt)	Lower quality than exported products
Skilled labour		
	Fast shift between different subcontractor firms	More diversified products range
Dependence on orders from a number of large-scale factories		Intensification of family and kinship relations
		Greater extent of informalisation

capital that was provided either by the principal firm or by the owner's ex-employer. In some cases, ex-employers encouraged their workers to establish their own businesses and work as their subcontractor atelier. In one case, an atelier owner who had been in the business for some years and worked for American firms such as Nike and Adidas supported his girlfriend in opening an atelier just to work for orders coming from his own atelier.

Even if in the early years of their businesses subcontractor ateliers work only for their former bosses, they quickly adapt to the garment business and find their own jobs in the market. Gaining fresh orders is not a difficult task, as a respondent reported that he called up firms on a long list of firms specialising in men's wear whenever his atelier was out of work to ask whether he could get any work. Despite the high turnover rates the garment business is a small one and everyone knows everyone. New ateliers operated by ex-garment workers are always welcomed, and are seen as a potential source for decreasing prices in the market.

4.3.3 Extra-global Commodity Circuits: Shuttle Trade in Laleli

The ateliers manufacturing garments for Laleli market are indistinguishable from those described below except where their products are sold. In the local business jargon, this production is called 'domestic production', but actually it is tightly connected to the 'informal' export market operating in Laleli, which is a neighbourhood in Istanbul serving consumers coming from Eastern Europe and the former Soviet Union. Called the 'shuttle' or 'suitcase trade', this has created a vibrant market in Laleli for 'tourists' coming to shop and shop owners selling consumer products. Laleli is an important node in the shuttle trade, specialising in the manufacturing and wholesale of apparel and other consumer goods. Thousands of stores selling garments and leatherwear to shuttle traders mushroomed in the neighbourhood during the 1990s, once freedom of travel was introduced in the ex-Soviet Union. Although there are no official records of the total amount of shuttle trade, it is estimated that it might be equal to the total of official exports, around 30 million US dollars. This channel of foreign trade has generated massive marketing opportunities for many garment firms, because the shuttle trade has mainly focused on the trans-national trade in clothes and other kinds of consumer goods.

Garment production for Laleli market is mostly informal and is dominated by small-scale and family-owned ateliers operating in *gecekondu* areas. The commodities produced are either sold directly to foreign customers, who come mainly from Romania, Russia, and Poland, or are exported through informal channels to Eastern Europe and Russia. These informal channels are crucial for collecting together exportable commodities from many small-scale producers and transporting them to foreign markets. Otherwise, these products would not be exported, since individual ateliers produce less than is feasible for export purposes.

Producing for the domestic 'informal' export market is well known among atelier owners, because the product quality is recognised to be lower than for the export goods market. This business is conducted totally informally with a larger scope for evading rules and regulations. Principal firms working for export markets require atelier owners to invoice their services so these exporter firms can benefit from export promotions and government tax exemption. This exposes ateliers to higher taxes and forces them to record their business transactions accurately. Many atelier owners told me that producing for Laleli is rather a good business because of the possibility of avoiding high rates of tax. The tax burden on small-scale industrialists is often criticised as being very high and is noted as one of the important obstacles that block the development of small-scale industries in Turkey (Taymaz 1997). Taymaz also claims that the tendency towards the informalisation of small-scale industry is intensified by this heavy tax burden, since firms try to keep their activities off the record. In the case of ateliers working for the Laleli market, the advantage of being less subject to tax regulations due to their independence and totally informal operations helps to keep production costs lower.

The informal nature of the Laleli garment business is supported by the existence of informal business networks organised around kinship and *hemşehrilik*. My informants claimed that the Laleli market is dominated by people originating from Malatya, Adıyaman, and Adana, and people with the same place of origin are more likely to stay in the business than those who are not. Kurdish migration has been the other significant movement of people to Laleli. Kurds, forced to leave their homes in the southeast since the late 1980s, make up the largest group of entrepreneurs and workers in Laleli[3]. The more resourceful and those who had start-up capital have opened wholesale apparel, leather and footwear stores to supply the shuttle trade. Poorer migrants meanwhile have become porters or workers in hotels and restaurants. It is not possible to estimate the number of Kurdish entrepreneurs in Laleli. Nevertheless, bankers, landlords and municipal officials who have observed the development of the market from the beginning said that at least two-thirds of the storeowners were from the southeast of Turkey (Yükseker 2003). These networks not only provide a ghettoisation of garment production in the Laleli market, but also increase the intensification of capital accumulation in a small group of people.

Relations of reciprocity, mutual support and solidarity based on kinship and familial relations are exploited and manipulated for purposes of competition in the market and to produce cheaper products.

The garment industry in Istanbul is a very dynamic sector and is shaped by very diverse influences ranging from macro-economic policies to international demand factors. Its integration into world markets has been achieved through formal and informal channels, as seen in the case of Laleli. However, the informality here not only refers to the international trading practices of Laleli market, but can also refer to the status of labour, the conditions of work, and the form of management of ateliers, as will be shown in the two case studies below.

4.4 Surviving through Informality:
Informalisation of Garment Ateliers

In his study of informality in Latin America, De Soto suggests that informality concerns more than employment and production and is almost a way of life for the poor in Latin America. Because migrants to urban areas were uneducated and unqualified for most employment and had few resources and opportunities, they devised extralegal means to fulfil basic needs. 'If they were to live, trade, manufacture, transport, or even consume, the cities' new inhabitants had to do so illegally' (De Soto 1989:11-12). One encounters the informality when wandering through a garment atelier in Istanbul where young boys and girls are crammed into tiny workshops that ignore labour regulations, the tax authorities and licensing requirements.

In Istanbul, informalisation is an integral and significant part of the garment production, and it has a relatively hidden, illicit, and under-reported character. These practices take many shapes, such as evasions of tax, health and safety, and social security. Especially small ateliers keep themselves officially unrecorded and therefore all of their activities stay informal and unrecorded. Atelier owners often reported that after registering the atelier's activities to a government office, they terminate the registration by declaring the closing-down of the business, which allows them to refrain from paying taxes. Then after a few months they register the atelier under another name as a new business, in order to be eligible for tax exemption. For example, two partners running a garment atelier officially registered one partner's name as the atelier owner. After a year or two, they closed down the firm and registered a new garment atelier in the name of the other partner. Another form of evasion is the way in which garment firms record their activities. Firms usually try to reduce their tax burden by under-reporting their price or volume of work. For example, in order to reduce their VAT and income tax, firms record the price of a garment as $5 instead of $10.

The avoidance of the regulatory framework for business is mostly practised in tax evasion and labour regulations. Most garment workers work without the social security coverage that provides access to health services for workers themselves and their families and pensions. The provisions of the Turkish Social Security Law require that every worker must be registered with the Institution of Social Insurance after a one-month trial period. However, only a very small portion of atelier workers were registered workers. Some atelier owners said that they could only afford to pay the national insurance contributions of their own family members working in their atelier. Many strategies are applied by atelier owners to overcome the inspection of tax officers and to hide their unregistered workers. In case of a tax inspection, workers are advised to say that they have been newly hired and are still doing their first month's trial. Workers are also hidden or sent out of the atelier during inspections.

In each atelier I visited a new story about how tax inspections were avoided was told. The most interesting one was in a two-floored atelier with one floor in the basement and the other on the ground floor. During inspections all unregistered workers were kept in the basement, which was locked and hidden from public view. The owner only showed his ground floor as the shop floor. Keeping away from the scrutiny of bureaucratic institutions was the reason why ateliers are operated in the basement of newly built apartment buildings, where windows—if there are any windows—are covered with thick paper or painted to hide the business and its workers from public view and bureaucratic inspection.

The intention behind locating garment ateliers in the basement and *gecekondu* neighbourhoods is not solely to escape from official inspections but also to take advantage of the cheap rents and labour in the area. All these factors lead to the informalisation and utilisation of cheap labour, and have actually helped the industry to be competitive in the international market. As competitiveness is achieved through the flexibility of labour and production relations, garment ateliers quickly spread into every corner of Istanbul to reach untapped and emerging resources of capital and labour. This is the development of the garment industry in Istanbul depicted by one of my atelier owner informants:

In the early 1980s, there were just a few places you could work as a *konfeksiyon* (ready-to-wear) worker. It was a very prestigious job. I remember that my father had asked a favour of his friend to get me my first job in a woman's outwear company. We worked from 9 to 5 and it took me a long time to be a skilled worker. Now, everywhere is full of ateliers and everyone is a *konfeksiyon* worker. If I had not had my working experience and the skills I gained in that factory I would not have dared to have my own business.

The informality of the garment industry presented here is not just a way of survival for the urban poor but also a way for the garment industry to be a globally competitive industry, providing ateliers with the ability to cope with and manipulate the formal rules, and to tap into cheap labour resources. The following two case studies of family-owned ateliers show how these ateliers are owned, operated and staffed by relatives, and are self-identified as family concerns. These ateliers are also a passage for the contribution of women to garment production, and provide employment for family members, increase and maintain control over family resources, and enhance the political and economic status and power of a family in a community.

4.5 Family-owned Garment Ateliers: Two Case Studies

The cases of the Timagur family and the Acar brothers examined through a methodology of participant/observation situated in households and workplaces revealed many of the economic activities of men and women and the day-to-day strategies of running a family establishment. The socioeconomic position of the two families is similar to each other as both are migrant families. Although they are not the poorest of the poor it is difficult to label them as middle-class families. Limited financial security and constant fluctuations in the business do not allow the families upward social mobility, as incomes are invested back into business rather than used to raise the consumption or living standards of family members.

Two commodity circuits dominating garment production in Istanbul are illustrated using these case studies, as the first family, the Timagur family's atelier, specialised in export production and manufactures men's trousers, women's skirts and suits, while the Acar brothers owned an atelier producing light garments for their shop in Laleli. The case studies are also significant in considering women's involvement in garment production. Not only as workers but also as family members, women play a pivotal role in the survival of these ateliers and the integration of their families into urban life.

4.5.1 The Timagur Family

The Timagur family resides in Gaziosmanpaşa, an area with many garment ateliers. They live in a three-floor building owned by the father, Hüseyin, who came to Istanbul from Bayburt, an eastern province, in the mid-1960s.

He was and continues to be a construction worker, and Hüseyin built the house where the family now lives. There are many relatives and others from Bayburt who now live in Gaziosmanpaşa. Hüseyin and his wife, Nazire, have three sons and two daughters. Only the youngest son is single; the others are married and have children. The eldest brother, İsmail, and his younger brother, Yaşar, live in the three-floor house built by their father, each having a separate flat. The daughters are married and have moved out of the house. The third brother, Ali, is single and lives with his parents.

After gaining experience and garment-making skills in different ateliers in Istanbul, İsmail decided to open a small atelier in his neighbourhood, where the rents and labour prices were cheaper than in the neighbourhood where İsmail used to work. İsmail told me that as Istanbul received migrants and expanded toward its outskirts, garment ateliers and factories also began to move to the city's edges. The old centre of the garment business, which now hosts marketplaces such as Laleli or shopping centres and office buildings, is an expensive place for small garment ateliers. The atelier is located near the family house, allowing the family to easily carry garments from the atelier home and back again. Because the area is replete with the Timagurs' hemşehris and relatives, the family is also able to recruit workers from among their kin and neighbours when needed.

Now, all three brothers, Ayşe, who is Yaşar's wife, and İsmail's daughters all work together in the atelier, and all are skilled workers. Gül, İsmail's wife and the eldest bride of the family, contributes to production by doing trim work from home and by organizing family members to help out when there is a need for extra labour. Gül's mother-in-law usually looks after the family's young children while the wives are working.

The atelier mainly works on orders from export companies. İsmail's area of expertise, shirt sewing, is also the atelier's specialty, since this is the area where İsmail can have the most control over the production process. Quality is very important for export-oriented production, and İsmail stresses his workers' high skill levels. He emphasises that becoming a skilled worker in his business requires almost ten years of working experience. His younger daughter, Semra, has been working with him for almost 6 years and needed, according to İsmail, 3 or 4 years' more experience to be a top-skilled worker.

Initially, the atelier subcontracted with İsmail's previous employer's firm, which supported İsmail in establishing his own business. Later, İsmail got to know many other firms, from which his atelier could also get work orders when needed. He told me that:

If you are in the business long enough, you get to know all the firms. Subcontracting firms, which are those that give out work, have a good knowledge of small ateliers and are very well aware of who is good and who is bad at their work, although there are always new people entering this market (*piyasa*). In the beginning, these newcomers offer cheaper piece-rates, but you need skills to stay in the market. Working for cheap prices is not enough to survive here, that is why you have to have the required skills for the garment business.

The trajectory of İsmail's atelier has changed often, depending on the general conditions of the garment business in Istanbul, and he has adopted different strategies to keep his business running. For example, he has established partnerships with other small atelier owners, and has expanded his business by adding more partners from his former workplace. At other times, he worked only with his brothers and immediate family members. As a subcontractor, İsmail's position literally shifts from employer to employee, depending on the requirements of production and the size of his atelier. As an owner-operator, İsmail's changing position had an effect on his family members, whether they helped in the atelier or went out to work for a wage in different ateliers or stayed at home.

The Timagur family's business is based on their garment-making skills, which depend on İsmail's expertise and skills. Because of İsmail's status as owner of the atelier and head of the family, the labour and financial contributions of other members of the family are under his control. He supervises the other members, manages business deals, and does the marketing. The gains from the business are distributed according to the contributions made by each family. As İsmail is the family head and makes all the decisions, he and his family take the biggest share, on the condition that he is fair to all members in allocating the money. In our conversation, İsmail stated that each family—including his own—gets only a worker's salary, which he thinks is too low. Yet small-scale production does not allow for large profits. Therefore, it is possible to say that this form of work is 'disguised wage work' (Bromley 1988).

4.5.2 The Acar Brothers

The second family I studied lives in the same area of Gaziosmanpaşa as the Timagurs. Four brothers from Adıyaman, the Acars run a garment atelier located on the ground floor of their house. The house has four floors, each used by a brother and his family. The youngest and oldest brothers came to Istanbul 10 years ago, staying for a couple of years with their uncle's son, who was a garment worker at that time. Shortly after the youngest brother, Mehmet, started working with his uncle's son, the brothers bought their first sewing machine and began making coats and jackets for sale in Laleli market.

As they were successful with their sales they decided to open their own atelier. The other two Acar brothers came from Adıyaman shortly thereafter to take part in the business. All the brothers moved to a shared apartment in Gaziosmanpaşa, where they took advantage of being from the east of Turkey and tapping into the networks of labour and business deals. Since people from Adıyaman and Malatya dominate the Laleli market, the Acars were able to reach the informal business network and export channels just through the informal connections afforded by being from the same place of origin and ethnic group. After a short time, the eldest brother's wife joined them and migrated to Istanbul to do the cooking, cleaning and washing in their shared household. She also helped in the atelier. The Acar brothers' atelier grew rapidly, and now has 14 machines and 20 employees.

The brothers have a division of labour based on seniority and skill level, which also reflects the hierarchical structure of the family, in which the eldest brother and his wife are the most respected. The eldest brother is in a kind of managerial position, deciding on issues related to finance and the spending patterns of the family members. All of the brothers ask for the eldest brother's consent before making most decisions, from buying furniture for their home to making a business deal. Structured around hierarchical lines, the Acars survive better in the garment business than others because they are able to access obedient and cheap labourers who devote their time and energy to maintaining the family business. The Acar brothers also have very intimate relations with *hemşehri(s)* and other relatives, offering yet another way to access informal business channels.

The Acar family live on a single collective budget, rather than separate budgets for each brother. The reallocation of household finances follows hierarchical lines, where the eldest brother is in control and makes sure the income is equally allocated between the households. This type of budget management is quite uncommon for families in cities and is mostly used in rural areas, where families might only have access to cash once a year after harvest and so need to watch expenditure closely. For the Acars, this type of budget control limits the family's luxury consumption and returns income back into the business. The corporate nature of budget control and labour discipline gives the Acar brothers a competitive edge.

The Acar case is interesting because it demonstrates both the benefits and conflicts of an extended family business. The advantages include having access to a ready labour pool and providing an easy coordination of family support in times of crisis and need. However, these relationships also generate conflicts of interest among individual family members, especially those higher in the family hierarchy. For example, the power to control the business has been source of some conflict among the brothers. Ali is the youngest brother, and he recently married Nazire. He has been in charge of the atelier's production and labour relations. After he got married, he wanted to have a more solid means of income, something he could possess himself. During my last visit, Ali told me that the property rights of the Laleli shop had been transferred to his name, and he was quite happy about it. Family relations are not free from conflicts or power struggles. Rather, members are aware of the benefits of working and living together, but they also are interested in advancing their own interests, which may challenge the interests of the collective.

4.5.3 Mobilising Resources: Comparing the Two Families
The two families discussed here have similar social backgrounds, being low-income and migrant families. In establishing and running their businesses both similarly dwell on the resources brought by their families and immediate kin and are also heavily dependent upon female labour. For managing the ateliers, the Timagur family rely on their garment-producing skills for European markets while the Acar brothers depend on kin networks to maintain their business and to have easy access to domestic markets. Given these similarities and differences, the Timagurs and the Acar brothers have mobilised in unique ways the resources necessary to become and succeed as atelier owners, as discussed below.

Investing in an atelier, even one engaged in informal and small-scale activities, is generally based on the capacity of a household to invest an increasing part of its income and savings in productive activities. As Pahl (1984) points out, relatively high-income groups are more likely to generate income through informal activities than low-income groups, which tend to be more unstable and have fewer resources to invest in informal activities. Indeed, the families investigated here are not the poorest of the poor in Turkish society. They are from working-class backgrounds. These families managed to channel their savings into a garment atelier. However, owning a garment atelier does not significantly elevate their social status or catapult them into the middle or upper classes. Rather, it makes them a better-off segment in the working-class neighbourhoods of Istanbul. In other words, informal activities are open to the better-off segments of the urban poor, those who are able to achieve some savings through hard work and frugal existence.

In the Timagurs' case, they established their garment atelier by drawing on family savings. İsmail's father provided his sons with a house where they could live rent-free. By living with his parents for several years after getting married and having children, İsmail was able to invest in sewing machines and other materials needed for the atelier. Having extended family and *hemşehris* living nearby enabled İsmail to tap into reciprocal assistance networks whenever extra resources were needed. When they are in need of money, the Timagurs borrow from people who earlier had borrowed from them. The availability of mutual help and solidarity between family members and kin exists as long as the reciprocity is perpetuated by each party involved.

Gold jewellery in the possession of women is seen as a financial asset that can be cashed in at times of financial difficulty. For the initial capital of the atelier, İsmail's wife, Gül, contributed her own seven gold bracelets, which were bought for her as wedding gifts. By using her gold bracelets to support the business, Gül proved herself a good wife and mother by showing sacrifice for the well-being of the family. This lifted her relative power vis-à-vis other family members, in addition to her seniority as the eldest bride in the family. This has resulted in Gül being more involved in atelier decision making and having the right to observe her husband's business more closely than she otherwise would have done.

The Acar family tapped into rural resources to generate the initial capital necessary to start up their atelier. First, they sold land their father owned in order to buy their first sewing machines. Second, they cut expenses on food consumption and other items by not buying luxury goods and by having foodstuffs sent from Adıyaman. For the Acars and many other urban families, material connections with rural areas are still of significant importance. Strong extended family structures can also be important resources, which can be utilised for business purposes. To do so, an individual (or family) has to be known to the community as reliable and trustworthy, important social capital in urban Turkey. In return, then, the community benefits by having a socially successful individual, who is able to provide—through job opportunities and financial credit in times of need—many externalities.

In the Acar family, the survival and success of the family is closely linked to the strict control of spending by family members. The tendency of urban families to increase consumption and use more luxury goods is eliminated by the Acars' collective budgeting. Household spending is planned very carefully, and shopping is done for all four families on a periodic basis. The eldest brother decides the family's individual and collective needs and each wife receives a small weekly allowance (*pazar parası*) to buy fresh vegetables for cooking; the amount given is calculated according to how many children the wife has. The eldest brother also pays all other expenses for the family, such as bills, schooling expenses of the children, and furniture, though these expenses are kept to a minimum.

When the youngest brother was getting married, the family bought everything necessary to set up his household, from refrigerator to television. The provision of all the items his home needed also set a limit for its level of consumption. After the marriage, his wife got 20 million Turkish lira[4] a week to buy fresh vegetables for the week's meals. The wife said that the other brides advised her to save some money for the future; since she did not yet have any children, she would not need to spend that much. In Turkey married women, especially if they are not engaged in wage labour, have limited access to cash called 'money for bazaar' (*pazar parası*), which is given to women to spend in the neighbourhood bazaars held once a week, and is provided by their husbands for foodstuffs and children's expenses. If women want to have their own money, they need to save it from their weekly allowance, which is usually allocated for household goods or for their children's needs.

Skill is the second component necessary for becoming an atelier owner. When families do not themselves have the necessary job skills or experience, they draw on the expertise of extended kin. In the early years of their business, the Acar brothers were able to learn from their uncle's son, a skilled worker who taught them sewing and how to make business deals with other firms. İsmail also had a skilled brother, Yaşar, who had begun atelier work after leaving primary school. By the time they decided to open a garment atelier, Yaşar was a highly skilled garment worker and became a helping hand to İsmail in dealing with the business.

Due to the fluid and fluctuating nature of incoming orders, shifting production deadlines and constantly changing labour requirements, ateliers depend upon a pool of reserve labour of family members and relatives. This core labour force[5] provides flexibility, allowing ateliers to easily draw labourers into and out of production. A reliable and loyal labour force willing to work long and unstable hours is vital to keeping the business running. This is why female members are so crucial to the garment atelier's success; women always have their homes and domestic responsibilities to look after when there is no atelier work.

Locating the business within a short distance from the home of the owner is vital to recruiting from among family, relatives and neighbours, and to staying in business. In one case, Osman, an ex-partner of İsmail, after moving his ateliers away from a neighbourhood where *hemşehri(s)* and close friends lived, had to close down his business. In the new neighbourhood, which was relatively better off, workers demanded higher salaries and his family members could not easily commute to the new place, resulting in the atelier's closure. However, such dynamics are not unique to Istanbul's garment industry and resemble case studies in Egypt (Meyer 1986; Singerman 1995). A large-scale survey of small manufacturing enterprises in Cairo, Egypt, found that slightly more than half of the labour force consisted of the owners, their immediate family members, and other kin. Moreover, immigrant owners were much more likely than those born in Cairo to employ members of their immediate family and other relatives (Meyer 1986). Immigrants, in general, appear to rely heavily on family and female labour in order to survive in a new environment.

4.5.4 Women's Labour in the Timagur and Acar Ateliers
As discussed above, in garment ateliers labour is acquired through informal channels of familial, kinship and neighbourhood relations. The importance of female labour for the maintenance and survival of businesses is not only due to the fact that women are easily available, flexible, and a cheap source of labour, but also because their labour presents an articulation of the social relations on which business success depends. Acquiring women's presence in these ateliers signals to society that their workplace is a secure family environment for women to work in.

In the Timagur family's case, Yaşar's wife, Ayşe, is a full-time skilled garment worker; Yaşar's mother looks after Ayşe's young children. İsmail's two daughters, Semra and Canan, work full time at the atelier, though his wife, Gül, does not. However, Gül is quite engaged in matters related to the business. Her status as the eldest bride, as well as the sacrifice of her gold wedding bracelets, invests Gül with more authority in the atelier's functioning, despite the superior garment-making skills of her daughters. Her roles in the atelier include allocating her daughters to different jobs and managing the labour of other family members.

Gül is also burdened with trimming and cleaning garments at home, and to finding and organizing her neighbours and relatives to trim garments, ensuring the work is completed on time. As such, Gül not only contributes to the garment business through her own home-based work, but also secures help when necessary from women relatives or neighbours for home-based piecework. Gül has also drawn on her own family resources to provide financial support when the business was in financial difficulty.

Gül's case is a good example of what Sharma (1986) calls 'household service work', in which domestic tasks extend beyond meeting the physical needs of household members to providing and maintaining particular ties with kin, neighbours, and friends, who are a source of information and aid. By combining her household work with actual atelier production and with organisation of that production, Gül plays a vital role in connecting the arenas of production and reproduction. Yet the Timagur family, and Gül herself, consider her to be just a housewife.

The example of Gül and her daughters highlights the ways in which women's bargaining power and social identities impact on how they participate in garment production, with daughters' and mothers' perceived contributions differing according to their relative positions in the family. So, while Gül's contributions to the atelier are not considered 'work,' she still has authority in the workplace because of her seniority and status. Semra, on the other hand, does 'work,' but she has marginal power. In this context, women's invisibility in productive work comes through the social values assigned to women's roles in the family, their marital status, and their status in the family hierarchy. Interestingly, the greater a woman's relative social status, the less her 'work' in the atelier is socially visible.

In the case of the Acar women, household duties and child-care are the primary responsibilities. Each of the wives occupies a strategic position mediating relations between the brothers, who must maintain close relations at home, as well as in the atelier, by transmitting domestic information and the private concerns of individual households. Although the women of the family are strictly confined to the domestic sphere and their behaviour is watched and controlled by other members of the family, all the women have garment-making skills.

Besides having weekly routines and work schedules, such as going to the bazaar once a week, they also participate in atelier production, by trimming garments, cleaning the atelier, or sewing at the machines. A wife's involvement in production varies according to how many children she has and her prior experience with garment work. The wife of the eldest brother works regularly in the atelier while the two younger brides—who have experience working in garment ateliers—are called to participate if extra 'help' is needed. These two women do not see themselves as atelier workers and do not acknowledge their work as contributing to the business, nor do they think of it as 'real work.' As the wives of the atelier owners, they are just helping their husbands. Likewise, the women's contributions to many aspects of production remain unrecognised by the family and themselves.

For example, the youngest bride, Nazire, is the most experienced worker among the female family members, having worked for more than seven years at her husband's atelier. After she married, Nazire was not supposed to work at all. Yet, whenever I met with the family, Nazire was at the atelier. Even after having her first baby, Nazire left her son with her mother to go and work in the atelier. However, none of the family members consider Nazire to be a garment worker, and not simply because she is not paid for her work. Rather, it is because she is married and has a child; she just happens to be helping her husband from time to time. It is not only society or their families that fail to see women's contributions to atelier production. Women's unpaid family work—masked by their roles as mothers and wives—is unrecognised by the women themselves.

4.5.5 Accounting for Gender in Garment Production

Family enterprises are characterised by a labour hierarchy. Positions within the family translate into working identities both for men and women, and family members usually participate in the family business by offering services that directly or indirectly contribute to the success of the family business. In return, some are unpaid family workers while others receive payments for their contributions. Women's contributions encompassed within their domestic roles and identities usually remain unpaid, invisible and unrecognised by the family and community.

Garment ateliers can generate 'gender-appropriate' jobs for women in the local community. This is especially beneficial for young girls. Because ateliers are located in their neighbourhoods and are owned by a neighbour or relative, unmarried girls commonly start their first jobs in a garment atelier. Families' opposition to a daughter's employment is eliminated through strict surveillance and control of girls in the ateliers. Before sending the girls to work, families make sure that their daughters will be strictly watched by the managers or owners of the ateliers. Girls are warned in advance that any improper behaviour will be reported to their parents. Consequently, employment outside the home shifts the control of family honour to those families operating garment businesses. Through these first jobs, families become accustomed to the idea that their daughters bring a substantial income to family budgets. Thereafter these girls keep working in other companies and in different types of jobs.

For married women atelier jobs have a different trajectory from those of young girls, as their labour is more often closely tied to household needs and family business cycles. If a family business closes down women go back to their homes and children, or if the business expands through partnerships with other ateliers and increases the number of non-family employees, the married women are excluded from the work and stay home. These shifts in ownership generate a separation between household and workplace, leading to the exclusion of married women from the workplace. As such, these partnerships draw attention to the line between the public and private sphere activities of women in Turkish society. As long as the workplace is conceptualised as an extension of the household, and as long as family members outnumber unrelated workers, the atelier is safe and secure for women to go and work there. Although a workplace is generally considered a public domain, its occupation by family members and relatives creates the illusion of a private sphere, freeing women to operate there as if it were a private domain.

For women, working in a family-owned atelier perpetuates the existing gender and social relations based on kinship. The intimate connections with kin and friends working at the same place are maintained outside the home. In every interview, my women informants emphatically expressed that a family or friend connection had helped them to get their current jobs, suggesting that women's entry into the labour market is constrained to the places where they have acquaintances. Moreover, women always feel obligated to those who have given them job opportunities, and to keeping those relational ties going. The sense of obligation and respect compelling them to work hard and show dedication to their employers creates a form of work ethic and commitment to the workplace, as if it were their own home. As a result, women sometimes find it difficult to change jobs, even when they have better opportunities elsewhere. White (1994:47) calls these social relations based on reciprocity and trustworthiness the 'power of debt,' which allows people to feel obligated to one another in return for a favour, such as offering a job or lending money.

In sum, the increasing number of garment ateliers has generated new employment opportunities for women, who comprise a pool of readily available, cheap and poorly organised labour crucial for firms to remain competitive in the market. As mentioned, women participate in production directly, either by engaging in full-time work at ateliers or by doing piecework from home. However, women also contribute to production indirectly by maintaining social ties with kin and neighbours.

Conclusion

Turkey has been one of the leading exporters of garment products. The industry has played an important role in economic growth, industrialisation and employment generation in Turkey. The high numbers of unregistered operations and informal workers is the main characteristic that allows the industry to be globally competitive and to remain flexible in its operations. This globally strong industry is supported by the extremely low-paid labour of women and children, whose work, under certain conditions, is unpaid or generally underpaid.

In Istanbul's garment industry, production for Western markets, domestic markets and the informal international trade has a significant role in shaping the structure of the industry, subcontracting relations and labour requirements. Besides fully export-oriented firms, on the one hand we see large-scale corporate firms manufacturing for domestic market consumption and offering formal employment opportunities for many, while on the other hand we see family ateliers working within chains of subcontractors for export and ateliers producing for the informal Laleli bazaar. The presence of these different market destinations shows that global industrial production cannot only be analysed in terms of production regimes created by companies working for European or western markets, but also that extra-global commodity circuits are a part of global industrial production in Istanbul.

Running a family atelier in Istanbul requires access to a rich pool of immediate family labour, as well as other kinship and *hemşehri* relations. By providing flexibility in production, these social ties enable firms to survive volatile and uncertain market conditions. While perpetuating social relations and networks based on mutuality, solidarity and trust, firm owners exploit their own and their family's labour and resources in order to be competitive. In this context, female labour is essential to atelier production, not only because it is cheap and flexible, but also because it mediates social relations in establishing ties of reciprocity and obligations among community members.

Employment opportunities for women in small-scale firms are diverse. They offer some women a degree of independence and increased bargaining power at home. Young girls, even though restricted, are sometimes able to move to better paying jobs. In contrast, the contributions of married and unpaid family labour are often 'invisible,' masked by their socially approved roles as dedicated wives and mothers. Since both women and their communities consider their participation as 'help' and render it invisible, being an unpaid family labourer provides only a limited degree of empowerment. Yet, while their productive activities may go unrecognised, their dedication as wives and mothers is socially rewarded by approval of them as 'good women' rather than workers. Moreover, by opting to improve their bargaining positions by perpetuating these primary roles as mothers and wives, women maintain and strengthen strong business and family relations. In the end, these activities can increase decision-making power in both the home and the workplace, as the case of Gül illustrates.

5

WOMEN WORKERS IN ISTANBUL
Factory Women, Atelier Girls and Pieceworker Housewives

I have been a factory worker for 15 years. In the early years, women rarely took factory work or any kind of paid work. After my husband and I got married we migrated to Istanbul. He had no work during the first couple months after we arrived. Then, he found a job in a factory. However, the money was so little and we had nothing to live on. Even the clothes we were wearing belonged to other people. Then, I decided to take up a job in a factory which was located near where we lived... We were village people and it was strange for us that a woman goes to work like a man... My husband always felt embarrassed by the fact that his wife was a factory woman. He used to keep it secret from his family and friends. In those days, it was not appropriate for women to go and work in factories. These days are different, everybody is in need of more money and days are harder. Now, it is not improper for a girl or woman to be a worker any more.

Sakime's story is a telling account indicating changing social perspectives on women's paid work. Although gradual, these changes have come hand in hand with increasing garment production in Istanbul. The socially constructed 'bad' image of factory women has been, to some extent, overcome by societal familiarisation with working women. Stereotypical portrayals of women exist not only in societies but also in the literature on women workers in the Third World. This image changes minimally across national contexts and industrial sectors. The female workforce is portrayed as homogenous: young, single, unskilled with rural backgrounds, a temporary workforce with little commitment to their wage-earning activities. These empirical generalisations and stereotypes ignore the diversity of backgrounds and uniqueness of women's responses to the realities of the environments in which they live.

The starting point for the research was to explain women's entry into the labour market in Istanbul, given the importance of the garment industry as a key source of employment for women in Istanbul. This chapter explores the lives and motivations of a sample of women working in Istanbul's garment industry in which the determining factors of women's labour supply provide the backdrop to the lives of these women workers. Exploration of the demographic characteristics and household structures of women who are engaged in three different work patterns, factory work, garment atelier work and home-based piecework, is an attempt to find out whether the differences and similarities in women's backgrounds and family lives have had any bearing on their different incorporations into the garment industry and the patterns of work they engaged in. The chapter takes up other important sociological contentions concerning low-income communities of Istanbul, household characteristics and women's domestic roles, as well as women's contribution to the household budget in the form of income-saving and handicraft activities that affect women's labour supply for garment production.

5.1 Istanbul's Low-Income *Gecekondu* Communities

'The city of rhythm' was the catchword in an advertisement used to attract tourists to Istanbul. The city is also an attractive destination for migrants coming from the countryside to find better living and working conditions. The immigrants inhabiting the *gecekondu* (squatter) neighbourhoods of Istanbul are obviously varied in terms of lifestyle, beliefs, and socio-economic positions, though all originally linked through similar social networks, yet nevertheless have significant similarities in the ways in which immigrant populations negotiate their adaptation to urban life in Istanbul.

Istanbul is the largest metropolitan city in Turkey, containing more than 10 million people. As the industrial, commercial and financial centre of Turkey, Istanbul is the city where the national income is most unequally distributed, and conspicuous wealth and consumerism coexist with severe poverty and deprivation; luxury apartment buildings and five star hotels are shoulder to shoulder with run-down structures and crumbling buildings (Aksoy 1996; Sönmez 1996; Keyder 2001). To absorb its growing immigrant population, Istanbul expanded its physical boundaries by pushing to the outskirts of the city. In Kıray's terms, this resembles the spread of a grease stain (*saçaklanma*) towards its limits (1999), resulting in the conversion of agricultural and public land into housing areas, which comprise the *gecekondu* areas of Istanbul. Originally regarded as satellite areas, these have now become an integral part of greater metropolitan Istanbul by establishing linkages, initially through public transport, and then by founding their own local municipalities.

The occupation of public land and the demands of immigrants for further dwellings have been among the important strategies that immigrants have adopted to survive in the city. As Işık and Pınarcıoğlu pointed out in their study of Sultanbeyli, a newly emerging constituency of Istanbul after the 1980s, the success of former immigrants in surviving is highly dependent on the number of new immigrants coming to settle in their locality and on their access to public land. In the authors' terms, 'rotating poverty' is the reliance of former immigrants on the rental income they drive from newcomers, in which they manage to transfer their poverty to the newcomers (Işık and Pınarcıoğlu 2001). However, this transfer of poverty not only takes place between former and new immigrants, but also involves more complicated forms of power relations that involve central and local governments, police forces and illicit mafia networks, which all have a stake in the process.

While the city attracted new migrants and the population continued to increase, land became scarcer. The occupation of public land to build *gecekondu*s has generated enormous amounts of rent for some groups. Therefore there emerged the *gecekondu* mafias, who illegally controlled the occupation of public land and sold it with high profit margins. Confrontations between police forces and *gecekondu* residents over the right to settle in the inhabited spaces have led to tragic scenes, reported in the daily news.

The occupation of land by the newcomers was considered an illegal act fit for the police to handle, but confrontations along the same lines quickly became daily events where the immigrants aimed to gain recognition and to secure minimal municipal services. This mode of struggle continued to be the principal means of articulating the demands of the new population, an established tactic with its own rules of conduct and expected outcomes. They involved all the heterogeneous strata sharing the same inhabited space (Erder 2001:163).

The highly heterogeneous cultural landscape of Istanbul is often referred as a mosaic of sub-cultures, reflecting the diverse lifestyles and values of the towns and villages from which migrants were drawn, as well as the lifestyles of the original city dwellers. Confrontations between different cultures and religious sects made sub-cultural and religious identities more salient, in ways related to the frame of migrants' places of origin. The Sunni Muslims, for example, developed ways of integrating Sunnis from different backgrounds by establishing a common religious identity and practices in the context of contrast with non-Sunnis such as Alevis. Religious schools (*Imam Hatipler*) and local mosques provided a medium in which the diffuse local practices of the Sunnis could be communicated and related to each other (Erder 1997). Ethnic, religious, and ideological differences in turn played their role in the history of the city as the instigators of urban antagonism and tension. The persistent inequalities existing between different groups and their access to public resources led to the development of social networks based on religion, local origin, and kin-based relations, helping to include some and exclude others. Thus, the *mallahe*s (neighbourhoods) of Istanbul are centres of pervasive conflicts and tensions between different groups, as well as places of solidarity, mutuality, and reciprocity.

Istanbul is divided into administrative units, which are locally represented as municipal constituencies. Over time, the expanding number of boroughs occupying new public land for newly arriving migrants to settle in the city has placed central and local governments under pressure to turn these new settlements into municipalities, resulting in the rapid expansion of Istanbul's new administrative units. Municipalities are also divided into *mahalle*s (neighbourhoods) and run by *muhtar*s (elected heads of neighbourhood). A *mahalle* may be considered as a cultural as well as an administrative unit. Particularly in the local settings of metropolitan areas and in small cities the *mahalle* is a source of identity, and *mahalleli* (neighbourhood resident) is a concept that defines people who live in the same quarter. The relationships between *mahalleli*s are based on norms and codes that show how people living in the same *mahalle* should behave towards each other (Ortaylı 1984; Erder 1996; Alada 1995).

This research took place in the numerous *mahalle*s located in the boroughs of Bakırköy, Zeytinburnu, Kağıthane and Gaziosmanpaşa. The historical trajectory of the settlement in a *mahalle* in Gaziosmanpaşa which I frequently visited began with the arrival of low-income migrants from other areas of the city and from the rest of Turkey after the 1960s. Initially, the *mahalle* was a *gecekondu* (squatter) settlement, which offered cheap housing for low-income families. At the outset there were no electricity, sewage, or water supplies, and transportation was provided through private minibuses, which ran to a single destination such as Beyazıt, where the *kapalıçarşı* (big bazaar) is located, and which is one of the oldest commercial centres of Istanbul. Given its closeness to the markets of Beyazıt and Laleli, Gaziosmanpaşa was an obvious alternative location for small-scale suppliers working for these central markets.

Gaziosmanpaşa became the most populated settlement of Istanbul and its access to public services and provisions increased, although they still remained inadequate in some *mahalles*. Most households have electricity, running water, sanitary facilities, and telephone connections. The area is most effectively connected to main motorways and other central areas of Istanbul. During the 1980s, the establishment of the municipality transformed the area from an unregulated *gecekondu* area to a regulated *varoş* area[1].

The initial settlers of the area were mostly wage workers, and the number of construction workers increased significantly due to the boom in large infrastructure and housing projects that took place during the 1980s and early 1990s. Currently small industrial and commercial establishments, and a range of jobs in construction and trade, form the main occupations of residents. From the end of the 1980s, the garment business took off in the area as the main provider of employment for the residents and for many women.

5.2 Factory Women, Atelier Girls and Pieceworker Housewives

Different segments of garment production have created a demand for different patterns of women's work in Istanbul, ranging from factory employment to atelier work and home-based work. These patterns are also strongly related to how the industry integrates with global markets and reveals the prevalent organisation of production today in one of the key industries of Turkey. Women work in factories and ateliers and at their homes to manufacture garments for the industry. The limited number of factory jobs available are undertaken by considerably lucky minority women who get nurseries for their children, free lunch or dinner, compensation for travelling or service buses, and bonuses three or four times a year. In any condition, factory work is preferable to the other forms of employment available to women of their class. It is a proper job. All factory workers remember very clearly when the opportunity of taking up a factory job appeared, the recruitment process and their first day at work, which represented a clear break from their past lives. This entitled women factory workers to an individualised income-earning capacity, handed to them as their pay-cheque each month.

Young age, being single and attainment of longer schooling years are the main traits of women's social background. Even though women start working at a young age the stability of factory work and the relatively better working conditions lead women to stay long years in factory employment. Employment in factories such as those in *Altıyıldız*, *Vakko* and *Bossa* and government jobs has been the single source of stable and secure jobs in Turkey, where the effect of permanent economic instability and increasing unemployment coupled with the marginalisation of urban jobs has been draining the opportunities for stable employment for working-class people.

The striking feature of the factory workforce is the employment of high number of ethnic Turks who have migrated from Bulgaria, among whom having a high-school diploma was much more common. Some other women workers ended up being factory workers although their hope was to find a government or office job. Eser was one of these women who struggled to find a decent job with her high-school diploma but could not find one. As reported by Eser, she felt discriminated against during her search for alternative jobs because her place of origin was eastern Turkey (*doğulu*). Ethnic differences accompanied by gender inequalities are the basis of the labour market disadvantage experienced by women in Istanbul's garment industry, which results in the exclusion of women from better job opportunities and confines them to a limited number of activities. The limitations placed on ethnic women and their labour market choices are a combination of ideological norms and exclusionary mechanisms operating in Turkish society, which give a handful of people the advantages of having better-paid jobs with fewer qualifications and skills, and exclude others from them.

Although much evidence is available in the literature showing the preference of factory managers for recruiting single young women (Nash and Fernandez-Kelly 1983; Joekes 1985; Lim 1983; Safa 1981; Elson and Pearson 1981), in Istanbul managers did not differentiate between married and single women as long as workers remained within the limits of the factory's specific age requirements. The attitudes of managers confirmed no discrimination against married women. However, the labour law in Turkey gives incentives to single women to give up work after marriage by providing the right to the full payment of severance pay. Under labour law, registered formal workers are entitled to the payment of severance pay only in cases of retirement and dismissal. Therefore, women's work is discouraged after marriage by a law that rewards women's withdrawal from the labour market with the payment of a lump sum of money. This situation is sometimes a concern for factory managers who try to encourage women to continue working after their marriage, as keeping a skilled labour force is crucial for production quality and effectiveness.

Defined as being in the 'twilight between regulated and unregulated economy' (Mitter 1986:63), ateliers sit at the heart of garment production in Istanbul, opening up a door of employment opportunity for many women. Atelier work, though identified with long hours of work, low wages, hard working conditions and being unregistered, attracts young girls and boys who have just completed their five years of primary schooling. Becoming a skilled garment worker takes long years of hands-on experience and going through every stage of garment production, so that recruitment at a young age is an advantage for employers in having access to cheap child labour. Young children initially are recruited as *ortacı*, whose job is to fetch pieces from the machines, redistribute them, and clean the atelier; as time goes by the *ortacı* becomes sewing machine operators or foremen/women. Therefore, the process of becoming a skilled atelier worker resembles the long established tradition of apprenticeship in skilled male occupations such as tailoring and shoemaking, where young boys are sent to work after primary education.

Women working in ateliers see their employment as a temporary stage, which is to continue until marriage or until a financial difficulty has passed. That is why almost all atelier workers in the research sample had no social security coverage and worked as unregistered workers. Even though it is obligatory for employers to register their workers after a month's trial period, workers are given a choice at the time of recruitment whether to get a higher cash income or to be registered with the social security system, which means that the employer deducts income tax from employees' pay. A worker opting to be *sigortalı* (a worker with social security) cannot receive a full salary. Especially, married women's preferences are for their husbands to be protected by social security, and if the husband is a *sigortalı* worker his whole family will be covered by health insurance, which provides free treatment and medicine in public hospitals. This also enforces the ideology of the temporary nature of women's work and its aim of generating cash for family needs.

A strong tendency for women to stop working exists among atelier workers too. Long and harsh working conditions at ateliers make it difficult for married women due to the pressure to devote more time to their domestic roles and responsibilities. Most of my informants reported that every girl quits her atelier job as soon as she is engaged. One of my informants, Dilek, is a good example highlighting this point. Two years earlier, Dilek had divorced her husband. Before her marriage, she had almost eight years of working experience as a sewing machine operator. When she married, her husband did not allow her to work. After the divorce, she moved back to her mother's home with her daughter and back to work as well. She was glad that her working experience helped her to make a living.

The married atelier workers are generally drawn from the family members and kin networks of atelier owners. However, claiming that all married women were the relatives of the owner would be wrong, as some women's atelier work was done due to extreme financial difficulties. One woman, Umman, 43 years old, with no financial support from her husband, began to do atelier work when her children were old enough to be left alone. Kudret is another example of how women make use of their working experience in garments in case of financial need after marriage. Kudret left home to get married to someone her parents did not give consent for, and fell out of her social support networks. Later when she had a baby she made up with her parents and her husband, and Kudret moved back to her parents' apartment. However, this did not solve her family's financial problems and she decided to go back to work in ateliers with her mother caring for her baby while she was at work.

In Istanbul's garment industry, atelier production and home-based piecework are close to each other in terms of workers' life histories. It is a common practice for a mother to do de-threading work at home obtained from an atelier where the daughter works. A worker might start to work in a workshop while she is young, and become a pieceworker when she gets married or becomes pregnant. All women in this category are dependent subcontracted workers (Carr and Chen 2002). Payment is generally piece-rate, and since there are no clearly established employer–employee relations, the usual labour laws covering wage workers are inapplicable. These women do not have any power to influence the terms and conditions of production, and the wage they receive is usually lower than the minimum wage. The pieceworkers are portrayed as passive and vulnerable victims who occupy the last ring in the chain of global production. Their labour is easily substituted and their labour market vulnerability is also reinforced by their personal characteristics, which are typically unskilled, poorly educated and married with children.

A significant characteristic of piecework in Istanbul is that women express their participation in group solidarity and membership through their engagement in piecework. Seen as a 'help' for their sons' or husbands' atelier work, sometimes doing piecework is just a way of taking over the workload of a friend's piecework. The demographic typology of workers is similar to the findings of previous studies (Çınar 1994, Eraydın and Erendil 1999). Being married and older with a low level of education are the prime characteristics of home-based pieceworkers in Istanbul. Piecework is not accepted as an appropriate occupation for girls and it is socially more favourable if they engage in their *çeyiz* making. They told me that the girls were better off if they only did their *çeyiz*, as piecework did not pay much and was 'back-breaking'. Through this, the pieceworkers not only devalued the work as a form of meaningful occupation but also downgraded their labour. As will be discussed further in Chapter 6, women's place in Turkish society and their future aspirations are strongly tied to their domestic roles and responsibilities. Activities enhancing this role are favoured over others. Paid activity is, therefore, not a common way for women to express their identity. The negative image of piecework being 'not a proper job' is supported by the economic gains and material satisfaction obtained through pay and work conditions. This is the reason why young women prefer to engage in *çeyiz* making, which will bring them more tangible gains through self-respect, dignity and status.

5.3 Migration and Urban Life in Istanbul

Home is not where you are born but where you eat² is a proverb meaning that home is where you have enough to eat and where you can earn a living, not where you were born. The main pull factor of urban migration is to obtain employment in the city and to live in conditions better than those in the village. Urban migrants see migration as a simple act of earning a living in the city. Perceived as a process of alienation, migration drives people away from their roots or homes, burdened with the responsibility of surviving in Istanbul. Migrants define Istanbul as *gurbet³*, and the place of origin, the homeland, as *memleket⁴*. Thus, earning a living is also a way of constructing an urban identity and overcoming alienation for migrants, which is built upon having a job and economic survival.

The experience of migration has for many meant living side-by-side with people from different social backgrounds, culture and religion, as well as the formation of alliances with those of similar rural origin. A newcomer initially stays with relatives or *hemşehri(s)* (people with the same origin), who have previously migrated and adapted to the city, until an income and housing is secured. For example, my own parents came to Istanbul immediately after they got married and stayed with my father's sister. After my father and mother found jobs and enough income to support themselves in a separate flat, they left my aunt's house. Their apartment was on the same street as my aunt's house and they remained close to each other even after they were living separately. After some years, my father's brother came to Istanbul and he stayed with my aunt and my family until he got himself a job. These networks of support are also important in finding a job in Istanbul, as my uncle began to work in the same atelier as my father, and earlier my mother found a place in a textile factory where my aunt was working. This survival strategy is a familiar experience for all first-generation urban migrants.

The need to preserve local identities that mediate easy access to material resources limits the interaction and communication that takes place between different groups[5]. Since survival is still largely dependent upon social networks and ties, the replacement of traditional social relations, such as kinship and *hemheşrilik* ties, has not been completed with more anonymous relations and formally structured institutional provision. As Mingione emphasises, informal relations, precarious work and family-based economies increase when there is a lack of public regulation, resources and provisions. The relations based on solidarity among low-income families help to bridge the gaps in institutional provision by generating a new basis for conflict, as explained below (Mingione 1981). The migrant communities of Istanbul, with the lack of institutional support and regulations, need to cater for their own needs, from housing to schooling. For example, despite the fact that schools are built from the central government budget, people living in the newly established areas of Istanbul sometimes need to build their own schools with the help of local *vakıflar* (religious charitable endowments).

The extent of utilisation of community relations and local identities in the struggle for urban survival enforces existing societal inequalities, power relations and conflicts between and within migrant groups. According to Pahl, the distribution of limited resources in cities is managed both by market and by bureaucratic-political systems, and local communities are shaped by the working conditions of urban life and regulations (Pahl 1970). In Istanbul, the distribution of and access to urban resources have been influenced by communities' duration of urban residence, the strength of their informal networks and more importantly their financial resources. Some groups have greater access to available resources than others. Without doubt, women, ethnic minorities, and religious sects form some of these disadvantaged groups, whose access to labour markets, property rights and public decision-making is curbed by their gender, race and beliefs.

5.3.1 Women's Migration Trajectories

Urbanisation and migration mean a great transformation not only for societies but for individuals as well. So, what do all these changes mean for migrant women and for definitions of gender in the migrant household? For women, the move to the city may open up new possibilities for redefining gender roles and relations. Migration may also give women the opportunity to use the city as a place to develop and affirm new identities and ways of living that were impossible back in the village (Brydon and Chant 1989; Buvinic and Chaney 1983; Tienta and Booth 1991; Jelin 1988). Tienta and Booth argue (1991) that women's position in society should not be defined exclusively in terms of economic exchanges but should include non-economic exchanges as well. In the Turkish context, Erman's study reveals that the vast majority of migrant women preferred to live in the city, despite the difficulties they faced. Thus, city life has offered some women diverse opportunities and more decision-making power (Erman 1998).

My attention during the field study was not directed at the reasons why people migrated, as migration decisions seemed to be overwhelmingly economic, but was more on the ways in which people migrated and how they adapted themselves to the city. As the fieldwork unfolded it became clear that families deployed different migration strategies. In some cases men migrated earlier, got a job, rented a flat, and then their family followed them. However, the most common pattern is joint migration to Istanbul shortly after marriage. Migration after marriage, however, reflects mainly women's experience because in some cases the men were already living in Istanbul. It is also common for men living in the city to marry one of the girls from their place of origin through an arranged marriage. Although single women migrants are a rare occurrence in Turkey, some single women who lived with their close relatives such as elder sisters and brothers in the city migrated on their own. However, the drive behind single girls' migration was not to search for a job or better living conditions, but to help their hosting relatives with domestic duties and childcare.

The case of Hatem, 24 years old, illustrated this point well. She came from Sivas to Istanbul to help out her sister with her first baby. Later on, she persuaded her family living back in the village to give permission for her to take up a garment atelier job. Another case similar to Hatem's was Nuray's experience of moving to Istanbul. Nuray, who is 26 years old, and had a high school education, came to Istanbul from the small village of Muş to look after her elder sister's child. Her sister was working as an official clerk in the municipality of Gaziosmanpaşa. After two years of childcare, when her sister's child was old enough to be enrolled in the nursery of the municipality, she decided to take up garment work.

> Our parents supported all my sisters and brothers to go to school and we all finished high school education in Muş. But there was no job there I could find. So I decided to go to Istanbul because it is better to be in the big city than to sit idle. There was not much agricultural work where I lived and I could not find any office work because our village was away from the Muş city centre.

Thus, single girls migrate in cases where female members undertake a paid job or need extra help with household chores and childcare. In other contexts such as Latin America and South East Asia, single women's independent migration is extensively documented and a well-known phenomenon (Fernandez-Kelly 1983; Chant 1995; Wolf 1992; Ong 1987); however, in Turkey women's migration is contingent upon other family members' needs and is not an independent act of seeking employment in cities.

Moving to the city together with the new socio-economic conditions in urban areas has diverse implications for the lives of women and their families. Despite the economic and financial uncertainties new migrants face during the initial stage of their migration, urban migration is seen by women as an opportunity to improve their lives and positions in their families. The women always emphasised migration as a significant experience and a kind of social status shift. One of my informants, Hatice, is a home-based garment worker and came to Istanbul from a small village of Malatya 21 years ago. Immediately after her marriage her husband, who was already working in Istanbul as a skilled shoemaker, took her to Istanbul. She said:

> There is nothing in the village but only hard work. You need to work in the fields all day and take care of animals. These are very dirty jobs. But, in the city one can live in clean homes and you do not have to go out and work all day under the hot sun. City life is very easy for a woman. If you are a housewife all you need to do is clean your house in the morning, take care of your children and cook for your family. In the village, you also need to work in the field.

The organisation of daily life for women changes dramatically, as Hatice's statement shows. Even though she is a busy pieceworker she still prefers it to being in the village. It was a significant experience for Hatice to leave behind the rural life, where she was closely observed by her mother-in-law and other extended family members; migration meant an increase in individual freedom expressed in the ability to manage her own domestic sphere. She and her family have also managed to construct their own house, which is something of a success story. Thus, the migration experience for Hatice has been a positive one, even though it has meant dedication and hard work, which paid off in the form of possessing a property, which in turn brought respect from relatives, *hemşehri*s and neighbours.

Although experiencing urban migration as a way of shifting their social status, women do not have a strong sense of identification with the city in which they live. Rather, their identities are constructed through group and family membership and gender. Interestingly, none reported themselves as *İstanbullu* (Istanbulites). Only in the case of lack of connections with relatives and *hemşehris* back in the place of origin did one woman consider herself as *İstanbullu* since her mother came to the city as a child with no other connections. Since people continue to live within social networks of local origin, women's identification with the city is rather weak. Although the length of settlement in the city might affect the ways in which those families had access to material resources and networks in the city, it did not, however, change the way they constructed and perceived their identity. Remaining as 'aliens', women could not transform themselves into *İstanbullu*s by establishing an urban identity.

As a structural basis for understanding women's changing lives and aspirations and the connections made between migration experience and garment work, migration was an important analytical tool. In this regard, migration, closely tied to the needs and expectations of the family, dramatically affects women's lives, and creates a pool of abundant labour for Istanbul's garment production. The hunger of the garment industry for cheap labour is fed by the availability of the labour of migrant women that is commanded by their families and communities. The meaning attached to migrant women's labour is socially structured in the light of women's domestic roles as mothers, wives and sisters, which also help to mediate women's entry into the labour market.

5.4 Household Size and Composition

Having emphasised the significance of women's domestic roles and responsibilities for their labour market activities, it is clear that the nature and composition of the households in which these women live occupy an essential place in the conditioning of the female labour supply in Turkey. While it is true that the primary locus of patriarchy is the household, the household is also where the relations of production and reproduction are maintained through ideologies emphasising male authority. Thus, the changing nature of household composition influences both the ways in which gender ideologies are exercised in the household and women's relation to the labour market.

Variety in household composition and domestic living arrangements forces us to move beyond statistically classifying households as nuclear or extended. Instead, the adoption of a lifecycle approach and the recognition of the dynamism in household forms help us to develop an understanding of the different solutions and strategies adopted by individual households in the context of social change. In this regard, Kıray conceptualised the family as a buffer institution, which meets the new demands created by social transformation through modifying its form and function, while continuing to meet its members' security needs in various ways (Kıray 1985). This approach also brings extra-household relations and kin networks into the analysis of household forms and functions as well as the structures of relations within the household. In this regard, I have identified three types of households in this research: nuclear family, extended family and single-parent family.[6] The aim of the section is to examine how households adopt and adapt to the changes brought by women's labour market activities, and how the changing labour demand of the household is met by bringing in new members and by transformations in household composition. In Istanbul a clear pattern can be established between women's work patterns and a specific type of household that has evolved in response to women's economic activities.

5.4.1 Nuclear Households of Factory Workers

Nuclear families are identified by their independent budgets for daily consumption. Residence and budget arrangements must be considered separately. In this regard, there are two types of nuclear family. The first is the full nuclear family, which is characterised by non-income pooling and independent residential arrangements. In the second form, families working together earn income from the same source but live separately. The Timagur family analysed in Chapter 4 was a prime example of the second type of nuclear family.

Nuclear families have some of the functions of extended families in Turkey and mainly maintain the roles of the extended family by remaining within a web of social networks. For example, the *gecekondu* housing in the metropolitan areas, especially in Istanbul, allows *gecekondu* owners to build their multi-floored apartment buildings, thus enabling parents to allocate to each of their children a residence in the same building. Each floor of the building then harbours an independent nuclear family, but actually they are a big extended family. This type characterises nuclear families with income pooling and independent spending budget under different homes.

Besides bearing the functions of extended households, nuclear households having their own budget and not pooling income with other families were the most common type among factory workers. However, the research has only recorded families' current form, that is whether they were nuclear or extended, even though some families had lived in other types during their life cycle. Therefore, it is difficult to say that nuclear families began their life cycle as nuclear and finish it as nuclear, when this may simply present a specific point in the domestic cycle. The popularity of nuclear households among factory workers is a sign of stability and well-being. Having a nuclear family is also a symbol of being able to have the financial resources necessary to form a nuclear family, which is evidently most frequent among factory workers.

Another form of household recorded among factory workers was the transient family in which a nuclear family lives with a relative (Rasuly-Paleczek 1996). The case of single girls who migrated to Istanbul to stay with their sisters' or brothers' families forming transient families was widespread among factory workers. This form of family is usually constructed with sons who live with their unmarried sisters and widowed mothers, or many brothers and a mother or a sister living together. Another example was families who had emigrated from Bulgaria, especially nuclear families, living with an old family member such as a grandmother, a grandfather, or old uncles and aunts.

5.4.2 Extended Households of Atelier Workers

The extended family usually refers to families in which the male head of household, married son and unmarried children live together. In terms of residence and budget arrangements, full extended families live under one roof and pool resources. I utilised this broad definition to describe families of at least two generations living together under the same roof. In this group, father and mother live together with their married sons' families and their unmarried children.[7] Timur (1972) uses the extended family to refer to the economic leadership of the father, whose sons are dependent on the male head of household, who controls economic resources. This form is characterised as the three-generational extended family. However, her definition best explains the relations of rural households. Urban extended households are more dependent on the economic contributions made by the younger generation. As Kıray acknowledges, the centre of gravity and authority has shifted from the older age group males to the active age group males as a result of migration and social change (Kıray 1985).

Extended households are more common among the atelier workers group as some of them work in their own ateliers. Family business in Turkey is not only peculiar to small-scale firms. The country's most elaborate capitalist enterprises, such as Koç and Sabancı Holdings, are also established on close family ties in which sons, daughters and sons-in-law are integrated into the management cycle. The frequency of extended families among atelier workers is, then, the result of pooling existing resources of money and labour in order to manage their family business. Having extended households is one of the important contributions to the success of small-scale ateliers in Istanbul. They not only provide an extensive network of labour, but are also a sign of a large pool of financial contribution. Money lending and borrowing between relatives and families is an important form of solidarity among them. This obviously enables families to manage their lives beyond their financial resources.

In Istanbul, families draw upon different forms of solidarity and mutuality to enable families to survive financially. One of my informants told me how she and her husband constructed a four-storied building with the help of her husband's relatives. It would have been impossible to do so with her husband's low wage, so they borrowed money extensively from their other relatives, to be paid back after they finished their house. Families support each other in other ways too. For example, one of the families I interviewed informed me that they lived in one of their relatives' houses when they moved to the city and stayed there until they had their own house. Moreover, the case of Zehra and her family is another interesting one. Zehra, her husband and children moved in with a family from the same village while their house was being built, so avoiding paying extra rent at a point when they needed to save extra cash for their own building. The existence of various forms of solidarity among immigrant families blurs the dividing line between nuclear and extended families.

In the case of Istanbul the domestic arrangements of the extended households owning a garment atelier are made in such a way as to release their female members for work, and usually older members take charge of childcare and other domestic responsibilities while the younger women are at work in the atelier. As expressed in Chapter 4, having an extended family and a strong family connection is the single most important source of forming and maintaining a successful garment business in Istanbul.

5.4.3 Home-based Workers:
Between Nuclear and Extended Households

Turkish nuclear families live within a web of social relations. The only exception to this generalisation is the nuclear families of the poorest households. The women living in nuclear families work mostly to meet the essential needs of their families, and their homes are often isolated from broader kin networks. This type of isolated household was more common among home-based workers who turned to piecework as the last refuge to make ends meet. Some of these households are either composed of internally displaced people from the southeast of Turkey or too poor to afford to become involved in social relations and networks. In Erder's Umraniye study in Istanbul, she identified those households from southeast Turkey as the poorest, and they had less access to established resources and networks.

Family members worked all the time and had no time or resources to invest in those relations and networks (Erder 1996).

Living in an extended household is one of the reasons why women take up piecework in the first place, for some of the extended families are the poorest group of my sample. Let me illustrate my point. Cemile was living in an extended family and had an ill and old husband. Her son's wife and children were living with them, also a divorced daughter together with her own daughters. She told me that it was crucial for her to bring home extra income, since it was impossible to live on the single income brought in by the son. Starting from Cemile's example, it is possible to argue that some urban extended families living under the same roof are relatively poor and have limited resources to support separate households. The functional difference between pieceworkers' and atelier workers' extended households is that atelier workers live in separate households and share a common budget, whereas pieceworkers often live in a residentially extended household and pool their incomes. For urban low-income families, establishing separate homes for their children when they marry is an indicator of economic well-being. As Özbay indicates, extended families are not a form of 'traditional way of life' in urban areas, rather living in extended households is a response to social and economic hardship. Therefore, one of the important survival strategies on which migrant poor families rely is the extended family in urban areas (Özbay 1998:170).

5.4.4 Single-parent Households

The single parent family comprises only a mother or father with children. In my sample, divorced or widowed women composed single-parent families. However, forming a single-parent household or female-headed household is not straightforward for women. Turkey is a predominantly patriarchal society, where social organisation is heavily based on the family unit. In this regard, family and marriage are important sources of identity, security and economic support. Divorce and bearing children outside marriage are considered strictly outside legitimate social arrangements. Even though there is an increasing rate of divorce among upper-class women, female-headed households are rare in the low-income urban areas of Turkey. Divorce is discouraged by family and kin as it may mean disruption of the cohesion of kinship and familial networks. Thus, even if staying in the marriage means experiencing domestic violence and economic difficulties, and in some cases living with a second wife (*kuma*), women do not give up their marriages. In addition, women are socially and culturally obliged to live within their conjugal contracts until their husbands leave them. By preserving their marital status, women trade off subordination to men's authority for protection and respectability in their social environment.

Divorced or widowed women find it hard to cope with the social and cultural trauma of being lone mothers in a patriarchal society, where a woman without a man is voiceless and socially vulnerable. One of the most significant ways women cope with being lone mothers is to go back to the protection of their own families or their husband's family, as the marriage is more of a social contract between families. If families are encouraged to see that the breakdown of the marriage is not the fault of the woman who acted as a 'good' mother and wife, they may offer protection. Two things undermine the options available for lone mothers other than the protection of their families. These are the negative image of divorced women still present in the society, as well as the kinds of jobs available to them as low-educated and unskilled women in the low-income neighbourhoods of Istanbul. Therefore, the phenomenon of female-headed households in Turkish society is hidden within extended households. Living in an extended household is one of the coping mechanisms after the breakdown of marriage, and this is also a way in which these women are rendered socially invisible.

There are a variety of living arrangements by which divorced and widowed women sustain their lives. If they are old, they live with their children and their families, and if they are young they have their own families to turn to. For example, Zöhre and her children were abandoned by her husband after he left them to work in Germany. She lived in the same house as her mother and in the same neighbourhood as her other close relatives. After some years, Zöhre managed to move out with her children who were now grown up enough to earn their own income. Now, she lives with her first married daughter, her son-in-law and her two other unmarried girls. For younger divorced women, it is a common practice to live with their own families rather than to form an independent household, due not only to financial inabilities but also to the social practices that scrutinise divorced women living on their own.

In summary, the households in which garment workers live take diverse forms, ranging from nuclear households, to extended households, to single-parent households. The changing structure of the household is a response to social transformations and the economic hardship experienced by migrant families, and also to women's economic activities. All the household forms examined here have to some extent enabled women's garment work, and the relationship between the organisation of household and women's employment is centred on the family-based networks and solidarities that often help to release women's labour for paid work.

5.5 Household Budgets:
Husbands' Occupation and Non-Monetary Contributions

Women's non-monetary contributions in the form of supplies of food and other kinds of materials such as clothes to the household budget have an impact on women's labour supply and on the economic activities women undertake in the labour market. These are basically the food preparation and income-preserving production of women, which takes the form of making different kinds of products for the use of family members, such as *kilims*, cardigans, jumpers, and socks. Instead of buying from the market, women prepare jams, tomato pastes and pickles at home. These contributions mean families spend less on their food consumption than if they bought these products ready-made in the market. Thus, women's income-saving activities provide the basis of the survival of migrant families in the cities where, although cash income is crucial for survival, non-monetary contributions make it possible to live on a low cash income, and even to save some of it.

The relationship between migrant families and their relatives in rural areas, preserved and restructured according to their new situations, is another way of helping families to survive in cities. Migrant families have connections with their villages, which are maintained in many different ways. A constant transfer of resources between the migrants and their relatives at home is a common feature of low-income migrant households in Istanbul. Winter supplies of food and other kinds of materials obtained from the village reduce expenditure on food and leave extra cash for other expenses. Moreover, by letting out their fields in the village migrants can derive an income in cash or in kind. These close contacts facilitate the successful migration and settlement of migrants in the cities.[8] Every woman in this research had some kind of connection with her home village that resulted in the transfer of food, materials or cash income through their fields. Some women even spent their vacations in their villages during summer time, working at harvesting. One of my informants went to Giresun every year to pick hazelnuts in her family's garden. In some cases, food packages including cheese, beans, honey, cracked wheat, rice, etc., were sent by their parents living back in villages.

In my sample, all households were in need of the women's financial contribution. Whether it was for their economic survival or their children's education, all women contributed immensely to the well-being of their families. In general, women's income was lower than their husbands', especially for those women working as home-based pieceworkers, who earned less than the minimum wage. During the fieldwork, the monthly average earning in the garment industry was around 180–200 million Turkish lira.[9]

However, this was for skilled workers, and the earnings of less experienced workers and children went down to 120–150 million Turkish lira.

The income level and occupation of male family members have significant influence on women's formal and informal work. Women's paid work is strongly related to the general income level of their families, which is mostly generated by male members—heads of household. Women's gainful employment is usually considered to be temporary and aims at providing security and stability until the family gets over its crisis, which could be a financial difficulty, needing to acquire a property, or redundancy of the main breadwinner of the family. Conceptualisation of women's work as essentially temporary leads us to investigate the nature of relations between women's work and household income level and husband's occupation.

The regularity of earning and the type of occupation of male breadwinners have important implications for women's paid work in general. No women among atelier workers and home-based pieceworkers in my sample had a husband or father/brother working for the government[j]. Having at least one member of the family working in a government job is a strong indication of stability and regularity of income for low-income families in urban Turkey. Fathers and husbands of women in my sample had jobs in many different categories. However, most of them were working as employees in small-scale firms. Construction workers, shoe-makers, pensioners, the self-employed and petty traders were among some of the jobs I recorded for male members of families. Married atelier workers were most likely to have their husbands involved in the garment industry, as either workers or owners. Factory workers were generally from stable income families that had at least one more stable-income-earning individual. In some cases, home-based workers had husbands who were unemployed or earning too little to support their families.

5.6 Women's *Elişi*:
A Path from Household to Labour Market

The invisibility of female employment manifests itself extensively in the dominance of women's domestic roles over their paid work. Thus, Turkish working-class women's engagement in income-earning activities is organised in their homes in the form of home-based piecework and their traditional activity of *elişi* (handicraft). *Elişi* is a common activity, covering knitting, embroidery, sewing and needlework, making a wide range of materials such as bedspreads, coffee table and table covers, cardigans, and socks. Making *elişi* has always been the basis of earning some cash for low-income women and also builds a bridge to the labour market in which women could always make some petty cash by making lace or other forms of *elişi* (Iktisat Dergisi 2002:3-17).

Turkish girls enter adulthood by acquiring skills of embroidery, knitting, needlework, crochet and sewing while they also learn how to cook, clean and serve. These skills, used to prepare an elaborate *çeyiz* (trousseau), are utilised to earn money in two ways. First, women make lace, embroidery and knitting for young girls' *çeyiz*, and second, women use their skills to take in piecework or to work in an atelier. Many women in the *gecekondu* areas in Istanbul who live on the income from either lace-making or needlework have similarities with the case of Mies's study in Narsapur in India, where lace makers working from their homes exclusively utilised their skills to integrate the Indian economy into the world markets of export production (Mies 1982).

Hanife was a lace-maker, who had two sons and an alcoholic husband, and lived in a one-room flat. Her husband has an irregular income and could barely support his family. Hanife's income from lace making was kept secret from the husband in order to force him to meet the necessities. She kept her money and saved it in a bank or bought gold for herself. Despite the fact she was engaged in lace making for many years her husband never realised that she was making money out of it because women's *elişi* (handicraft) is always seen as a hobby and a non-monetary activity.

Filiz, a former garment worker, quit her work when she got married. However, although her husband had regular employment, his income was not enough to support his family. Thus, Filiz started making *elişi* for her neighbours. She said:

His salary is all right but just enough for rent and food. I want to buy carpets and curtains for my home… Making *elişi* is better than going out for work. I earn some cash and do my household chores (*evişi*) as well. My husband never knows whether I make money with *elişi*. He thinks this is a thing I try to pass my time and entertain myself with… If I work hard I can make 50–75 million a month and spend some of this money to buy things for my house. It is not that I want to hide money from my husband but I do not want to make him to feel like he is not capable of earning money to support his family.

Her earnings are dependent upon the price set among the women who demand and supply these products that create a kind of local market for *elişi*. For example, there is an approximate price for a ball of yarn (*yumak*). Setting up the price of the lace maker's labour, two women, the buyer and seller, negotiate and determine the price each time. A well-known fact among local women is that the prices for *elişi* are very low. Low prices for *elişi* can be explained by the fact that customers and lace makers are both from working-class families. If the price is low women can afford to buy, otherwise they would make it themselves, since every woman has similar skills of lace making. Thus, these reasons for low prices make income from *elişi* very low and marginal. My interviews with women engaged in *elişi*-making show that there is always a demand for *elişi* either from other women or from traders who specialise in the marketing of these products.

The *elişi* trade takes place in two different channels. Firstly, there are shops that sell trousseau items and generate a demand for women's *elişi*. They buy from women and sell the items in their shops. There are also middle (wo)men who collect items from other cities around Istanbul such as Bursa, Balıkesir, etc., and bring them to Istanbul. The second channel is more outward oriented and internationally marketed, with Arab countries being the main destinations especially for women's headscarves, which are tediously decorated with needlework or lace-work.

Engaging in *elişi* (handicraft) is a way for women to express their identity. Women's *elişi* skills, which are normally devoted to making girls' *çeyiz* (trousseaux), are often turned into an income-generating activity that provides a significant support for household survival. Whenever women need extra cash they can easily rely on income from *elişi*. This work has the advantage of 'invisibilising' incomes, as in the case of Hanife, and building nest-eggs. In some cases, this income becomes vital if a woman is trying to establish financial security for the future. However, women's contribution to the household budget does not drastically alter the patriarchal nature of gender relations and the women's perception of their primary roles as mothers and wives.

Conclusion

Factors conditioning women's labour supply range from women's demographic characteristics to the structure of households and household income level, which all determine the type of work women undertake in the labour market and women's entry to paid employment. This chapter has outlined some of these factors, as Lawson argues, in order to show that an 'understanding of women's experiences as wives, mothers and household heads is crucial to understanding their particular experiences with manufacturing' (Lawson, 1995: 441).

Low-income communities that have migrated to Istanbul to find better living conditions and employment opportunities offer a rich source of labour for Istanbul's blooming garment industry, which is located in *gecekondu* neighbourhoods. Women's manufacturing work in the industry in the form of factory, atelier and home-based piecework is shaped by their demographic characteristics and those of the households in which they live. Turkish women do garment work for different purposes at different stages of their lives. A girl may start to work in a workshop then become a pieceworker when she gets married or becomes pregnant.

Place of origin is a strong identity reference for people in working-class neighbourhoods of Istanbul, and this identification governs personal contacts and networks. Women's identities are still strongly bound to their places of origin, as most live in communities and neighbourhoods surrounded by people from the same locality. Ethnicity also makes a difference, especially for Kurds and Turks who had migrated from Bulgaria, in accessing certain jobs. For Kurds, it was harder to go into regular, well-paid jobs, whereas Turks who had migrated from Bulgaria found it easier to have access to those jobs, due to their stereotypical images as diligent workers and their better education levels.

Household characteristics and women's domestic roles in those households were discussed as central factors affecting women's labour supply. The size and composition of households have conflicting influences on the release of women's labour. Most women workers live in nuclear households. However, this tendency is higher among factory workers. In the case of factory workers, nuclear household composition is a sign of well-being and of having access to a regular and secure job. In other cases, however, this household structure may be a sign of isolation from other material resources and personal connections. Women in these relatively poor households are to be found engaged in home-based piecework or low-paid unskilled atelier work. For home-based workers, the extended household structure could be an indication of poverty that requires the pooling of the labour and earnings of different families, whereas for some atelier workers it is a survival mechanism for their family-based businesses in the garment industry. Divorcees or widows are usually absorbed into extended households, as female-headed households are rare in Turkey. The absence of security underwritten by male protection could mean the degradation and isolation of lone-living women from the community. Thus, these women are hidden from the public eye and hardly ever form an independent household. They manage to form an independent household only in cases when they have a son who is old enough.

Women's contribution to the household budget in the form of income-saving and handicraft (*elişi*) activities is an important element that puts downward pressure on women's labour market entrance. Women's activities in food preparation and production for their own use involve making different kinds of material for the use of family members, such as *kilims*, cardigans, jumpers and socks. Moreover, migrant families' economic connections with their home villages, from which families obtain free or cheaper food staples and sometimes financial support, help them to save cash. The rural resources that migrant families rely on are quite important, at least until survival in the city is secured. The resources migrant families receive from rural areas may be important contributions for the budgets of these families, and the extent of this contribution affects women's decisions about labour market participation.

6

PATRIARCHY, GENDER AND LABOUR SUPPLY IN *GECEKONDU* NEIGHBORHOODS OF ISTANBUL

The social meaning attached to women's work is a reflection of the perceived role and place of women in a society where not only the community but also women themselves affect the way in which the meaning of women's work is established. The invisibility and temporariness of women's garment work are associated partially with the nature of the work women do, and partially with the way that the identities and priorities of women are oriented around their domestic roles, which are the signals of the meaning attached to women's paid work in urban Turkey.

The dominant ideology of *evinin kadını* (women of their homes)[1] overshadows women's every paid activity and also their relationship with the labour market. This chapter continues the analysis of the supply factors conditioning female employment by looking at gender relations, women's working identities and the social meaning of women's work, and the justification of women's paid work in Istanbul's garment industry, and at how all these factors mediate women's entrance into the labour market. This analysis will be dependent upon how women conceptualise their working experience and their roles and identities, and the ways in which traditional gender relations are challenged, renegotiated and modified by the strategic struggles adopted by women themselves and their communities when an opportunity of employment comes up.

6.1 Strategic Struggles for Power: Gender Relations
The prevailing ideologies of gender in Turkish society not only outline what it means to be a man or a woman but also affect the ways in which women's garment work is made invisible. Women's domestic roles, which

assign them to motherhood and wifehood, suppress the way that labour market opportunities are undertaken and perceived by women. Emerging opportunities for informal work and the economic pressures to generate extra income are always challenged and negotiated through women's traditional roles, which ultimately affect the meaning and value attached to women's work.

One of the major theoretical contributions for an understanding of gender relations in Turkey came from Kandiyoti, with her concept of 'bargaining with patriarchy' (1988). In her analysis, the classic patriarchal family appears to represent the actual structural arrangements of family life even though it may vary in form and shape. It embodies the forms of control and subordination associated with the patriarchal family system in which women receive 'protection and security in exchange for submissiveness and propriety' and 'adopt inter personal strategies that maximise their security through manipulation of the affection of their sons and husbands' (Kandiyoti 1988:280).

Although Kandiyoti's reference is mainly to patrilinearly and patrilocally organised peasant households, low-income urban households are organised around similar ideologies regarding gender and intergenerational relations. The pervasive male dominance in Turkish society is perpetuated by a social organisation based on the family unit (Duben 1982). Even with the urban relocation of many rural families, the Turkish family has retained its authoritarian and patriarchal character.

Despite the fact that families live in separate households and are nuclear in structure (Timur 1972; Güvenen 1999), the extended family remains a powerful cultural ideal (Kandiyoti 1988:278). Thus, it is clear that the relations governing nuclear households remain very close to those in the extended family. Abandan-Unat calls this form of nuclear family the 'functionally extended family' (1986:186). It continues to be characterised by a sexual division of labour between two differentiated and relatively isolated spheres of activities, which society clearly defines and assigns to men and women (Olson 1982).

The allocation of roles and responsibilities in the household is made among family members on the basis of gender, age and seniority. In the extended family, senior men have authority over all members of the household, including younger men. The young bride is brought from her family, through marriage, to another male-headed household in which her husband's close female kin—mother, sister, brother's wife— exercise considerable power over her. Therefore, women can establish higher status in the household and gain their economic security by having sons. The hardship that younger women endure is eventually superseded by the control and authority they exert over their own daughters-in-law. During their lives, women have changing degrees of power and status. At younger ages, women are in a subordinate position to an older woman in their families. It is also argued that women have not only been submissive and passive victims of patriarchy, but have also acted strategically in obtaining recognition within the existing ideological framework of gender relations. Women's power of manipulating their husband's and sons' affection in return for enduring lifetime security makes them active agents of the perpetuation of the patriarchal order (Kandiyoti 1988).

Kandiyoti stresses that the bargaining process is between men and women in the household, whereas White, in her ethnographic study among low-income families in Istanbul, recognises the importance of the relations taking place between women and the community. Therefore, women not only bargain with their immediate family members, but also negotiate with their communities. She writes that:

> [Bargaining] could also primarily be seen as a bargain between the individual and the group, of which the conjugal family is a subset. In meeting the moral and labour requirements of her roles as wife, neighbour, mother, a woman signifies her willingness to participate in the web of reciprocal obligations on which group stability and security rests. (White 1994:61)

Thus, community relations are extended to interact in the construction of gender relations in which women are enmeshed in a complex web not only of exploitative relations, but also of relations of solidarity and reciprocity based on kinship. White's analysis provides a significant analytical tool through which emerging forms of gender relations can be conceptualised in migrant families in urban areas. It is fundamental to recognise the implications of kinship and other community relations in Turkey, where the rural–urban transformation of society is still ongoing, yet where almost all social relations are based on face-to-face interactions and informal networks.

Ethnographic studies of changing gender relations and household formation in urban Turkey remain limited. A few of these studies have focused on the labour market participation of women migrants, including women in the informal sector and home-based piecework (White 1994; Bolak 1995; Hattatoğlu 2001; İlkkaracan 1998); however, their focus was mainly on women's work and its outcome. Erman's work on gender and the distribution of power in the migrant household significantly contributes to an understanding of the ways in which migrant women manage or fail to change the power dynamics in the household that has been disturbed by urban migration. She draws attention to different factors affecting women's bargaining power, such as paid work, the ability of male members to earn a living in the city, religion and age (Erman 1998; 1998a). According to Erman, 'the urban context opened up new bargaining potentials for rural migrant women, nevertheless, in their bargaining with patriarchy, they have remained highly asymmetrical' (1998: 162).

My research suggest that changing socioeconomic conditions and new employment opportunities for women affect the way in which authoritarian and protective patriarchy is constructed in Turkish society. However, it does not mean a general transformation of the relationship between men and women or a radical reform of what it means to be a man-husband or a woman-wife; the reproduction of familiar traditional practices continues in new social contexts. What changes instead is the way women manipulate and negotiate patriarchal relations in urban settings. By remaining confined to traditional gender relations women are effectively bargaining with the patriarch and larger patriarchal structures. The internalisation of those traditional roles also results in how the gender system is perceived not only as oppressing women but also as a string of cultural practices that are equally exercised and internalised by both men and women without questioning its gender-based inequalities, and that also brings access to social membership, certain social roles and responsibility, as well as to rights and material resources.

Although Bolak (1995) argues that women accept patriarchy as a cultural script without necessarily internalising it, a woman without a man remains voiceless in Turkish society. Women's identity and position in society are primarily derived from their position within the family and from their roles as daughters, mothers, sisters and wives, which assign them a socially acceptable role of 'good women'. As will be argued further, these choices are manipulated by women to gain power and status in society.

6.1.1 Strategic Gender Negotiations

There is a variety of ways in which women enforce existing gender roles and relations, depending on the context they are in. In some cases, it is the effort of keeping husbands in the marriage by manipulating social pressure against them, while in others it is the utilisation of their husband's authority to stop sexual harassment in the workplace. Sometimes it takes the form of women's efforts to uphold the traditional division of labour in household chores, even when they are employed full-time.

The story of my informant expresses how male protection is important for a woman. Leyla is a married factory worker. She has worked in the same factory for over 15 years, since she and her family emigrated from Bulgaria. She was sexually harassed by one of her male colleagues and the factory management did not act upon her complaints. However, a few days after the incident, her husband came to the factory to physically challenge the person who harassed her. After the husband backed her case, the factory managers decided to fire the culprit. This case is rare but important in pointing to the position of women in Turkish society. Leyla's demand was only met by the factory administration when it was voiced by her husband. As the only woman among my informants who mentioned sexual harassment in the workplace, Leyla's case represents the way in which a woman's claim was only upheld when a man stood up for her. Although this might not have altered her bargaining power in the household, it is evident that she was powerful enough to stop the harassment and to punish her harasser.

Women sometimes uphold existing gender relations and norms against husbands who fall short of meeting the demands of masculine responsibility. In this case, gender roles are practised in the form of a series of responsibilities and obligations in the family where women develop strategies to force men to honour their expected roles and duties. Let me illustrate my point with one of my informants' cases: Ayşe, 26 years old and a mother of two children, has been going through an unhappy marriage. However, Ayşe refused to divorce her husband and by her refusal gained the approval and support of her husband's and her own family. In Turkish society, great social support is provided for staying married. Although exit from the marriage contract is always available to every individual, it is severely punished by the rejection of the person as a group member. At the time of the interview, her husband was running a garment factory in another city and she was working as a forewoman in a garment atelier. She described her situation as follows, 'I am like a divorced woman but I am able to subsist and look after my children and stand on my own feet.' As a highly skilled garment-atelier forewoman Ayşe earns as much as her husband does and whenever her husband comes up short in providing for the family she can easily support her children.

Ayşe's efforts to sustain and keep her family together and her resistance to her husband's unwillingness to live up to his responsibilities as a father and husband brought her social status as a 'good' mother and woman and earned her financial and childcare support from her in-laws. Her position was also backed by her gainful employment as a forewoman in the garment atelier. Women's internalisation of the patriarchal system by conservative choices that cannot be seen as a simple act of women's lack of autonomy and power vis-à-vis men is a way of constructing women's role as active agents of their own social environment in affecting the framework in which the patriarchal system is practised and negotiated. In the words of White:

> If the patriarchal contract is seen as a general social contract that links men and women as a group, then women's conservative choices are not only a form of pressure to make men live up to their obligations to their family, but also an accentuation of women's identities as group members, and an appeal to the rules of reciprocity underlying group membership. (White 1994:61–2)

My case studies show that women are not simply victims of patriarchal oppression but are aware of the best possible options available to them within a given setting. Therefore, women strategically support the patriarchal system in such a way as to manipulate it to alter the situation working against them. Brought up to be 'good' and respectable daughters and mothers, social expectations and approval are mostly available to those women who live up to these expectations, when in charge of their households, and caring for their children, and when women of their home (*evinin kadını*). Women holding on to those roles and making claims and demands through those roles are the most powerful in Turkish society, since their demands are perceived to have legitimacy.

At this stage, the question of why women live up to social expectations that end up enforcing unequal gender relations in the society is an important one. In the light of these cases, the answer lies in the very limited options available for women outside the household. In a social setting where women are considered as a mainly peripheral and temporary urban workforce, economic activities are pursued only in the case of financial necessity and are seen as predominantly marginal. In her work, Şenyapılı points to the negative aspects of women's economic activities in *gecekondu* areas. For these women, work never will be a source of social unification, equalisation or satisfaction. Instead women will be subjected to further exploitation due to the basically unorganised, marginal nature of the labour force (Şenyapılı, 1981:212). Şenyapılı's analysis is significant in indicating the exploitative and marginal character of urban jobs available for low-income women. Thus, women are less likely to see these jobs as central to their lives and an alternative to their roles as mothers and wives. Nevertheless, there are many opportunities for women outside the household to work and earn their living, but these are exploited at great cost: loss of the protection implicit in the patriarchal system. The only option left to women is to operate within the parameters of relationships over which they can exercise a measure of control. As long as women remain dependent on men, not only for economic needs but also for social protection, they are socially acceptable. However, living outside male guardianship usually results in the social vulnerability of women. Thus, women prefer to engage in forms of behaviour that easily meet with the approval and support of the community. 'Patriarchal risk' is an ample concept to capture the fact that women have marked dependence on men for social protection and economic need. The absence of this protection would leave women particularly vulnerable to what Kabeer terms 'patriarchal risk':

> The risks and uncertainties attendant on women's dependent status within such systems paradoxically engender in them greater incentive to comply with, rather than challenge, male dominance, and to manipulate the norms of male obligation and protection to shore up their own position within their families. (Kabeer 2000:42)

The relevance of 'patriarchal risk' in shaping women's ability to make choices can be illustrated with Gönül's employment trajectory.

Gönül's case shows that female employment is closely related to husbands' job experience. In her interview, when she told her job history, it became obvious that whenever her husband changed his job she adjusted or changed her work accordingly. For example, after he opened a restaurant she quit her job in a small textile atelier and started to cook in her husband's restaurant. After a few years, following the closure of the restaurant, he bought a small shop, where cigarettes, alcoholic drinks and newspapers were sold. This time she gave up her current job to take care of her young daughter and to provide cooked food for this shop. The constant shift in her husband's and Gönül's occupation continued until her husband found stable work as a taxi driver. Then Gönül got herself a regular job in one of the biggest textile factories in Istanbul.

Even in cases where women can earn a decent salary due to their skills and experience, it seems difficult for them to perceive paid work as permanent. Women's identities constructed around the roles of motherhood and wifehood and responsibilities in the reproductive domain are always the prime point of reference for women and their families. Women's eagerness to perform all household duties on their own without asking for much help from their husbands can be evaluated as a strategy to protect the household as their own sphere of responsibility and to strengthen their control over it. The perception of home-based work and other forms of informal income generation as an extension of domestic work is also a reflection of this value. This false perception of home-based pieceworkers about their work is extensively cited in the literature (White 1994; Cınar 1994; Hattatoğlu 2001). Similarly, Hattatoğlu's work on home-based pieceworkers points to the ways in which women strategically avoid putting too much emphasis on their work, thereby creating an environment in which their husbands could feel incapable of taking care of their own families (Hattatoğlu 2001).

My findings show that even when women take up gainful employment the relationships between men and women are not radically challenged. Women, however, adopt strategic manipulations to protect their positions and expand their power both in the public and private domains. Turkish women are keen to protect their relative power at home, which is only maintained by taking on responsibilities related to household chores, childcare and by being a woman of honour (*namuslu*). The perpetuation of these roles and identities thus provides women with space for manoeuvre in which the exercise of power in decision-making processes in the domestic domain and other aspects of life is attained. Therefore, overemphasis on women's domestic roles and identities ends up hiding women's roles as workers and agents of income generation.

The attaining of power in the domestic and public spheres through the internalisation of traditional gender roles gained through marriage is a manifestation of women's adulthood in Turkey, where marriage for women is the celebration of the elimination of the patriarchal risks that women face in the absence of a male authority. Let me turn my attention to how the women in my sample experienced and perceived their marriages.

6.1.2 Mitigating Patriarchal Risk: Power of Marriage

When I first met Hanım and her daughter, Reyhan was an 18-year-old single girl. Hanim was eager to marry her daughter off as soon as possible. Arranging a marriage for her daughter with a suitable candidate from a relatively well-off family within their own social network or from the same region of their origin was her duty as a good mother. When I asked her whether her daughter was too young to get married she said:

> Sooner is better. When girls get older they do not want to marry any more and become more choosy. Getting married at a young age is good because you learn to become a woman sooner. I myself married my husband when I was 14 years old.

Hanım's daughter was a skilled garment worker and she worked in an atelier located very close to their house. Hanım occasionally did piecework for the same atelier. Her family also had a good relationship with the owners of the atelier. Hanım was also aware that her daughter was flirting with a young brother of the atelier owner. She supported her daughter's wish to marry him and even allowed her to date and to have phone conversations with him during his military service. She said, 'If her father finds out about it he would kill us both.' However, she gave her daughter full support in dating him. After his military service, the man told his brothers that he wanted to get married to Reyhan, whom his brothers knew very well. After some time, Hanım encouraged her husband to accept Reyhan's boyfriend as a candidate for marriage. Later on, his family came to Hanım's house to arrange the marriage details and soon after Reyhan got married. Three months later, Hanım took me to Reyhan's home, which was located 15 minutes walking distance from hers. She was quite proud to take all her relatives and neighbours for a visit to Reyhan's new flat, which was in a building owned by her husband's family and where his two brothers lived as well. When we arrived, she showed us every detail of Reyhan's home. She also knew what new couples needed to establish a proper home. In conclusion, Hanım managed to marry her daughter to a well-off family and fulfilled her duty as a 'good' and caring mother.

Hanım's effort to arrange a marriage for her daughter is not a peculiar case but an interesting one to point to the energy that parents put into their children's marriage affairs. Marrying is conceptualised as a passage to *dünya evi* (the house of the world) and every individual is educated to believe that marriage is a necessary component of their identity as adult men and women. As Hanım's case shows, marriage is an obligation to one's family and to society, as well as necessary for biological reproduction. Turkish social practices require that everyone should marry; if not, enormous social, personal and economic pressure is brought to bear to ensure that an individual does so. Otherwise, strong public exclusion and censure are applied to individuals who choose to remain single or to divorce.

In working-class neighbourhoods of Istanbul, women tend to marry either one of their kin or someone from their village or region. The reason for the custom of marrying someone from the village of origin (*hemşehri*) or network of kin is that the families know each other. This gives families certain knowledge about the character and qualities of the prospective bride and groom. For example, mothers try to find a groom with secure employment or income who will support their daughters. Families with sons try to find obedient girls from 'good families' with good labour skills.

While through marriage a woman secures the protection of her husband in the form of personal security and financial support, a man establishes his role of patriarch as head of the family. In respect to practical needs, a man marries to be cared for by a woman because men are considered to be incapable of taking care of themselves. The idea that a man must have a woman to look after his daily needs is reinforced through childhood training. A boy is served by his mother and sister(s) and all of his housekeeping needs such as food, laundry, cleaning and ironing, are provided by a woman. When men marry, this role passes to their wives. Men's involvement in housekeeping activities is socially discouraged and ridiculed. The enforcement of men's lack of interest in household chores is also a way of keeping men tied to the marriage contract (White 1994).

A girl is taken as a bride (*gelin almak*) to her husband's family to bear sons and serve him and his family. Marriage ties subordinate women to their husbands, his kin, and especially to their mothers-in-law. Attaining adult status through marriage, she is transformed from a child to an adult through the protection, control and care of a man within the conjugal contract. This transformation could be clearly observed in Reyhan's attitude. Before her marriage she was keen to act as her parents wished and she seemed very obedient and respectful by accepting everything during her marriage arrangement. When I visited her house after her marriage she told me:

> I am not old Reyhan any more, who said yes, OK to everything and everyone. I behaved very obediently (*yumuşak başlı*) and I accepted everything, whatever family elders and my parents promised to do for me. But now, I am not going to act as I used to do. I want to openly demand things from my husband and from his family and I am going to speak up as I wish.

Reyhan's story is not merely an individual manifestation of being an adult; it highlights the social practice that establishes a framework for giving a married woman a certain degree of status and decision-making power at home. Thus, a married woman is a respectable woman whose opinions carry weight among her peers and family members. Marriage gives her a certain status, although in a controlled and restricted way. Delaney (1987:42) suggests that 'Unmarried women are socially invisible' in Turkey. The relationship between husband and wife is based primarily on duty and obligations, men are the main breadwinners and responsible for the economic well-being of the family, while women are confined to the domestic sphere by the ideologies of mothering, caring and nurturing.

The wealth and labour exchanged between families are transferred through the cultural practices of *çeyiz* (trousseau) and *başlık* (bride price). The bride is expected to bring a considerable amount of *çeyiz* (trousseau) items such as such as lace bedspreads, quilts, pillows, night-clothes, slippers and hand-woven cardigans and jumpers that represent girls' handicraft (*elişi*) skills, when she marries. The items involved in *çeyiz* have drastically changed over time; cookers, refrigerators, vacuum cleaners, food processors, washing machines, televisions, and carpets are now added to the *çeyiz* list, since these items make women's life easier at home.[2] The amount of *çeyiz* presented before the marriage shows the welfare of the bride's family and handicraft skills of the bride.[3]

Bride price is a widespread customary practice, which involves the transfer of wealth to the father of the bride in the form of *başlık*[4]. In some regions, this transfer is made in the form of cash, but in some in the form of gold bracelets that are presented as a wedding gift to the bride. Despite the consideration of the gold bracelets as a gift, families negotiate on the number that the bride should be given. The difference between the customary practice of *başlık* and gold as a gift is that the bride has possession of those gold bracelets, whereas the possession of *başlık* is kept in the family of the bride as the price of bringing up a woman who is given away to the service of the groom's family. The exchange of gold bracelets and their number are always negotiated before the marriage and are seen as the provision of financial protection for the daughter in case of breakdown of the marriage.

In Turkish society, marriage is a medium of labour and wealth exchange between families. Families make alliances through marriage to bring an extra strand of security into the web of reciprocity that supports the system of related families. The alliances between families of similar social class not only establish a right of access to extra labour and economic resources but also access to social relations and networks. Marriage, according to White (1994), is the single most powerful way of declaring membership in a community and also a signal of the willingness to remain in the community.

6.2 Uneasy Definitions: Work and 'Work'

The invisibility of women in Turkish labour markets is not only a result of measurement problems and gender biases inherent in the nation-based surveys but also a result of how women define and differentiate their income-generating activities. Women engaged in informal production, home-based activities such as knitting, sewing and assembly work that revolve around the demand of childcare, housework, and other obligations of a home, see their income-producing activities as a mere extension of their domestic responsibilities. The type of work women do, the location of their work, and the social context and social relations of their work have tremendous implications for how they define themselves and the meaning of work in their lives.

Jenny White's study (1994) of a group of squatter settlement women in Istanbul, who engage in home-based piecework or work in family and neighbourhood ateliers for export and local markets, demonstrates married women's concentration in the informal sector by its easy accommodation to women's family responsibilities. White presents a detailed analysis of why the women she studies, although intensely engaged in income-producing activities, maintain a fiction of 'nonworking' and deny that they actually 'work' by conflating their income-producing labour activities with household labour. This conceptualisation of the self as 'nonworking' becomes even more striking for those women who work away from home, in neighbourhood ateliers, and are employed as non-family workers. They, too, insist that they are not working because, White explains, capitalist small-scale commodity production, even when intimately tied with the global market, operates with a kinship logic in Turkey, where labour is organised 'according to ideology of the traditional family, which links labour with role identity and responsibility' (1994:14).

Since for these poor and low-income families the family and community constitute a substantial source of support and security, giving labour or other resources without expectation of immediate monetary return is seen as the basis for forging firm bonds of mutual aid and indebtedness. But more importantly, within this framework, not only is women's labour seen as the property of the group but a woman's gender identity is largely defined by her labour, in the sense that her income-generating labour is conflated with her social roles. Thus, the unpaid or poorly paid nature of women's labour is legitimised by a cultural construction of 'giving' labour as a contribution to family and community and an expression of identity. In this regard White expresses that:

> A woman who engages in a capitalistic wage-labour relationship is involved in an impersonal relationship and deviates from the model of womanhood that entails giving without expectation of immediate return as a wife, mother, and daughter. Such a betrayal of femininity can also betray her reputation as a good woman... By conflating their labour for money and their family duties and household work, they maintain a sense of self-respect and dignity in the face of the degrading status of working for wages. As long as individual production,

piecework, and atelier labour are seen to be an expression of group identity and solidarity, rather than 'work', they remain morally and socially acceptable (1994:113).

White (1994:16) concludes,

> If women (men) do not recognise a difference between women's income-producing labour and household labour, there is no obvious way for income-earning activities to substantially affect their lives in terms of greater control over their resources and decision making. Women gain no individual control over their economic or productive lives from the work they do because their labour is in a sense the property of the group

White's account is a powerful one in addressing the ways in which women's invisibility in national surveys is culturally constructed through the entangled relationship between women's work and social identity.

Women's invisibility in the labour market produced through the uneasy definitions between work and 'work' that intertwine women's work and their social identity was observable among the garment workers in Istanbul. Especially home-based workers, traditional handicraft makers and some of the atelier workers described their activity as a hobby or help to the family business and did not consider it as 'work'. Therefore, women regard their work as the extension of their traditional housewifery activities by perceiving it to be an expression of group identity and solidarity.

Women's unpaid or under-paid work expressed as highlighting their social and group identity was also seen by my informants as a means of earning money. Although the expectation and demand for a fair financial return were not publicly expressed, all women I interviewed were well aware that their work, even as 'help', meant a financial gain and directly or indirectly contributed to the family budget. The financial returns were highly appreciated by women and their families. Despite women's confinement to the role of housewife and the marginality of their income, all the pieceworkers in my sample were conscious of how much money their work made and the dependency of their families on their income for survival. Women's awareness of financial gain from their work does not, however, translate itself into women's perception of themselves as workers and breadwinners for their households.

The case of my informant Ayla illustrates the extent of appreciation of financial gains made through home-based piecework. Ayla, who was 32 years old and a mother of 3 young children, was a regular pieceworker for an atelier located in her neighbourhood, and said that:

> No one pays you money for sitting idle at home. My husband and everyone know that I earn money for my children and my family. We even managed to save money for the future. In case of illness or an emergency, we at least have some money so we will not be in need of financial help from other people (*elalem*).

Ayten was one of my key informants. I lived close to her and had long hours of conversation with her. She has three sons and a husband who does irregular jobs and often shifts from one job to another. Even though he is usually not unemployed, the money he makes remains very marginal because of the irregularity of his occupations. Thus, Ayten began to take in piecework from a large-scale textile factory eight years ago. She said that:

> I know that it seems like petty work but I make as much money as my husband earns each month. Without my contribution we would not have been able to support our sons' education. We also have built the house we live in with my contributions. Although it is very hard and irregular work, everyone knows without it we would be starving out in the streets. My husband's income is only enough to feed us but the rest is done through the money which I make from the piecework.

The significance of women's income for the survival of low-income families in Istanbul has not helped to change how women's work is perceived and valued. The uneasy definition that women's paid work is not seen as 'work' is also a result of the nature of garment work, which is mainly done at home or in family establishments. For women, the classic meaning of work requires being present at a workplace and working fixed hours, which is easily observable in the case of factory workers. However, piecework and *elişi* (handicraft) activities are usually perceived as not being 'work' but as just passing time and making some cash.

Preserving a sense of self-respect and their identity of motherhood in the face of the perceived temporariness and marginality of their work is managed by expressing the priority of their family duties and household work over their work. In Istanbul, women's social identity as mothers and wives does not stop them turning their skill into an income-generating activity that contributes to making ends meet and provides a significant contribution to the family budget. The pervasiveness of women's identity as the 'women of their homes', through which women refrain from carving out a work identity, is also a result of the negative social image attached to working women.

6.3 Defining Workers and Working Identity

The self-definition of 'work' as not work is the reflection of women's own perspective on how they conceptualise their income-generating activities, which provide a significant financial contribution to the family budget. However, this view falls short in explaining the social meaning attached to women's paid work and the identities of those who earn a living through waged work in Istanbul's garment industry.

In Turkey, single girls are called house-girls (*evkızı*) and married women are housewives (*evkadını*). Men are automatically defined as the head of households (*aile reisi*) regardless of whether they are the providers or not. The identities of men and women, defined according to their positions in the household and marital status, shift a little when their workplace identities are considered.

The profiles of garment workers in terms of mode of employment and autonomy in the labour process suggest that modes of employment in garment production have significant implications for the formation of work identities. Different workplaces attach to women different identities such as atelier girls (*atölye kızı*), factory women (*fabrika kadını*), or pieceworkers (*el işçisi*). In Turkish, work identities are gender-neutral as long as the subject is a man. For example, *işçi* means worker and a garment worker is *konfeksiyon işçisi* and their simultaneous reference is a man. However, these definitions change when the gender of a worker is a woman. Not seen as *konfeksiyon işçisi*, women are called *atölye kızı* or factory woman, which bears a negative social connotation attached to their roles as workers.

Recall that the majority of women in this study have applied different strategies to get permission from their family members for their employment in different segments of the garment industry. Some of them mentioned the negative image of the 'working women'. One of my informants, Sevim, told of her father's refusal to let her work in an atelier. She said that:

My father objected to the idea with no intention of letting me work in that atelier. He kept repeating that he cannot make people talk behind him that his daughter was an atelier girl. He said that nobody knew what they did all day long working in the same place with boys. People think that all *konfeksiyon* workers are loose women and bring shame to their families.

The negative social implications that women's work identity carries are one of the reasons for women's perception of their work as not 'work' in Turkish society, which also results in women's invisibility in the labour market and pushes women's work into the realm of the informal economy.

Engaging in a capitalistic wage-labour relationship is seen solely as a male domain, and for women it always involves deviating from their roles as wife, mother, and daughter with a danger of losing respect and socially degrading their status by working for wages. Overcoming these negative meanings is made possible in the garment industry through women's employment in family-run ateliers or by their working with family and friends in the same workplace, employment that reinforces patriarchal definitions of women's identity. Releasing women for paid work necessitated finding a way of getting over the negative social meanings attached to female employment in Turkey, managed through the different reasons given to justify women's work in the garment industry.

6.4 Justifying Women's Work: *Ekmek Parası* (Money for Bread)

Once the social structural conditions are established, such as working as a pieceworker or in a small neighbourhood atelier or working with family members and friends in a big factory, under which women's labour is channelled to garment production and traditional patriarchal gender relations can be sheltered and nurtured, women and their families use a string of reasons to justify women's paid work. Through these reasons, employment is experienced as not being problematic and is seen as an extension of traditional work rather than a radical departure from it. As long as families and husbands can maintain the traditional forms of control over women's work and provide socially acceptable justifications, such as that women's work is highly tied to their domestic roles and family responsibilities, women's paid work is accepted.

In contrast to women's work, which is perceived as temporary, men's work is seen as permanent. Earning money for bread *(ekmek parası)* encapsulates the economic activity of male heads, in which bread, the single most important food staple eaten at every meal, is earned. The cultural meaning attached to male earnings is similar to the model of male breadwinner developed within the framework of the post-war European welfare states (Fraser 1997; Folbre 2001). In Turkish society, men's work is symbolically as essential as bread. Thus, men are socially mobilised to obtain a stable job, whose attainment, preferably in the public sector, can eventually lead to long-term security and retirement.

Investigating household survival strategies is the only way to analyse how migrant families and women adopt different employment strategies in Istanbul, where low-income families have no provisions from the welfare state and survival relies heavily on the effective use of those strategies. Household studies focusing on employment strategies in the industrialised countries reflect the state and welfare system as important agents influencing decisions about employment, survival strategies and the allocation of household duties (Pahl 1984; Morris 1987; 1990). In Turkey, welfare state provision generally has little to do with people's employment decisions and day-to-day monetary resources except for creating, for a limited number of people, stable employment opportunities in the public sector. The absence of state-based social safety nets is offset by the manipulation of kin or family-based agencies. The survival strategies are therefore dependent upon having access to those agencies and also to households' abilities to use those individual and community resources.

For a working-class family, a regular income derived from formal sector employment, home ownership, and access to kinship and *hemşehri* networks are among the most important factors that families rely on in establishing a sense of security for the future. In the first place the intentions are to meet the basic needs but later families stretch their resources to secure families' long-term well-being in the city. Among garment workers, financial difficulty was the most commonly cited reason for women's labour market participation. However, only a few women worked to meet basic needs of foods, clothes, etc., while the rest had the aims of securing a better future for their families such as buying a house, children's further education. Interestingly, none emphasised any long-term projections of having an independent business or any other development in their labour market activities. A clear-cut conclusion is that the meaning of paid work for women is to meet their families' needs and future aspirations rather than to be a manifestation of self-expression and personal development.

Meeting basic needs was the main reason for widowed, divorced and women without a man's financial support to take up garment work. For example, a widowed woman who came to Istanbul three years ago with her 20-year-old son and a married daughter and was working as an unskilled garment worker was only able to pay the rent and buy basic food for her family, which were almost equal to her salary. Working as an *ortaci* (all-purpose helper, unskilled garment worker) was the only job she could do due to her age and lack of skills; she earned very little money in return for her manual labour. My second informant is a 32-year-old divorced woman who now lives with her mother and two other sisters. She began to work in a garment atelier immediately after her divorce. She said that she had to look after her daughter, and her work helped with the budget of her mother's household. Having work experience prior to her marriage gave her an advantage and she was able to earn a skilled worker's salary, which is a bit higher than that of an unskilled worker. She said that it would have been impossible for her to survive as a divorced woman if she had not had her mother. Another woman who worked to meet the basics, Zahire, was a middle-aged married woman whose husband did not bring home a regular income and sometimes stopped supporting his household altogether. Thus, Zahire decided to work while her daughter, 16, was at home taking care of domestic work. Her income is devoted to meeting the family's daily needs and she said that she could only think of making ends meet.

Buying a house that seals the success of immigrant families is a convincing and socially acceptable reason justifying women's work among garment workers. Every family aspires to have their own house, which is perceived as a secure provision for future. In Turkey, the narrow national social security system covering only a limited number of formal-sector employees allows a privileged few to have old age pensions. Home ownership acts like a long-term safety net and offsets the insecurity of not having a pension. Therefore, families with a relatively regular income and with some financial help from their families or kin build and/or buy their own flat. In this context, women's paid work is usually justified as a temporary measure until house or flat ownership is secured. Women make enormous efforts to put together all of their resources to own a house. Lale, who is a 35-year-old factory worker, told me how she manages her house and works to save money to pay off their debt:

> I work 8 hours a day and also take in piecework from the factory that my husband, daughter and I do during the nights. I also tried to make everything at home in order to spend as little as money as possible. I make our jams and tomato paste at home. When we go to our village during our vacations in summer I bring cheese, olives, rice and beans from our village. So we try to make our living. But I do not know when I will reach the good days of my life.

The contribution of women to building a house is not limited only to providing financial means, but also covers their physical involvement in the actual building process. Carrying bricks and cement during the construction, cleaning, and providing food for construction workers are among the different contributions. When their husbands are away working all day, they help on the construction site so that their labour may save them from hiring extra manpower. The process of owning a house makes women's paid work socially acceptable, since the whole community aims to reach the same target. Therefore, married women's paid work is expected to continue for a certain time until they have their own house, and then they can give up work and be 'woman of their own house' again. During my conversation with Ayten, her husband was complaining about her work as a garment pieceworker:

> After we finish paying all the money that we borrowed from my brothers I want her to stop doing this work. I hate to see garments lying around and she sometimes works until morning to get the work done on time.

Providing for children's education is another reason justifying women's employment. No women, however, reported their children's education as their initial reason for taking up employment. Investing in children's education, which was envisaged as a lifetime income security for the children and financial protection for their parents in their old age, is usually directed at male children. However, many women in my sample showed their insistence on providing higher education for their daughters as well.

Education and the welfare of children are considerations among the married women working in formal factories rather than being a main concern for atelier workers or pieceworkers. If workers have a long history of work, provision for children's education is the only valid reason for women to continue working. For example, Kadriye, who is 35 and has been working for 15 years in the same textile factory, invoked the welfare of her daughter to keep working as a garment worker. At first, she found a job to save up some money to buy a flat. After that she wanted to work because she felt that her husband's income did not stretch far enough to cover their own needs as well as their daughter's education expenses. She said that:

> My husband and I worked hard for so many years and he sometimes worked two shifts a day from 6 o'clock in the morning to 10 at night. When I had night shift we could not see each other for a whole week. We used to leave written notes to each other. After so many years of struggle, we finally managed to build our three-floor house. I want

to continue working because I am going to retire soon and I want my daughter to go to university. My only aspiration in life is to see her working as a professional and I don't want her to earn her living working like me.

Thus, investing in the social mobility of future generations is an important target that keeps women in employment.

The main reasons for young girls' employment are to provide a substantial income for their families and to buy items necessary for their *çeyiz*. Working for *çeyiz* is popular among young girls whose family cannot afford to make *çeyiz* for their daughters. Kerime was a 19-year-old garment atelier worker and she had got engaged to a male garment worker three months before our interview took place. She began to work five years before when her parents decided to build a house. They allowed her to work because they were not able to give her any money for her *çeyiz*. She told me that she bought everything necessary for her *çeyiz* and even additional items such as washing machines and food processors. Although Kerime's work is legitimised for making her *çeyiz*, it was evident that her income was also vital for her family to be able to build their house.

Women's testimonies defuse the widely held notion that migrant women take up paid work only for the sake of the survival of the family in the face of economic uncertainty. Society justifies women's work only if a link with family survival is recognised, even when these justifications can change from providing for essential means to buying a house, through which women establish wage work as a permanent part of their lives. A high level of commitment to paid employment does not, however, undermine women's identities as mothers and wives or their devotion to the homes and families that remain the centre of their lives and identities.

6.5 Barriers for Work: Permission, Children, Age and Image

As Delaney puts it, 'Authority, except for the elder men… is always outside the self' (1991:172). In the context of Turkish culture male authority thus manifests itself in the concept of permission, or consent (*izin*) for women's work. Getting permission is women's first step in taking up paid work in garment production. Earlier research showed that the consent of the household head is the crucial issue keeping women out of the labour market or leading to their concentration in home-based piecework activities (Ecevit 1991; Cinar 1994; Eraydın and Erendil 1996; İlkkaracan 2000).

Bargaining to enter the labour market and overcoming opposition to paid work activities have different results; for some the outcomes are co-operative, and for others conflictual. Co-operative forms of decision-making refer both to an absence of opposition and to an active consensus. The absence of opposition tends to indicate the level of poverty or the loss of the male breadwinner. Co-operation between couples or family members concerning women's entrance into the labour market draws attention to common concerns about necessary living standards, priorities about children or the family's future prospects. Conflicts in the bargaining process in decisions related to women's employment reveal the nature of the relationship between gender, power and conflict within the family (Sen 1990; Agarwal 1994; Kabeer 1994). Therefore, the conflictual form of bargaining is more likely to clarify our understanding of power and gender relations in the family.

In this research, the factory workers had no opposition from their families when entering their current jobs. The relatively high benefits and bonuses they receive make factory work appealing. Being recruited for a large-scale factory is welcomed among working-class families since the work is much more regulated and workers have benefits and are covered by social security. Şenay is a garment worker in one of the largest textile factories in Istanbul and she told me her methods of finding her present job. Rather than facing opposition from her family members, Şenay had open support from her family for her recruitment:

> The strongest opposition to my work came from my parents before I took my first job, which was in a small garment atelier. They could not believe that I wanted to work but after long days of negotiations I managed to get permission at least to work for a short period of time... However, it was hard to get my current job. My sister's husband provided me with a personal connection. The doorkeeper's sister-in-law was working in this factory and we contacted her to help me to get this job.

Permission to work is not a major obstacle for factory workers because of their previous working experience. Since families get used to the idea of their daughters and wives working, it becomes easy to take another step for a second job.

Pieceworkers are thought to be free of husbands' disapproval since their work takes place at home, allowing them space to attend to all their domestic duties and childcare. According to Cinar's findings, some 54 per cent of pieceworkers could not get their husband's permission to work outside the home (Cinar 1994). Concerning the pieceworkers in my sample, all women felt the need to get approval if the work took a large amount of their time, such as 15 hours or more. One of my informants told me that when she first saw the advertisement that a garment factory was giving out piecework in neighbourhoods she and her husband went there together to get her first job. A case is the young single pieceworker, Sultan, living with her four brothers, who was the only one who managed to hide her work from her brothers. She was staying alone at home all day long, cooking, cleaning and washing for her brothers. At first she started with helping women in the neighbourhood and then secretly began to work on her own account. Her family was far too conservative to allow her to go out on her own, let alone do any paid work.

For the home-based pieceworkers, their husbands' permission was not the only obstacle preventing their employment in a factory or atelier. Childcare, old age and being unskilled were also cited as obstacles. A commonly encountered problem is the care of small children. Working only becomes possible when proper childcare facilities are available in the workplace; otherwise a family needs to find alternative methods of childcare. For example, the help of other family members or private crèches, even though costly for a working-class family, are other means of sorting out childcare while the mother is out at work. Using these options is viable only in the case of lucrative and stable employment. Women prefer to do home-based piecework if only marginal and temporary employment options are available for them. The testimony of one of my informants clearly singles out childcare as an obstacle to women's entrance into the labour market:

> How could I go out to work? I have two small children and my husband works all day and comes back late in the evening. I do not have anybody from my family who can look after my children while I work. My husband's family is far from where we live now. So I am doing piecework and looking after my children at the same time. We live in a one-room flat which was transformed from a kind of storage room or *dükkan* (shop), so it is hard for me to have a relative with us to look after my children. I wish I could work in better paid work so we could buy our own flat and live better.

Age and being unskilled are other reasons for doing piecework. Six women said that they began to take in piecework because they were too old to go out to work. In fact, these women could have found some kind of unskilled job in small garment ateliers, but thought that they were too old to go out to work. Married women, especially those with children after their thirties, defined themselves as too old for factory or atelier work. The perception of women about their age is related to the fact that women gain status with advancing age. Therefore, women themselves attach a degree of status to being an elderly woman who is not to go out and search for a paid job. As seniority is acquired through age and marriage in Turkish households, being old is in fact a subjective factor.

For most of the pieceworkers, their husbands' permission before labour market entrance is of crucial importance. However, some of the women in my sample preferred to focus on other obstacles such as domestic duties and childcare responsibility that prevented their employment, rather than on the opposition of their husbands. The emphasis on those duties and responsibilities puts women in collusion with their husbands in constructing and preserving their roles as wives and mothers. The perceptions of gender roles and meanings attached to being a man or woman are internalised equally by men and women through a set of cultural practices that help to hide the unequal socioeconomic outcomes of confinement to these asymmetric gender roles.

The negative image of being a 'factory woman' is an obstacle for women's work, as shown by Ayten overtly telling the story of how her prospect of taking up and maintaining formal employment in a large-scale textile factory was prevented by her husband and his family:

> One day, one of my husband's relatives informed us that his wife's factory had begun to recruit workers and I applied for the job and got accepted. As soon as I began to work a rumour was spread that our relative's wife was having an affair with a man in the factory. So immediately, my husband's family and my own family asked me to quit the job and so I did… While I was working in that brief time my husband kept complaining that there was no food when he came back from work and the children were all alone at home all day long. But now I regret that I quit it because I struggle too much to make money. And more importantly I missed the opportunity to get retirement benefits and the chance of being on pensions now.

The rumour of alleged 'immoral' behaviour at the workplace significantly affected Ayten's employment trajectory 15 years ago when there was a more negative public view of women's employment. The recent spread of small-scale garment ateliers has altered this negative public image of 'factory woman' to some degree. Although a total overhaul of this view has not yet emerged, having a significant number of women engaged in paid work makes it more difficult for other women to be criticised for working. Having a close relative or woman friend working also helps women wishing to take up employment to negotiate more actively for the consent of their families.

The literature on Turkish women's waged work points to the lack of permission from husbands or male members of the family (Ecevit 1991; Cinar 1994; Eraydın and Erendil 1996; İlkkaracan 2000). Each of these studies emphasises that opposition is mainly from male heads of the household. However, permission is tied not only to male members but also to older female members who are influential in decisions made, whether negative or positive, regarding women's entrance to the labour market. For example, Gülben, a 19-year-old garment worker, thought at first that it would be impossible for her to get permission. But she said:

> I cried every day that I want to go to work. It seemed to me like playing a game, going to work and earning money. I insisted every day and I told my mother that her sister was working as a garment worker, why shouldn't I have worked as well?.. And, when my parents decided to construct our house then they allowed me to work. The atelier was just a street away from our house and my parents had known the owners of the atelier for a long time. They were our neighbours. After all this effort, I got permission. But what I think is that if my mother did not want me working I would have never been able to work in any way.

Including the influence of elderly women or mothers in the analysis enables us to comprehend the workings of the patriarchal system more fully. Since senior women have control over younger women, their influence on younger women's working prospects is decisive. In Gülben's case, once her mother was on her side it became easier for her to get her father's permission. As Kıray showed earlier, women have a great deal of involvement in decisions related to their children, especially during rapid social transformations such as rural–urban migration, and she also indicated the progressive role played by mothers in support of sons leaving villages for work or education against their fathers' will (Kıray 1976). Thus, women' key position in the decision-making process at home reflects a different aspect of patriarchal gender roles in Turkey.

Permission for women's work reveals the nature of the authority structure and the bargaining process in Turkish households, where the consent of senior male prepares women's passage into the world of paid work. Evidently, bargaining not only takes place between men and women but also includes hierarchical positions related to age and seniority among different members of families. Therefore, women not only bargain with male members to get permission for work but also negotiate with senior female members in their families and other authority figures in their communities.

Conclusion

The factors conditioning women's labour supply, such as marriage, gender relations, justification of women's work and barriers for work, examined from women's own perspectives have highlighted the ways in which women's labour is released for paid employment and how women conceptualise their work and working identity. In Turkish society, where social organisation is heavily based on the family unit, family and marriage are important sources of identity and security as well as economic support for women. Women mitigate 'patriarchal risk' through marriage and confining themselves to traditional gender roles and relations. Publicly voicing themselves through the roles of motherhood and wifehood, women can only gain status and decision-making power when they most ascribe those roles. Thus, the confinement of women to their roles as mothers and wives is the only way for women to attain power in both private and public spheres in the low-income communities of urban Turkey. Only through the manipulation of these relations can women effectively negotiate with their husbands, father and other members of their family and community.

Marriage is also a strong institution in which women and men are expected to perform certain kinds of duties and roles with respect to each other and to society. Women are usually expected to play a major role in marriage arrangements. They are eager for marriage, as Kandiyoti (1988) argued, as a conservative choice against the uncertainties of the future. Women step out of childhood and enter into womanhood through marriage. Thus, marriage and motherhood are sites in which women's patriarchal bargaining constantly and consciously goes on. Although women may end up internalising the classical patriarchal system, my argument is that women consciously alter the existing roles and relations by utilising these roles to protect themselves against insecurities and also to gain status and power. By following the same line of argument, it is suggested that the emancipation of women needs to be perceived as a journey rather than an ultimate destination that is to be reached.

Women's employment is significantly influenced by gender roles and identities in Turkish society. Women's decision to work is extensively connected to their families' needs and to the joint aspirations of the family. This nature of women's employment leads to the temporariness and invisibility of women's work. Therefore, women's characterisation as a temporary and invisible labour force is the result not only of the nature of the work that women undertake but also of the way in which women themselves construct their work, as well as of the way in which women set their priorities as 'woman of their home'.

7

WOMEN IN THE WORKPLACE
Recruitment and Mobility

The invisibility of women's work in Turkey is a reflection of gender ideologies that construct women's primary roles as wives and mothers. Women's engagement with paid work is never prioritised over their major roles at home and in society. In this regard, women's participation in labour market activities is constructed around their domestic roles and also the needs of their families. Gender ideologies exercise a powerful influence over how women have access to employment opportunities and why women take up paid work. Moreover, gender ideologies shape the conditions under which women enter into labour market activities as workers.

Gender-biased labour markets are argued to discriminate systematically against women. Labour market segmentation confines women to mostly poorly paid, repetitive, unskilled and labour-intensive jobs (Anker and Hein 1986; Beechey 1987; Elson and Pearson 1981; Humphrey 1985; Scott 1986 and 1990; Walby 1990). Therefore, women's domestic roles find a reflection in what women do in workplaces, resulting in the devaluation of women's work. Labour relations as 'bearers of gender' are structured to reflect the gender relations of the society in which the labour market is embedded (Elson 1999).

This chapter consolidates and develops the themes that labour markets are the bearers of the relations and institutions of the societies in which they are embedded. This is most explicit in the recruitment practices in the garment industry in Turkey, in which identities and hierarchies are constantly renegotiated and reconfigured. Recruitment processes not only carry existing hierarchies into the workplace but also generate new forms of seniority, surveillance and authority between workers. Moreover, recruitment through 'word of mouth' helps a smooth transition of skills and shifts control over workers from managerial groups to the workers themselves.

The mobility of women and the location of firms and ateliers are examined to assess the impact of women's labour force participation. Specially provided transportation and the clustering of the garment industry in neighbourhoods enable the firms to have easy access to female labour. The increasing mobility of women has changed private surveillance over women to public surveillance, and transformed women's secluded private sphere by generating special gendered arrangements in transportation and location. These measures are not only used to prevent sexual harassment and protect the reputation of women commuting to work, but also help to create the subordination of women. The role of social networks that manipulate recruitment processes and help to perpetuate gender ideologies is delineated through qualitative interview data. The ethnography examines how gender ideologies, cultural practices, and local discourses on women's work translate into wider processes of cultural justifications for the release of women's labour, and also examines how these processes are acted out and sustained in people's everyday lives and the way that they are reshaping social relations and the notion of gender in low-income communities in Istanbul.

7.1 Disciplinary Power of Social Relations: Recruiting Women Workers

The investigation of the recruitment process not only reflects workers' job-seeking strategies and employers' recruiting strategies, but also provides insights into the gender ideologies that shape women's experience in workplaces. A variety of recruitment strategies employed in different firms reveals why and how women are employed and the influence of gender and familial networks on labour market relations in Turkish society, which contribute to the entrenchment of patriarchal structures in local labour markets. While Harris and Morris (1986) point out that recruitment is rarely the direct result of formal rational and public procedures on the part of either worker or employer, the assumptions and attitudes of key decision makers at managerial and supervisory levels undoubtedly contribute to the perpetuation of the ideas and values of existing gender ideologies.

The strategies adopted to recruit workers in Istanbul's garment industry are directly linked to efforts to extend kin-based familial relations into workplaces. These efforts have proved to be beneficial for employers through giving them access to a cheap and docile labour force. Two basic recruitment strategies have been adopted in the garment industry. The first is to recruit from the labour of the immediate family and kin members of employers, and the second is to employ people known to current workers. This word-of-mouth recruitment strategy allows employers on the one hand to reach a cheap labour pool, and on the other hand to establish a form of power that helps to exercise easy control over the workforce. Leading to a kind of chain of control, this power gained through recruitment not only provides for the control of workers and their surveillance by managerial methods, but also forces workers to be accountable for their behaviour in the workplace to the people who initiated their recruitment. Thus, obedience, hard work and submissiveness are the elements of the code of behaviour required from workers. In addition, the strict control mechanism over workers managed by the word-of-mouth recruitment strategy is crucial for the performance of this labour-intensive industry. Seeking a job through one's own personal connections explicitly necessitates the perpetuation of relations based on obligations and responsibilities in the workplace. For example, if a relative, friend or neighbour helps a person to get a job in the same factory where she or he is employed, the person feels the obligation of properly fulfilling the requirements of their job. This puts the 'grantor' worker in an accountable and responsible position to factory management for the performance of the newly recruited worker.

Reciprocal bonds generate symbolic indebtedness among individuals. Relations between creditor and debtor, patron and client, master and apprentice (usta-çırak) are dependent on the 'power of debt' (White 1994). The acceptance of reciprocal obligations for both parties is repaid in the form of respect, loyalty, work, service and homage, helping to enforce the perpetuation of social networks. As argued earlier, access to various forms of social networks and community is an important means of survival in Istanbul. It is, however, evident that relations based on reciprocal ties are not free from domination and power. As White argues, 'the construction of un-repayable debts is a source of power and domination not only within the family but throughout Turkish society.... Individuals are usually dominated and dominant depending on their position in the strands of reciprocal relations that have been activated' (1994:101).

The position of individuals within the web of social relations can change and shift according to their gender, age and social status. Reciprocal relations also offer every individual the chance to practise power and domination over others when the opportunity arises. Thus, all members of Turkish society have access to some degree of power through the manipulation of reciprocal ties. Helping a member of the community to be recruited for a job creates a debt that can be paid back by being an obedient and loyal worker. If, as Bourdieu (1977) suggests, giving is a way of possessing, then it becomes clear that workers exercise asymmetrical power relations over each other.

Asymmetrical relations of reciprocity in the recruitment process serve to discipline workers in workplaces by partially transferring disciplinary power from managers to peer workers.

Relations of reciprocal domination in the sphere of economic behaviour and within the family have significant implications for the ways in which women participate in labour market activities. Women are extensively controlled and constrained not only by the systemic exploitative relations of capitalist production, but also by the patriarchal relations perpetuated in the workplace. Earlier studies on female employment in Turkey have shown that relationships between male workers or managers and female workers are established on the basis of kin relations, such as father/uncle–daughter or brother–sister (*bacı*). Thus, the usage of familial-kinship idioms creates a metaphor of the family in the workplace, with which labour relations are associated. This provides a safe and family-like environment in which women work[1] (Ecevit 1991; Eraydın and Erendil 1996; White 1994).

Familial relations in the workplace are maintained not only through the use of kinship idioms, but also by prioritising the recruitment of individuals who already have a personal connection with the workplace. Even though opposite interests are at stake this is beneficial to both employees and employers, which gives extra negotiating power to both parties for different reasons. For example, a girl can ensure permission to work in a workplace that belongs to a relative, while the employer acquires cheap and docile female labour. What follows in this chapter are the findings from the fieldwork, where the focus is on the different recruitment practices applied by different garment producers.

7.2 Recruitment of Factory Workers

The Turkish Employment Agency is an official state institution whose function is to match vacancies with job seekers. In practice, however, the institution is rarely used either by private or public sector firms. Daily newspapers are likely to receive more job vacancy advertisements than the Employment Agency. Newspaper advertisements and the Turkish Employment Agency are the only two anonymous channels available for seeking a job in the labour market. Other ways used to seek a job or recruit workers are always based on personal connections and word-of-mouth introductions. The job vacancies section in the daily newspapers has, in recent years, mostly been devoted to vacancies for white-collar workers. Therefore it is rare to see an advertisement in a daily newspaper looking for a garment worker, since this is an expensive method of recruitment for garment firms. Garment factories use newspaper advertising only to fill professional vacancies, and rely on word of mouth for filling jobs on the production line.

Word of mouth was an extremely common recruitment method, used by nearly all of the employers interviewed in this research. Seen as an efficient and inexpensive recruitment method, word-of-mouth introductions are embraced enthusiastically, and at least 90 per cent of factory jobs were filled through this method. Vacancy announcements made through noticeboards placed in easily recognisable areas in the factory such as cafeterias show the factory management's tendency to recruit people who are recommended by their current employees.

Another way of recruiting workers adopted by garment factories was to place an advertisement at the factory gate; garment ateliers use this method as well. If the factory is located close to a busy neighbourhood, this method may effectively draw the attention of people living close by. However, some large-scale factories located in the outskirts of Istanbul, far from the residential areas, recruit workers using the method of placing large posters in the working-class neighbourhoods where the potential workers live. These posters indicate which company is seeking workers, what kinds of workers are needed, and what the benefits and bonuses of the job are. For example, 'A jeans factory located in Güneşli is looking for qualified and unqualified workers, the positions are well paid and lunch, transportation and social security provided.' This method is usually utilised when factories initially recruit large numbers of employees.

The word-of-mouth recruitment method worked like a reference system, and, although informal and face to face, was mostly preferred by employers who found it more secure to employ someone brought in by an employee than to hire a total stranger[2]. Moreover, some employers mentioned the difficulty of assessing prospective employees in what they felt to be an increasingly uncertain and dishonest world. Being unable to judge the honesty of applicants encountered through other means of recruitment such as newspaper advertisements was a great concern for the employers. Thus, using personal contacts to recruit is a way of creating a stable, disciplined, productive and homogenous workforce. Another reason for recruiting through current workers' contacts is to promote the smooth transmission of skills on the job. Workers are more likely to provide efficient, informal and on-the-job training to people they have brought to the workplace than they are to strangers[3].

This recruitment technique signals the ways in which industrial production is socially organised by the mobilisation of urban kinship networks in

Turkish society. A strong connection in each factory between the place of origin (memleket) of managerial personnel and that of the dominant group of workers was found to be common in Istanbul's garment factories. For example, when the factory manager was from Kars, so were almost half of the workers in the factory. People from the Thrace region of Turkey dominate some factories, and those from Karadeniz (Northern Turkey) dominate others. This, of course, helps to keep relations of domination and group identities intact in the workplace, as well as reinforcing them. Moreover, these identities and forms of domination are valued more than ever before, as they are the principal means of survival in the cities.

Recruitment through word of mouth and personal connections tends to reproduce existing gender roles and occupational segregation based on gender and ethnicity. As individuals in particular groups have and circulate information about certain job opportunities, word-of-mouth recruitment perpetuates the gender-biased character of labour markets. Using the personal contacts – friends, neighbours, kin – of present employees to recruit new workers promotes the spatial clustering of employees, which prevents women from breaking through the boundaries of existing patriarchal gender roles and identities by keeping them bound to their communities. Thus, I shall focus on how the women factory workers in my sample experienced the recruitment process.

All of my informants working in garment factories mobilised a personal contact to get their current jobs. The types of personal connections range from their family members working in the same factory, to an acquaintance who either has a position in the managerial section of the factory or has personal connections with the factory management. The ways in which the oldest factory worker in the sample, the mother of three daughters and a son, used her position in the factory to recruit her daughters was an interesting case. Shortly after she got married her husband developed heart disease and never attempted to work again. She then became the sole supporter of her family, and began to work in her current job. As her daughters gradually grew up she took them to work with her. The eldest daughter got into the factory, then the second daughter began to work with her mother after she graduated from primary school, and then the youngest girl also started working in the same factory. The mother told me:

> My two daughters work with me and I got them the jobs. When they
> finished primary school the factory was looking for workers. I told
> the *ustabaşı* (foreman) that I wanted my daughters to come and work

with me. Since then, 7 years now we have been working together. This is better than them sitting idle at home and I can also watch over them. In turn, they keep me company. They also save up money for their *çeyiz*. Otherwise it would have been very difficult to afford their *çeyiz* spending because my husband cannot work and my salary is just enough to feed us. But I support my son to study and become a lawyer when he grows up. I want him to go to university.

Evidently the hierarchical authority relations between mother and daughters were perpetuated in the workplace, and she made sure that her daughters behaved submissively, obediently and 'appropriately'. Observation and supervision were evident not only among close kin but in other patron–client relations. The following example demonstrates this point.

Sunay was a 26-year-old divorced woman and had been working for four years in one of biggest garment factories in Istanbul. She had two children and lived with her parents in a small flat in Esenler. After her divorce, she got fed up with her father's complaints that she and her children were a burden, and that if she had been a good woman she would have stayed with her husband. Even though her husband was a violent man who had been convicted for robbery, her family only grudgingly accepted her separation from him. She told me that her parents were quite religious and had married her off when she was 17 years old to a man who lived in her hometown, Tokat. After her marriage Sunay lived with her in-laws for four years. She separated from her husband when he was in prison, and then moved back to Istanbul to her parents' house. In order to stop her father's complaints about her own and her children's presence, Sunay decided to work. One of her neighbours helped her to get her current job in the factory.[4]

> I know that she helped me to have my job. But I am a hard worker and could get any kind of job to earn a living for my children. This woman thinks that she is my boss. She always watches every move I make and tries to make me feel I owe her everything. She even gets angry with me if I make friends here and she tells my parents whatever happens at work. I cannot even have lunch without her being around me. But I know that somehow she is very jealous of me because I learnt the job quickly and became a hard worker. I even got promoted. After I got the job I got my divorce and I tried to buy myself a flat. She may be jealous of what I have done so far on my own and she may be doing all these things because I am a divorced woman.

The identities women acquire through marriage inevitably remain with them in every aspect of their life; they are not like possessions that can be left at the door of the factories. Their workplace relations with other colleagues and friends are contingent upon those identities. In Sunay's case, it is apparent that her friend could not have patronised her as much as she did if she had still been a married woman. Therefore, women's identities can only be altered by shifting the nature of their relations to men. At the end of our conversation, Sunay told me that she is going to marry a man who is almost twice her age. She said:

> This is the only way that we have a proper place in society. Otherwise I keep fighting with my parents and feeling unwelcome. However, now I can have my own house and look after my children. He accepted to marry me even though I have two children.

In some cases, recruitment through personal contacts is utilised to eliminate the ideological conflicts and prejudices that the factory management has towards people from different ethnic groups. Although diversity in background and ethnic origin exists in Istanbul's garment industry, during recruitment workers with different ethnic origins, religious sects and political activities are made to feel threatened and vulnerable, so that they do not dare to make trouble. Two women workers reported that their job applications were about to be refused because of their origin. However, their connections at the factory persuaded the management to employ them even though they were Kurds.

Eser was one of these workers, and was discriminated against because of her place of birth. She was from Diyarbakır, had a high school education, and came to Istanbul 10 years ago to find better work and life options. Initially she stayed with her brother and his family and worked as a secretary in small offices. Since she did not have any specific qualifications, her jobs did not last long. She later worked in a small cosmetics production atelier. When her brother's friend informed her about a vacancy in his department, she enthusiastically applied for the job in the hope of finally having a stable and decent job. Her contact was a very influential figure in the factory and promised to pursue her application. As Eser puts it:

> When I applied for the job it was kind of certain that I would get the job. But the management made a big hassle because I was from Diyarbakır. Our friend really tried hard for me and in the end I was

recruited for the job. Since we are from *doğu* (the east)[5] everyone thinks we are all rebels.

During our conversation, Eser often reiterated her connection in very deep appreciation and called him Remzi abi (older brother). On every occasion she showed her appreciation to him. If there was a celebration in his family, for his daughter's birthday for example, she always chose her gift with great care, showing her feeling of indebtedness. Therefore, power relations and hierarchies in communities reinforced through recruitment strategies have different implications for different workers; for some they are empowering, while for others they limit women's behaviour and future prospects at work.

In sum, these recruitment strategies help to euphemise the tension of class conflict and the exploitative relations of capitalist production by shifting disciplinary control from the management of the factory to fellow workers. As Granovetter suggests, labour markets reflect constraints associated with the social networks and other social structures in which economic behaviour is embedded (Granovetter 1988). Thus, existing patronage relations and also gender relations are integrated into the capitalist system of production so as to generate an obedient, submissive and cheap labour force. The nature of hierarchical relations may provide individuals with the opportunity to move further in the hierarchies of power within the community by gaining seniority and working experience. However it seems that this shift does not work to change the fundamental nature of capitalist exploitation. It rather reproduces those very relations.

7.3 Recruitment Strategies of Garment Ateliers

Mobilisation of family labour is the basis of the labour force working in garment ateliers. Not only unpaid family labour but also members of kin groups and neighbours comprise the core workers in garment ateliers. The composition of the workforce has created an environment in which labour relations are more intimate and face to face, and family idioms are used to enforce this family-like workplace.

Having an extended family is the basic foundation of a garment atelier, and most ateliers are run either by brothers or with the cooperation of immediate relatives, such as partnerships between elder sons and brothers-in-law. The terms of partnership vary depending on which partner provides capital, labour and skill resources. For example, Ahmet was an atelier owner, and the initial establishment of the atelier was a partnership of ex-colleagues, as Ahmet's partner had the skills of garment making. Later he married a skilled garment worker who had been working since she was 12. After their marriage, he established his own business with his wife. Eventually his two younger brothers became involved in the business. He told me that while he was dealing with outside jobs, his wife managed the production and labour relations within the atelier.

Within this setting, the labour force working in garment ateliers can be categorised into two groups. The first is 'core' workers composed of family members and relatives. The second group is the 'peripheral' workforce, rather flexible and with higher turnover rates. The flexible workforce is more likely to perform unskilled jobs, and home-based pieceworkers can also be considered as peripheral workers of garment ateliers. The core workers are people who have blood ties with the owner's family and remain the dedicated workers of an atelier for as long as it survives. Children, the wives of atelier owners, the owners themselves and immediate relatives such as sisters, brothers, nieces/nephews and cousins are members of the core workforce. The atelier owner, Ahmet, had his two daughters, a son and his wife involved in the business, and he trained his two nephews to be skilled makinacıs (sewing machine operators). With regard to his nephews he said, 'I trained them until they were the best and I taught them everything I knew so that we could do our best performance together. They worked with me almost 10 years and then they left my atelier when there was an offer for higher pay. As they are very skilled workers they get the best pay in the market.'

7.3.1 Invisible Workforce of Garment Ateliers

The examination of women's positions and their roles in the categorisation of core and peripheral workforce in garment ateliers shows the ways in which women are the invisible informal labour force of global industrial production in Istanbul. This invisible labour force is in both the core and the flexible belt of the workforce such as home-based pieceworkers. Women who casually engage with garment production after the male members of family (husbands, fathers, brothers) have established their businesses are the core workers of garment ateliers.

In a traditional extended family, the wife of the eldest son is the first gelin (bride) of the family. She is expected to gain status by age and childbearing and is the most respected woman in the family after her mother-in-law. Her status is transferred into the workplace as a dedicated 'helper'. These women do not have any specific skills for the work itself, but their contribution ranges from trimming finished garments and cooking lunch, to cleaning the atelier and machines. Their involvement makes the atelier a homely place and attracts other women from their community and neighbourhood as workers. However, their work in the garment industry is strictly bound to their husbands' business trajectories and they drop out of the labour market when the business ends.

Beyhan was the 38-year-old wife of an atelier owner with whom I spent a lot of time during the fieldwork. She married 20 years ago and had four children, three sons and a daughter. She had lived in the same flat with her in-laws for almost ten years. After adding a flat to the family's house, her family moved into their own home. She had not done any kind of paid work before her husband opened his atelier. She was not paid for her work in the atelier but considered the business as her own. In fact, she never asked for money for her contribution since it is considered an awkward situation to be paid for helping out your husband. Thus, Beyhan's social status came not from being paid, but from being the wife of a respected man who managed his own business. Her power is derived from being a mother and wife as well as being the eldest gelin of her household, not from earning an income. The degree of devotion to her family and her husband seems immense. Her presence in the atelier as a woman standing beside her husband gave her respect in the community, and her role helped her husband's atelier to attract cheaper labour from their community.

Beyhan also had a certain degree of power over matters related to the business. Burdened with the organisation of piecework and the cleaning of garments at home, she had the power to give orders to people around her. Beyhan not only provided an important support for garment work in the atelier but also provided financial support from her own family circle when her husband's business was in financial difficulty. Socially, she is seen as a housewife, but it is obvious that she has a very important role that clearly connects the areas of production and reproduction of social life, which resembles what Sharma (1986) calls 'household service work', in which domestic tasks extend beyond providing for the physical needs of household members, to the provision and maintenance of, in particular, ties with kin, neighbours, and friends, who are a source of information and aid.

7.3.2 Skilled 'Wife' Garment Workers

The second group of women are the wives of owners, whose garment-making skills either led to establishment of the atelier or resulted in the expansion of the husband's garment business. These women proved to be a valuable asset for their husbands' entrepreneurial capacity, as having access to skilled labour through the wives' engagement in garment manufacturing is a crucial element in establishing a successful business in Istanbul.

An interesting commonality of this category of women in the research sample is the way they exerted power over their families' decisions on their marriages. By putting a lot of pressure on their families to accept their own choice of husband, these women managed to shift away from arranged marriages. This was more evident in the case of the marriages between different religious sects, where two of my women informants married Alevi husbands although they themselves were Sunni Muslims. The shift in marriage decision making is a powerful measure of working women's emancipation, and women garment workers are able to exercise some control over their marriage arrangements. Therefore women gain a certain degree of power through paid work, which enables them to marry the people they want, rather than their parents' choice.

The contribution of skilled women workers to their husband's businesses is extremely crucial in several aspects. In some cases, the marriage itself led to the decision to establish a garment atelier. In other cases, it reinforced the success of the existing business by enabling access to an unpaid, reliable and skilled workforce so that the ateliers become more flexible, efficient and cost-effective. In this regard, three of my informants told me that their husbands decided to establish their garment ateliers after they got married. As the small-scale garment business is heavily dependent upon the collaboration of ex-garment workers, it is unlikely that one person can operate an atelier without any help from family members and relatives. Therefore, a skilled garment-worker wife who can control workers and the quality of production makes the business operate more efficiently. For example, Zeynep told her story as follows:

> My husband, Kemal, and I worked in the same atelier for many years. After we got married I stayed at home for three years. In the meantime I had my first child. During these years, Kemal tried to establish his own atelier with his other friends and worked for his ex-workplace as a subcontractor. He had many problems with his partners over work issues. Then, when my in-laws supported us financially, we decided to open our own atelier. Since then I work here as *makinacı* and control everything in the workplace. I am like the *ustabaşı* (foreman) here. Kemal is always out trying to get work. He does not even know how I make things work here. Even when an instructor comes from the subcontracting firm to teach us how to sew new models, they teach

me first and then I show our workers how to do it....Although I work hard for the success of this business, no one calls this place Kemal and Zeynep's atelier but it is only Kemal's place. So, our labour always remains invisible.

Esma, who is 31 years old and has two children, is also the wife of an atelier owner. Before her marriage she worked for almost 10 years in different ateliers. After she got married she became a housewife until her husband and his brother decided to establish their atelier. At the time of interview, she worked there full time along with her husband and her brother-in-law. Both of her children were of primary school age and were taken care of by their grandmother when they finished school every day:

> My husband and I worked in the same garment atelier for some years. After we got married he did not allow me to work. I did not want to work either. Because my husband brought home enough money to make ends meet and then there were children. I enjoyed being home after working for so many years. But now, we have our own business so I need to work and help my husband. I am a skilled *makinacı*. You cannot trust other people to come and do your work nowadays. Hiring a good and skilled *makinacı* is very expensive and they tend to quit the job or they are often absent some days of the week. Why do we pay for someone else when you have your own people to work for you?

Reyhan, a 18-year-old informant, was newly married after working for 6 years with her husband in the same atelier. Almost a year ago, she got married. Her husband was from the same *hemşehri* network as her family and also his family was relatively well off. Thus, it was easier for her to persuade her family to accept him as son-in-law. After her marriage, Rehyan did not work and was considered as a housewife. However, my conversation with her revealed a different story. She often went to the atelier to help when there was need for an extra hand:

> Last week, I cut some models and sewed them together. My husband said that customers liked my models very much and he sold many of them at the shop... When there is work (*iş*) I go to the atelier. I am a skilled worker and can do every kind of work at the atelier so there is no need to hire someone to do the work.... But I don't want to work full time. It is good to work sometimes so that I can cook, clean and

take care of my household duties.... Sometimes work is very busy, and we need to meet the deadline. However you cannot make people work all night. This is our work and *ekmek parası* (bread money) and so I work all night without sleep to finish the work off.

Reyhan's labour is an extra resource and obviously obviates hiring an extra hand, which enables the atelier's organisation to be more flexible. Access to flexible and unpaid labour is not only important in reducing the cost of production but also saves the time and energy of hiring a suitable workforce for the job. Easily subjugated family labour is the major factor in why small-scale ateliers are the dominant actors in garment manufacturing in Istanbul, and the discipline of workers is mostly provided by generating a familial attachment to the atelier business. In this regard, the appropriation of women's skilled and unskilled labour to perform different activities in the workplace provides flexibility for ateliers. Also, whenever and for whatever reason their labour is needed, they are ready and willing to help.

7.3.3 Atelier Daughters

Many atelier daughters, working in their fathers' ateliers day in day out since their early teens, are the core workers of small ateliers. Most work until marriage. Canan was one such atelier daughter. She began to work when her father opened his business, which was right after her graduation from primary school at 12 years old. After working for 7 years in her father's atelier, she married a garment worker. The marriage did not change her employment trajectory very much, for, after having a long break for the birth of her first child, she went back to work. The only difference this time was that she was employed where her husband was working. Her employment history shows that the patriarchal control of her has smoothly shifted from her father to her husband. Discussing her working experience Canan remarked that:

> If my father had not had his business my family would not have let me work. In our atelier, we worked all together, it was like our home. We just had a few hired people and the rest were family members and relatives. So, it was better for me to work among family members than with complete strangers.

Canan's working experience gained in her father's atelier, which provided her with the ability to earn an income whenever she needed it, was a major financial contribution to the family's budget. Although her work conditions and options seemed limited to the places where her husband or father was employed, Canan had the skills to earn an income. However, this does not cancel out the fact that Canan's work is under the strict surveillance of her family. Women being pulled in and out of the labour market whenever their families need their contribution or not makes their labour a contingent element of garment production. Despite this control and surveillance over women's labour, women gain status and power when they enter paid work activities, and their power becomes more apparent when a monetary contribution is made to the household budget. Thus, the material gains derived from work help women to modify and reconfigure their bargaining power at home and in society[6].

Another atelier daughter was Seda, a 17-year-old girl working with the rest of her family in their atelier. After her graduation from primary school she began to work as a full-time worker, and gradually gained garment-making skills and learned how to operate a sewing machine. Her father was proud of her garment-making skills and of the fact that she was a very diligent worker. Seda seemed satisfied with her situation at the workplace, but our in-depth interview revealed that her labour was drawn into the family business by blocking her educational prospects:

> I was in primary school when my father opened the atelier. I used to help out in the atelier after school and I got used to doing little things. After my graduation my parents asked me to work in the atelier so I stopped my further education. My older brother continued his education until he failed the university entrance exam but now he has a high school certificate. My parents sacrificed my education to have me as a worker. Everybody thinks that girls would fly out of home when they marry so it is meaningless to spend money on their further education. I regret now that I did not go to school. I am just a worker in my father's atelier and have never worked anywhere else.

Decisions over children's education show differences according to whether they are girls or boys. It is generally the case that parents are more willing for boys to continue their education rather than girls. During our conversation, when Seda's father talked about the future of his children, his main concern was for his sons. However, he was not too much worried about his sons, who could run the atelier if they failed in education. The different attitudes developed by parents concerning their children's education, in the case of families engaged in garment manufacturing in Istanbul, are the result of how the labour of girls and boys is valued. Seda's parents were more eager to appropriate her labour than her brother's because females' labour is easier to discipline and control and always remains under the strict control of their families.

The employment of young girls under their families' strict scrutiny is not unique to Istanbul's garment ateliers, but is prevalent in many societies. The association of female labour with lower skills and wages is, therefore, the result of a complex alliance between gender and kinship ideologies, which determines the terms upon which women enter the labour market. Like men, women are bearers not simply of labour power, but also of gender attributes grounded in the prior division of labour enacted in specific family and household arrangements:

> The terms upon which women may compete in the labour market are thus dictated by the social relations within which they operate as daughters, wives, mothers, widows, etc…and which impose ideological sanctions upon their identification as 'free labour'. (Standing 1989:1078)

In a ground-breaking study on industrial sub-contracting and women's home-based work in Mexico City, Beneria and Rolda (1987) illustrate how women are not part of an open labour market and do not have the same relationship to the means of production as men. Gender ideologies identify women with certain characteristics such as docility and tolerance, and men with attributes like restlessness and impatience. These ideologies mediate production relations to create a demand specifically directed for female and male labour. Along the same lines, a study of black and minority women working in family enterprises in Britain reveals that labour power is gendered and that this determines the conditions under which women and men sell their labour power. 'Women's domestic roles in reproduction (servicing the household and family) are articulated with roles in social production that generated wages' (Westwood 1988:4).

7.3.4 Flexible Belt: Peripheral Workers

A circle of peripheral (flexible) workers, other than family members and relatives, works in garment ateliers in Istanbul. 'Flexible workers' are those with a high turnover rate but with little attachment to a special workplace. Therefore, flexible workers are mostly those who specialise in the manual and unskilled parts of garment work, and are easily made redundant when the business is slowing down. Atelier owners often complained about the unreliability of flexible workers and the weak attachments developed towards their work. These complaints are not always realistic as the women in the group of peripheral workers usually remained in their first workplace until their atelier went out of business, or they sometimes changed their jobs because they wanted to get a new position and a higher salary. One of my informants, Ayla, told me that her first job was in the same workplace where her brother was working as *makinacı* and she worked there for more than a year as an *ortacı* (manual worker). She recalls her first day at work as follows:

> My brother was a skilled *makinacı* when I began to work. We usually worked more than 9 hours a day and I used to come to work with my brother. The atelier was not really far from where we lived. I was so shy in the first weeks and rarely talked to people. The boss and workers ordered me to do every kind of chore and I went shopping for them, I served water and lunch for them, swept the floor after work hours and distributed garments between the workers. After a few months I came to recognise that I need to learn how to sew so that I could get better paid, and stop people ordering me around. Thus, I began to practise every day during my lunch and tea breaks. When I found my progress satisfactory I went to another atelier and began to work as *makinacı*. If I had stayed in the same place it would have been more difficult to be a *makinacı* for me.

The flexible workforce also has other characteristics. The workers in this group are usually outside the circle of personal relations and contacts established in the atelier, which means having weak connections with the workplace. Thus, as the first to be made redundant in times of crisis, unskilled manual workers and children, whose labour is greatly exploited in garment manufacturing, are the flexible workers of Istanbul's garment ateliers. Regarding ethnic origin, these workers, who are alienated from the community relations at the workshop, are newly migrated ethnic Turks from Bulgaria and Kurds from the Southeast of Turkey. Women in this group of workers form the most deprived and impoverished clusters of Istanbul's mosaic-like communities, as they remain outside the networks of kinship and *hemşehri* and are too poor to develop these relations. Home-based pieceworkers can also be seen as the most flexible layer of the labour force of the garment industry. Following is an example of the recruitment strategies used to employ home-based pieceworkers.

7.4 Recruiting Home-Based Pieceworkers

A global surge of new forms of flexible labour relations and fragmentation of the labour force are often associated with feminisation of the labour force (Standing 1989). In both developed and developing countries women seem to have been more affected by this trend than men (Mies 1982; Beneria and Roldan 1987; Standing 1989; White 1994). An increasing number of home-based pieceworkers is another phenomenon of the feminisation of the global workforce. The characteristics of pieceworkers and the nature of home-based work are better researched in Turkey than other components of the female labour force (Cinar 1994; White 1994, Hattatoğlu 2001). Although some of this research has shown the high number of women engaged in piecework, little effort has been made to highlight the relationship between industrial production and women's piecework (Cinar 1994; Hattatoğlu 2001). The role of women pieceworkers in garment production analysed in this chapter, together with the recruitment strategies adopted to employ them, aims to show that recruitment creates new forms of hierarchy between co-workers and further flexibility of production relations for employers.

Kinship and community relationships play a significant role in accessing subcontracting work and the labour of home-based pieceworkers. In Istanbul's garment industry, some tasks are subcontracted directly from a workshop to women and others are allocated by middle-women, who are sometimes relatives of the workshop owner. There was a distinctive difference between how larger-scale factories managed their subcontracting, and how garment ateliers organised their relations with home-based pieceworkers. Garment ateliers are the mediators for large-scale factories in distributing garment pieces to home-based workers. As it is a time-consuming and costly activity to deal with home-based work, large-scale factories preferred to subcontract the work to garment ateliers. Despite some factories subcontracting piecework to ateliers, the ones that specialised in designer and high fashion production had direct relations with home-based workers, as the tasks required highly delicate and skilled handicraft, such as embroidery or making ornaments on garments. In order to find the right women for the work, factories establish an efficient network of subcontracting.

Here is an example of how a large-scale factory directly managed its subcontracting relations with home-based pieceworkers. Two workers were allocated to distribute garments to pieceworkers, who were all women and lived in neighbourhoods close to the garment factory. One of these workers was the driver of the van, and he was also in charge of carrying the garments. The other worker was a woman who was in control of the women pieceworkers. She demonstrated to the women what should be done to the new pieces, and kept records of the garments distributed and the payments each worker should receive. She could decide independently how many pieces to be subcontracted and to whom. This woman, Serpil, who was 35 years old and the mother of two children, told her story of how she became the middle-woman of the factory.

I am good at maths and also a high school graduate. Most of my colleagues are primary school graduates and I was quick to learn every job at the factory. So, our manager (*müdür*) asked me to do this job when they decided to subcontract some tasks to women instead of doing them in the factory. Now, we have 50 women in different *mahalles* around here and some of these women have been working for more than 8 years. What I do is very difficult because if a piece is missing or something is wrong with the quality of the work I am responsible. I try to work with women whom I trust and have known for a long time. In the beginning, there were just a few women whom I reached through my own personal contacts and mostly from my own family and neighbourhood. We need to make sure that women have skills to do the job. Even though most women have skills of sewing and embroidery it is more important to follow the designs and be precise, clean and on time.

Although Serpil was an ordinary worker in the factory, her role as a middle-woman of the factory gave her decision-making power over the pieceworkers. Serpil was like a manager with pieceworkers, and demanded information about the process of their work. She often reminded the women that the timing of task completion was very important and if the work was not completed on time payment would have to wait until the following month. She was certainly the boss of the pieceworkers, for whom having a good relationship with Serpil was the channel for getting access to regular piecework.

The relationship between middle-women and pieceworkers is constructed on the basis of 'fictive kinship' (White 1994). Most women get to know about these opportunities by word of mouth, and through existing kin and non-kin networks in the community. Thus the relationships take on kinship overtones, as most women emphasised the important role of middle-women in giving access to a regular supply of work. Thus, daily survival requires maintaining membership in social relations and community networks and in continuously nourishing a web of reciprocal arrangements (White 1994:133). A form of 'mutual indebtedness' is maintained among women to manipulate social relations in order to ensure a steady supply of work.

The irregular nature of piecework and the strict rules of work completion have resulted in the composition of a complex alliance between women pieceworkers and middle-women, which shows the extra-economic relations underlying the social organisation of piecework in Istanbul's garment industry. This irregular structure of work has developed a network of women in which a pieceworker, for example, is the main subcontractor of the factory but also shares her quota with other women in her household or neighbourhood. In cases of surplus work and under time pressure, a pieceworker uses the help of her neighbours and pays them later. This practice of collaboration among women generates further flexibility in the organisation of piecework, and shifts the responsibility of middle-women, in terms of finding new subcontractors, to pieceworkers.

I joined Serpil on one of her visits to her pieceworkers where she distributed some work and collected the finished pieces. In one of the neighbourhoods, there were two women pieceworkers whom Serpil had known for a long time. When we arrived the two women were together making their garment pieces. Serpil gave them the new garments and explained what was required, and then a third woman suddenly appeared and carefully listened to what Serpil had to say. Later, I asked Serpil who she was and she told me that the other two women shared some of their work with her. When there was too much work and too little time to finish all the pieces, Serpil herself gave work to the third woman. This was one of the ways that the factory's circle of subcontracted women enlarged over time.

Garment ateliers establish their network of pieceworkers through using the personal connections of the women in their families. Extended families always have some untapped labour of women that can be drawn into production whenever necessary. For example, the grandmother of the family usually stays in charge of childcare during the day, while other family members are working in the atelier. Sometimes she also does the finishing of garment pieces by cleaning stitched edges, or, in some cases, she acts as the middle-woman in their immediate environment by distributing garments to other women. Ateliers that are unable to utilise their own family labour usually have a number of pieceworkers who have worked for them for a long time. These women establish a small network of pieceworkers in which they have the leading role as distributor. Their networks can be as small as four or five women.

While piecework is an individual activity and each woman is paid individually for her work, it is common in the literature to argue that women work collectively in their homes (White 1994; Cinar 1994). Often a neighbour would come in and join in the work for an hour or so and leave. There was a clear sense among all the women interviewed in this research that piecework is low paying and extremely tedious, and all subcontracted tasks are repetitive, time-consuming and require very little skill. That is why pieceworkers are those who are in extreme economic difficulty with few other available sources of work. As very little is paid per piece, the total monthly income of a pieceworker is much lower than the minimum wage.

Although pieceworkers make a substantial contribution to the global garment manufacturing in Istanbul, their income is conceptualised as *pazar parası*[7] (bazaar money), which is seen as charity to poor women. This conceptualisation was made clear in one atelier owner's statement, where he explained how and why he subcontracted to women:

> We subcontract only to women and they sometimes come and ask us whether there is any work. Most women are regulars and all are from this area. In the past, we hired women to do hand-work of the pieces as full-time workers but the garment business is irregular. Sometimes these women had nothing to do for weeks and we had to pay their salaries. Later on, we decided to subcontract women at home so that we delivered pieces to them when there is work and pay them on a piece basis. For women, it is better to do piecework than sitting idle at home so they earn their *pazar parası*. I think that this work is good for women because *fakir kadın* (poor women) need to feed their children and at the same time they can watch over their children. Times are hard for families so people are trying hard to make ends meet and everyone has to do something in order to survive *(hayatta kalmak için)*. Piecework gives the opportunity to live without depending on anybody *(el açmadan yaşama)*[8].

Usually associated with the neediest women in the community, piecework is done by women who are known to have no economic support from husbands, such as divorcees or widows; those whose husbands are not providing for them for a variety of reasons; or those who need extra cash for other reasons such as investing in home ownership. Such a woman was seen as a *fakir* (poor) woman, who is usually pitied *(yazık)* in her community. This also reflects how a woman without a man's economic support is conceptualised in society.

In summary, piecework in Istanbul's garment industry is defined as women's work because of the assumed characteristics of patience, endurance, lack of mobility, and dexterity associated with women, and also because of the low amount of money paid for each piece. The networks of collaboration created among women are the main element of recruitment of pieceworkers and a further aspect of flexibility in garment production in Istanbul.

The different forms of recruitment used in different branches of Istanbul's garment industry have enforced pervasive forms of gender relations as well as power relations in society. The investigation of recruitment strategies reveals how the capitalist relations of industrial production interact with the existing forms of gender hierarchies, and use them to provide a more docile and submissive workforce. Additionally, recruitment helps to shift the control of workers in the workplace away from managerial staff to fellow workers. In the next section, the issues of location and mobility and their implications for women's labour market participation are examined.

7.5 Transporting the Private Sphere: Location and Mobility

Space and place are important in the construction of gender relations and in the struggles to change them. The symbolic meanings and gendered messages of space and place are transmitted in a culturally specific division of public and private spheres. Space and place are not only gendered themselves, but in being so they both reflect and affect the ways in which gender is constructed and understood (Massey 1994). The attempt to confine women to the domestic sphere is both a specifically spatial control and also a social control on women. The spatial separation of home and workplace as analytical categories are themes that illustrate women's place in society. As a source of anxiety in eliminating the public–private divide, women's access to the workplace tries to overcome this separation. In this part of the chapter, an effort will be made to identify how this anxiety is handled in Istanbul's garment industry.

In their seminal work, Hanson and Pratt showed that women workers spend a shorter time committed to their workplaces and that the decisions women make about where to work tend to reflect their limited mobility (Hanson and Pratt 1995). Women's work in their local communal territories is a reflection of their willingness to juggle the roles of housewife and worker together. Working near home saves time and energy for women who avoid commuting long distances to work. Some writers have pointed out that, besides women working close to home, the spatial segregation of industrial production reflects the gender-based segmentation of labour markets. Storper and Walker (1983) have argued that segmented labour markets have a clear spatial expression. The fact that employers with specific labour requirements seek out different areas is way of understanding how gender-based labour market segmentation is mapped onto places. The studies show that city size and the industrial mix in a metropolitan area have an impact on women's labour force participation rates and on the types of work that women do. Places where most of the jobs have been in traditional male manual work (mining, steel making, ship building) have had low rates of female participation in the paid labour force, whereas places with many job opportunities in female-type work (assembly of garments, electronics assembly) have higher proportions of women in the work force (Massey 1984).

In this regard, the garment industry in Istanbul, whose location is organised in residential neighbourhoods, can be considered as female work. The locational characteristic of the industry facilitates women's access to garment work by overcoming the limited physical mobility of women, which in turn enlarges the available source of labour for the industry. For a woman, being a worker means a further step into the public sphere, to which women have limited access in Turkey, and also means overcoming the socially constructed separation between public and private spheres by not disturbing existing gender roles and ideologies. Therefore, the anxiety created by women moving into the public sphere is solved by the attempts to extend the private sphere from the household to the workplace.

The transfer of control over women's behaviour from families to the community is a way of extending private patriarchal control to the public sphere. The private gaze over women's behaviour becomes a public one, which watches and oppresses women in the public sphere. This transformation by 'privatisation of public' in the case of garment manufacturing is made possible by employing women in their local areas and through the enforcement of social networks and relations in the workplace. Thus, women's work under such conditions is more easily socially approved than situations in which women have more interactions with 'strangers' in the public sphere.

In Istanbul's garment industry the most common way of 'privatisation of public' is the use of special buses (*işçi servisi*) which transport workers from their homes to factories and ateliers. No women in the research sample used to commute to their work by public transport: they walked instead, or used a special bus (*işçi servisi*) provided by their factories or ateliers. *İşçi servisi* are mostly used by large factories located in specially designated industrial areas such as Güneşli, İkitelli, Yenibosna and Halkalı in Istanbul, away from the city centre and residential areas. With a population of over 10 million, Istanbul has chronic public transportation problems. As the city's central municipality is unable to provide regular transport to these areas, such firms arrange their own means of transportation for their workers, creating a parallel transport system to enable an easy commute. By having their own transport, factories ensure the timely arrival of their workers when the shift begins, and also provide the flexibility for having workers to do overtime without being concerned about their transportation. With these buses women are transported to workplaces without coming into contact with 'strangers' on the streets and avoiding overcrowded public transport.

İşçi servisi are an efficient way of connecting workers to their workplace. A firm with 150–200 employees has 6–7 buses running between their employees' residential areas and the workplaces. Bus routes are usually arranged according to where most employees live in the city, from where the firm recruits most of its workers. The clustering of workers in a number of neighbourhoods saves time and energy and provides for efficient running of the bus system. At first sight, these buses make it easier for women to commute, especially when it is so difficult to catch a public bus during the rush hours and it is troublesome for women to be present in an environment dominated by strange men. Moreover, on public transport women are often subjected to sexual harassment and disturbance. The women interviewed in this research were pleased to have buses provided. Nazlı was a worker in one of those large-scale textile factories located away from the city and told me about her route to work:

> The factory (fabrika) is outside the city and there is no public transport to the factory. When I am late I can take a taxi to get the factory but it costs a lot. If you have a car it is like 30 minutes to get there but I need to get up like 5.30 so I can make for the servis which is running from my area at 6.15 and it takes till 7.30 to reach the factory because the service picks up many people living in this area and stops many times. What I can tell is that it is much better to have a *servis* otherwise it would be impossible to go to work. You know how terrible the public buses are during rush hours. Men are always quicker to catch buses and you just stand hours and hours to get an empty bus. If you cannot get a seat men can make life miserable for you on the bus. You know many stories about how women get disturbed during rush hours on the buses.

The domination of public transport by men, especially during rush hour, alienates women as customers of the city transport system. Nazlı also mentioned her experience when she was commuting to work one morning.

She squeezed into the overcrowded bus. As no seats were available she had to stand. When she asked the man standing next to her to make a little bit of space her he told her that if she was not happy she should not have taken the bus but rather a taxi. Men's attitude reflects the view that it is only men who take the bus to go work, and women are overcrowding the buses for their leisure. In the *gecekondu* areas of Istanbul resources are scarce and many people, mostly men, try to get to work and put much effort into finding a bus at the overcrowded bus stops. This day-to-day struggle to catch a bus makes women to opt for the *servis* buses provided to go to work.

Locating ateliers in the neighbourhoods of Istanbul partially overcomes the limited mobility of women workers. The neighbourhoods are the most popular sites to locate an atelier, offering an easy hide-away from government surveillance and control and easy access to a female work force. Women's preferences for working close to their homes provide insight into women's attitudes towards labour market activities. The factors shaping women's decisions about where to work reflect the choices and constraints women have during this decision-making process. Women's decisions are mostly the result of how they can most easily combine their domestic roles and the responsibilities of paid work. Women's access to information about what kind of work is available to them is constrained, and when women seek work they usually consider finding a job in their immediate vicinity. The distance between work and home is the subject of a great deal of consideration for women and their families. This was the case for one of the married informants, Umman, who had two children and was 43 years old, who decided to work when she was around 35 years old. She found a job in a garment atelier where her close friend was working. The atelier was in the same neighbourhood as her residence but she had to walk approximately ten to fifteen minutes to work. She recalled her first day at work as follows:

> I went to work with my friend and worked all day long. In the evening I knew that the atelier was near my home but I could not find my way around. I was so embarrassed to ask where I was and kept walking around. In the end, I arrived somewhere and it was already dark and someone told me how to get home. As my first experience was scary afterwards I decided to walk to work with my friend or I asked my husband to meet me until I got used to finding my way from work to home or home to work.

As seen in Umman's case, women are not confident enough to commute long distances, not only because society or their families restrict them but also because their experience of the city is often limited to their close neighbourhood or local area. Thus, the decisions of women about where to work should be seen as rational choices rather than as a constraint that women are unable to overcome. The deliberate choices made within the context of constraints such as unreliable transportation, inadequate child care and husbands who are not equal partners in homemaking and childrearing affect their decisions to work close to home. Moreover, the available work opportunities for women in local workshops can help to ease the tension of getting permission from their families, since the workshop is also easily accessible to family members. To overcome the difficulty of gaining permission for work, women generally try to connect their families to the workplace by having a friend or relative working in the same place, or by working in a relative's or acquaintance's garment atelier.

Women are reluctant to travel further to get to work. The atelier workers in the research sample spent less time getting to work than the factory workers who usually commuted by a service unless they lived within walking distance of the factory. Evidently commuting times are based on the location of the factory, but the research findings indicate that factory women travel for between 20 minutes and an hour to get to work, while women workers in the ateliers spend a maximum of half an hour. Most of the atelier workers walked to their workplaces or took one short trip on public transport. However, none of the women said that they took public transport, whereas men are commuters on public transport.

The most immobile group of workers are home-based pieceworkers. Physical immobility is one of the main reasons for undertaking piecework. Companies usually provide the distribution and collection of piecework, so women need not go out and fetch it. This explicitly helps to utilise women's immobile labour as a pool of cheap labour that remains strictly tied to the home. Most pieceworkers emphasised that this service provided by the companies made their work possible, as the physical mobility of middle-aged women with small children remains restricted to walking distance, and their activities to a very narrow sphere.

In conclusion, the utilisation of women's labour in the garment industry generates a string of difficulties for women, their employers and their community. One of the ways in which these difficulties are overcomed is through the employment of women within their local areas. In addition, a service bus to the neighbourhood is provided if workshops are not located in the same vicinity, in order to easily transport women workers to their workplaces. These measures are used to avoid not only sexual harassment on the way to work, but also a bad reputation for the women. Therefore, women's physical immobility and confinement to the private sphere are related to culturally specific ways in which the segregation of urban space and women's access to the public sphere are connected to gender relations and ideologies in Turkey.

Conclusion

This chapter set out to examine the conditions in which women enter into and participate in the world of paid work. Portraying the relationship between women and labour markets has led to the conceptualisation of labour markets as bearers of the relations and institutions of the societies in which they are embedded. In this regard, Kalleberg and Berg (1988:5) point out that:

> Labour markets are the arenas in which workers exchange their labour power, creative capacities and even loyalties with employers in return for wages, status and other rewards. Labour markets are intimately related to the institutions and practices that govern the purchase, sale and pricing of labour services; they are thus markets wherein labour force inequalities are mostly directly generated.

The implication of gender relations for the ways in which women participate in labour market activities is most explicit in recruitment practices in the garment industry. The recruitment process reflects the social embeddedness of labour markets in Turkey, in which identities and hierarchies are constantly renegotiated and reconfigured. Recruitment processes not only carry existing hierarchies into the workplace but also generate new forms of seniority, surveillance and authority between workers. Moreover, recruitment through 'word of mouth' helps a smooth transition of skills and shifts control over workers from managerial groups to the workers themselves.

There are different layers of family labour that garment ateliers draw upon to generate a reliable and cheap labour force. Mothers, wives and daughters of the family and relatives provide the main labour supply. As the most invisible source of labour in the Turkish labour market, these women's participation in production ensures the survival of garment ateliers. Home-based pieceworkers are recruited through the utilisation of neighbourhood networks of women, in which some female pieceworkers perform the role of middle-women in order to reach other women in their family and community. All these processes not only enforce existing hierarchies, but also create new ones in which new types of identities and hierarchies are imposed on women.

The mobility of women and the location of firms and ateliers are examined to assess the impact of women's labour force participation. Special transportation provided by *işçi servisi* (buses) and the clustering of the garment industry in neighbourhoods make access to female labour easier. The increasing mobility of women has turned the private gaze over women into a public one and transformed women's secluded private sphere by generating special gendered arrangements in transportation and location. These measures are not only used to avoid sexual harassment as well as a bad reputation for the women commuting to work, but also help to create the subordination of women. Thus, gender relations and ideologies reflect themselves through the culturally determined segregation of urban space and women's access to the public sphere.

8

CONCLUSION

This book began with two central questions: what is the nature of women's employment in the garment industry of Istanbul, and what are the supply and demand factors conditioning women's entrance into garment production in Turkey? Women's work is not sufficiently reflected in the official statistics, and subsequently remains highly invisible. Therefore, the aim has been to show the role of women in the industry in order to challenge this invisibility by focusing on the organisational structure of garment production, women's role within it, and the interaction of gender relations and women's work in Istanbul, where the majority of garment production takes place at small ateliers in low-income neighbourhoods.

This research located itself within a large body of literature that draws heavily on the interrelationship between the role of global production, flexible production methods and women's labour force participation (Harvey 1989; Pearson 1998; Elson 1999; Standing 1999; Sassen 2001). There is a large consensus on the emerging trend of women playing a major productive role coincided with the increasing mobility of global capital and the introduction of new production techniques, such as subcontracting and out-sourcing labour, have created a rising demand for flexible and informal labour. The rising number of women moving into paid employment has been observable in different parts of the world and has taken many different forms. The same phenomenon has taken the form of increasing part-time female employment in the post-industrial world, whereas it has appeared as rising industrial female employment or informal work in the Third World. These different forms were based on a dialectical relationship played out at different geographical locations between the supply and demand factors of female labour, determined not only by the trend related to production but also by supply factors such as gender relations, family organisation and social networks.

The first objective of this research was to challenge women's invisibility in the labour market by exploring women's role in the garment industry. Exploring this question through almost seven chapters, the answer seems straightforward: that women's labour is an essential part of global garment production in Turkey. The employment opportunities created for women by the integration of the garment industry into the global market are shaped by the intersection of two sets of factors, demand and supply, that keep women's work within the informal economy, rendering their labour invisible. Women's income-generating activities have been more important than ever both for their families and for garment production in Turkey. This research has, therefore, shown that women are actively working at different levels of garment production. They have been drawn into the labour market in a variety of ways. It has also shown how traditional gender relations in conjunction with the labour demands of the industry keep many women in a subordinated position.

The second and third objectives of this research were to explore the supply and demand factors affecting women's labour in the industry. Female labour demand was examined in relation to the way in which the industry is organised, including its place in global commodity chains, its relations with the domestic markets and the informal market, and what impacts these markets have on production, subcontracting and home-based work. The supply factors of female labour were identified as gender relations, household structure, migration and community in urban areas and the need for economic survival at the household level. The intersection of these two factors determines the form and level of women's participation in Istanbul's garment industry. The overall objective, therefore, was to examine the ways in which the dialectic between supply and demand factors conditioning women's work has generated a geographically specific example of women's industrial work in Turkey.

8.1 Feminisation of Informal Work

My interest in analysing women's industrial work in Turkey was stimulated by the fact that women's labour force participation has been decreasing in the last couple of decades (Özar 1994; TÜSİAD 2000; World Bank 2000). This shows an opposite outcome to the feminisation of employment that has occurred in many of the countries that adopted export-oriented industrialisation policies. In Turkey, where rather a trend of de-feminisation of the labour force was recorded in urban areas (Cagatay and Berik 1994), the measured labour market activities of women have appeared to be stagnant for the last 20 years, even though some of the socioeconomic transformations taking place have been similar to those in other developing countries, where the participation rates for women have been rising.

I argued that the story presented by the official statistics regarding the degree of female employment is a partial one, and needs to be challenged for several reasons. As discussed in Chapter 3, the interplay of different factors contributed to the invisibility of women's work in urban areas where official statistics recorded most women as 'inactive' housewives, and focused mainly on the economic activities of educated women, who are the only visible females in the labour market. While the official figures illustrate decreasing rates of female labour force participation, an increased role in informal income-producing activities is observed by many scholars (Cinar 1994; White 1994), and these activities have taken different forms ranging from home-based industrial piecework, traditional handicraft activities, domestic services and unpaid family work, to atelier work. My research aimed at providing an extensive investigation into the role of those women classified as 'inactive' in garment ateliers.

My research data also revealed that atelier production and home-based piecework attract many women into production. The success of small family-run ateliers in Istanbul is due to their ability to have access to a source of cheap female labour from their own family and relative circles, and to mobilise their labour in order to achieve survival, competitiveness and flexibility in production. A network of daughters, mothers and wives is a passport to the success of the garment business, where women's work has no public recognition, most of these women remaining invisible in the labour market.

The hidden nature of urban women's work in the informal economy has been partially the consequence of data collection problems in official statistics. Additionally, the inconsistencies between different data sources and gender biases involved during data collection have resulted in the total invisibility of women. Despite the self-assessment nature of labour force surveys, which should capture all forms of economic activity, women's work remains unreported or under-reported either because they do not get involved in the data collection processes or because of their perception that their informal work overlaps with their domestic roles. Moreover, especially married women's income earned through home-based work and traditional handicraft activities is usually hidden from husbands and fathers and kept in safe places unless an urgent need for its use arises.

Women engaged in informal production, home-based activities and assembly work see their income-producing activities as a mere extension of their domestic responsibilities. White (1994) powerfully demonstrated why women are inclined to see their work as 'nonworking' and deny that they actually 'work'. This is due to the fact that women's paid work is socially and morally unacceptable unless it remains within the limits of a cultural construction of 'giving' labour as a contribution to family and community and an expression of identity.

A consideration of all these factors creates a challenge to the official figures suggesting that export-oriented industrial production has not influenced women's labour market participation in Turkey. The increasing level of women's participation in the informal economy and the increasing demand of the industry for informal labour lead at least to a conclusion that feminisation of informal work has been occurring in Turkey since the implementation of export-oriented economic policies. Low-income women living in the suburbs of Istanbul are the main actors in export-related production and they have not only substantial but also diverse roles in garment production in Istanbul. Labour-intensive sectors such as the garment industry have provided different types of opportunities for women to generate income through informal activities. This is clearly observed in the case of increasing home-based piecework in the manufacturing sector, unpaid and underpaid labour in small-scale family-owned business and also women's informal employment in the service sector[1].

Thus, the question remains as to how women's activities could be better represented in official records and gain public recognition. No straightforward answer exists. However, making women's work visible is a feminist agenda that include a complex set of actions and targets. Evidently the consideration of different forms of work other than wage work, together with the adoption of better measurement and data collection methods, would lead to an accurate measurement of women's work in Turkey. Therefore, an easy target to help eliminate women's invisibility in the labour market is to scrutinise existing data collection methods and develop different categories that can capture women's different range of informal and home-based activities. As illustrated by Anker *et al.* (1988), appropriate survey techniques and questionnaire design can result in an accurate and complete measurement of the female workforce. Asking specific questions on subjects such as animal husbandry, knitting, sewing, etc., rather than abstract and general questions such as main activity and secondary activity would work better in measuring low-income women's economic activities.

In the agenda of making women's work visible, the role of ethnographic studies is significant. Data produced about labour-intensive, 'unskilled and informal working activities by using ethnographic research methods and case studies, instead of country-based surveys can prove vital in making women more visible actor in the labour market. Revealing key issues in the informal sector by showing its value in the economy and highlighting women's participation in the productive labour force (Çınar, 1994) increases the visibility of women's informal sector work at national and international levels. Therefore, information on women's informal work can serve policy advocacy aiming both to improve the conditions of informal work and to influence national policies on the informal sector in general, or women's informal work in particular.

8.2 Demand Factors Conditioning Women's Work

My research examined the structure of the garment industry, the different niches of markets for which the garments were produced, and the impact that these market have on production, subcontracting and labour requirements as the demand factors affecting female employment in Istanbul. The way in which the garment sector is integrated into global markets and supply chains through the processes of industrial production and trade has affected women's employment in the industry.

The demand factors that the industry has created have offered many employment opportunities for women in low-income households in Istanbul. An analysis of the structure of firms operating in Istanbul showed the dominance of small-scale firms in garment production. The clustering of firms in a number of migrant neighbourhoods, in which Merter is the centre of Istanbul's garment production, and other nearby areas has provided easy access to migrant female labour. The analysis of product specialisation of firms showed that standard garments such as T-shirts and sweatshirts are mostly produced with simple techniques. Production of standardised products also pointed to the easy training of the workforce and the repetition of similar activities due to a distinct division of labour in the workplace.

The structure of the industry in Istanbul is highlighted by its relationship with three distinct markets and the impacts that these markets have on production, subcontracting and the labour requirements of the sector. Factories produce garments for up-market domestic consumption, and there is also production that targets European markets, as well as the Laleli market production for the markets of Eastern Europe and the former Soviet Union countries, which all together have created a differentiated demand for female labour.

Factories that produce for up-market domestic consumption are usually owned by formal and large-scale corporate Turkish firms, with prestigious brand names such as *Vakko, Altınyıldız* and *Bossa,* and provide formal employment opportunities for women. After the 1980s, these firms managed to compete with foreign brands in domestic markets and enforced their brand identity through extensive advertisements and marketing. The factory production conducted in the realm of the formal economy offers employees all available rights and liabilities within the regulations and requirements of state legislation. The subcontracting relations of those formal factories have remained restricted to certain kind of activities such as some hand stitching or embroidery that must occasionally be performed outside the production complex.

The second type of production, targeting European markets, undertaken by massive producers and exporters of standard products such as T-shirts and sweatshirts, offer women employment mostly in small-scale ateliers. As it stands at the heart of global commodity chains, this type of production uses the networks of production linking labour, production, and distribution processes together, resulting in one commodity. In Istanbul's garment industry, the main actors are small-scale garment ateliers working for orders coming from large-scale factories and employing mainly family-based cheap labour. Atelier production is an effective way of connecting women's informal and home-based work into the global commodity chains. However, the skill and timing requirements of export-oriented production differentiates these ateliers from those ateliers producing for the informal international trade, which is the third form of production process in Istanbul's garment industry.

As mentioned above, production for the Laleli market, a neighbourhood in Istanbul serving people coming from Eastern Europe and the former Soviet Union, is organised informally on an atelier basis, employing mostly unskilled or semi-skilled labour. The products for the Laleli market are either sold directly to the foreign customers from the transition countries or are exported through informal channels to those countries. The informal international trade established in the Laleli market is crucial for the export of commodities collected from many small-scale producers and the transportation of them to the foreign markets. The ateliers producing for the Laleli market have a limited subcontracting relationship with other firms in the production process but utilise home-based workers.

Istanbul's garment industry is characterised by its extensive use of subcontracting relations and its ability to diffuse into untapped resources of labour. My fieldwork findings show that while large-scale producers are independent agents of garment production, ateliers are more dependent on orders from other companies. All the ateliers included in my sample worked on orders from other companies. In addition, subcontracting relations between Istanbul's garment firms are not always vertical but sometimes horizontal, meaning that garment ateliers subcontract to their counterparts, and sometimes act as mediators and distributors of piecework to home-based women workers.

The flexibility of garment production based on the utilisation of subcontracting networks, small-scale ateliers and home-based workers has resulted in the informalisation of production. Informalisation is practised not only by hiring labour with no social security but also through the relations between subcontracting firms and the misreporting of values and volumes of production. Informalisation has been the hallmark of garment production in Istanbul due to its hosting of the market for informal international trade located in Laleli. Additionally, the degree of informalisation is best observed in the ways in which the industry and small ateliers have access to female labour and base their survival in a very volatile market on having access to a cheap and reliable female labour force. Therefore, female labour involvement in small-scale garment ateliers in Istanbul is an important element of production, since these ateliers rely mainly on the exploitation of both unpaid and underpaid labour provided by family and kin.

My case studies in Chapter 4, focusing on two ateliers in Istanbul, one producing for the European markets and the other for the Laleli market, revealed how families pooled their labour together in order to succeed in the sector, and also the extent of women's labour used in the production. Family-run ateliers are highly dependent upon immediate family labour, as well as other kinship and *hemşehri* relations. These social ties enable firms to survive by providing flexibility in the production process under volatile and uncertain market conditions. With the perpetuation of social relations and networks based on mutuality, solidarity and trust, firm owners exploit their own and their family's labour and resources. It was also evident that women's role in the maintenance and nurturing of these networks had enabled family-run businesses to tap into the financial and labour resources of their communities. In two cases, the generation of a web of flexible labour resources was based on the role of the senior women in these two families, where women from their own families and neighbourhoods were channelled into production either as 'helpers' of piecework or as cheap atelier workers.

Women like Gül played a mediator role in connecting the atelier work with their larger community. These women are not only burdened with trimming and cleaning garments at home, but also organise their neighbours and relatives when extra labour is needed. Although remain housewives, these women extend their domestic tasks beyond meeting the physical needs of household members to providing and maintaining particular ties with relatives, neighbours and friends, who are, in turn, a source of aid and reserve labour. Their involvement in the atelier made the place homely, further helping to attract women's labour. The family-based nature of atelier work made possible the utilisation of labour of women like Gül, whose work remains invisible but still at the core of the flexibility of garment production in Istanbul.

Employment opportunities for women in small ateliers are diverse, and women's involvement in atelier work, whether it is directed to European markets or to the trans-national trade via Laleli market, has been crucial for garment production. Being an atelier worker for European markets requires longer years of skill acquisition and dedication because of the more stringent quality control of products. This has led to skilled women's involvement in the production process, whereas production for the Laleli market requires more of women's manual labour. Due to the masculine nature of the trading activities in Laleli market, women are almost absent from marketing, but their contribution to the production was nevertheless immense, ranging from atelier work to piecework. The domination of garment production by small-scale family firms has resulted in an overlap between women's workplace and domestic activities, creating opportunities in which women's unpaid family labour could be exploited easily for the sake of families' well being.

8.3 Supply Factors Conditioning Women's Work

The analysis of demand factors conditioning women's involvement in the labour market in Istanbul facilitates an understanding of the structure of an industry that offers a wide range of employment opportunities to women from low-income households. The most distinctive forms of these employment opportunities are factory work, atelier work and home-based piecework. However, the role of women in garment production is best understood in the light of the supply factors affecting women's entrance into the industry, as women's work is always mediated by the prevailing culture of Turkish society and its gender relations.

With regard to supply side effects, women's personal characteristics and household structures are important in determining women's entry to the labour market. Education, age, ethnicity and marital status are the cornerstones of women's personal characteristics in the garment industry. Age is in itself a strong element influencing women's entry to the labour market and the forms of work they engage in. Home-based pieceworkers were older than the women who did atelier or factory work. Young women are generally more advantageous than older women as older age may bring status in the household, which is accompanied, in some cases, by more decision-making and management power in the family-owned businesses. Years of schooling are one of the important factors affecting the supply of women's labour. This is evident not only for my case studies but for the general trend in the labour market. This trend represents an increasing number of women's participation in the labour market after the completion of longer years of schooling. This research demonstrates that women's education level changes in accordance with the type of work they engage in. Factory workers have the highest level of education, whereas home-based workers have the lowest level of education and poor literacy. Less educated and older women are more likely than better educated young women to engage in informal income-generating activities whether these are home-based piecework or traditional handicraft activity (Chapter 5).

Marital status has a strong influence on women's decisions to do paid work and the availability of jobs for them. This research illustrates how some jobs, especially formal factory jobs, are totally closed to married women; however, some married women also felt that they were too old for seeking work in ateliers or factories. Employment for young girls is socially more acceptable, as their work is expected to terminate when they get married. Women's employment in Turkey is perceived to be temporary whether women are single or married. Women's work is meant to tide their families over financial difficulties, and the returns are usually invested into projects that provide families with long-term security in the city; their work is destined to end when all these exceptional conditions are over and the financial future is secured (Chapter 6).

Ethnicity is a rarely studied topic in Turkey and there are no significant studies connecting discrimination against people of certain ethnic origins in labour markets. In this research, people who identified themselves as Kurds mentioned the difficulties they had in finding stable and secure jobs. On the other hand, the managers of large-scale factories emphasised their preference for hiring Turks who had emigrated from Bulgaria because of their superior work discipline. Besides ethnic discrimination, place of birth origin is a strong identity reference for people in working-class neighbourhoods of Istanbul. This identification governs personal contacts and networks that are fundamental for access to jobs. None of the women in my sample describe themselves as *Istanbullu* (Istanbulites) although they had been living in Istanbul for a long time. This indicates that women's identities are still strongly bound to the places of their origin, as most of the women were living in communities and neighbourhoods surrounded with people from the same localities (Chapter 6).

Household characteristics and women's domestic roles in those households were discussed as central factors affecting female labour supply. Most women workers live in nuclear households. However, these nuclear households, as seen in Chapter 5, function as extended corporate entities since strong connections continue to exist with non-co-resident kin. The type and structure of households have conflicting influences on women's entry to labour markets. In some contexts, women living in nuclear households have a higher tendency to work, since this household structure may be a sign of isolation from other resources and connections. Women in these relatively poor households are to be found engaged in home-based piecework or low-paid unskilled atelier work. Yet in other contexts the extended household structure could be an indication of poverty that requires the pooling of the labour and earnings of different families. Moreover, living in extended households is an indicator of being unable to afford to live as a separate unit.

Female-headed households are a rare occurrence in Turkey and the most of divorcees or widows are usually absorbed into extended households. Hidden from the public eye and hardly ever form an independent household these women move into the patriarchal control of their families. The only case of forming an independent household is together with a son of working age. Under the condition of the absence of security underwritten by male protection having a female-headed household could mean moral degradation and isolation from the community. This is a heavy price in a context where community solidarity and reciprocity are one of the only resources on which migrant families can rely during economic hardship and difficulty.

Women's contribution to the household budget in the form of income-saving activities is an important element that puts downward pressure on women's labour market entrance. This study shows that household income heavily depends upon women's contributions, whether monetary or in terms of kind. Beside food products, women are involved making different kinds of material for the use of family members such as *kilims*, cardigans, jumpers, and socks. Moreover, migrant families, through their economic connections with their home village, families and kin obtain free or cheaper food staples and, sometimes, financial support, helping them to save cash.

In determining the degree of women's labour supply, I focused on migration, gender relations, marriage, bargaining power and reasons for work, in order to highlight the factors affecting women's work that are prevalent in the private sphere. Kandiyoti's 'bargaining with patriarchy' is a fundamental conceptualisation in explaining women's role and position in Turkish society, as well as in analysing their relation to paid work. Women's internalisation of gender roles and relations has significant implications for their access to paid work. On the one hand, women in Turkey gain power and status by confining themselves to traditional roles and responsibilities. On the other hand they manipulate gender relations in order to provide long-term security and respectability. Thus, marriage and children are the main assets that grant women the power of exercising and manipulating gender ideologies for their own benefit.

Within this context, women try to expand their leverage and power position through expressing their roles as mothers and wives. This is the only arena where they can effectively negotiate with their husbands, fathers and other members of their family and community. Throughout this research, I structured my argument from the perspective of women who are defined as *gecekondu* women of Istanbul, and pointed to the reasons why women stay within the confines of oppressive and exploitative gender relations. However, this does not necessarily mean that the domestic sphere is free from conflict; it is indeed a place where women are subjected to exploitation, physical and psychological violence. Women strategically struggle to gain power in the domestic and public sphere by enforcing existing gender roles and ideologies. It is a constant and conscious struggle to maximise outcomes within their given environment. This system leads women to conceptualise their paid work as an addition to their main duty of motherhood and wifehood. This is also why they prefer to engage in home-based informal activities, which make it easier for women to juggle domestic roles with income generation.

An analysis of the social construction of work helps to understand the ways in which women participate in income-generating activities in Turkey. Household survival strategies facilitate women's entry into paid work in an environment where there are no social safety nets. As women's work is identified as temporary, the main impetus for women to take up paid work is to save for home ownership or prepare their trousseaus for marriage. These reasons generate legitimate excuses for men to give permission their wives or daughters to work. Since the need for work is constructed as generating 'extra' income, men still protect their main breadwinner role. Thus, letting women work for money does not damage men's honour. In the Turkish cultural context, men work for bread (*ekmek parasi*), as the main bread earner. This corresponds with the system of the 'family wage' in which male workers earn a family wage whereas women's income is 'secondary' or complementary (Fraser 1997; Folbre 2001). Thus, women's work is additional to the 'family wage', which is to meet other financial needs. This socially constructed meaning of work for men and women results in men getting secure and permanent jobs while women are over-represented in marginal informal jobs such as home-based work or domestic handicraft activities.

Women's *elişi* (domestic handicraft activities) constitute a central theme in analysing women's informal income-generating activities as it is an element in contributing to women's invisibility in the labour market. Although *elişi* is a good source of income generation women never see it as 'work'. Husbands are rarely aware that women can earn some cash from their *elişi* since it is as normal as cooking for a woman to do *elişi*. Engaging in *elişi* is seen as a way for women to express their identity and pass the time. These skills, which are used to prepare an elaborate *çeyiz* (trousseau), are also utilised to earn money in two ways. First, women make lace, embroidery and knitting for young girls' *çeyiz,* and secondly women use their skills to take in piecework or work in an atelier. The skills used for *elişi* also provide a transition to the labour market, whereby women become a cheap labour source for home-based industrial piecework (Özbay 1990; Cinar 1994; White 1994). The invisibility of *elişi* as an income-generating activity, together with its identification as not being 'work' is a passage for low-income women in gaining access to extra income without becoming visible workers.

Obtaining permission for paid work is one of the obstacles to women's labour market entry. Different strategies are adopted by women to overcome this obstacle and women's bargaining for permission to work takes place between women and men and also with the larger community. This is not, however, to suggest that there is a homogenous approach to women's work in terms of obtaining permission and/or facing oppression. There are co-operative forms of decision making in which women face no opposition due to the degree of poverty of their families or the absence of the male head or breadwinner from the family. Moreover, the stability of the job and the extent of financial gain help women to obtain permission easily. Once women have done some paid work it becomes much easier for them to remain involved in work.

8.4 Interaction Between Supply and Demand Factors: Women at Work

The meeting point of supply of and demand for women's labour is the workplace. The workplace is analysed as a place in which the interactions of culture and economics generate a particular type of work culture. This approach stems from the view that labour markets are gender-neutral institutions, which are 'bearers of gender' (Elson 1999:611), 'in the sense that there are social stereotypes which associate masculinity with having authority over others in the work place and social stereotypes about what is 'man's work' and 'women's work'. Such stereotypes are not matters of individual preferences, but are inscribed in social institutions. The formal and informal rules which structure the operation of labour markets are instantiations of the gender relations of the society in which the labour market is embedded' (Elson 1999:611-12). Women's workplace experiences are good indicators of this point, which was analysed in my research through recruitment and mobility in the garment industry in Istanbul.

Recruitment is an area where the social embeddedness of labour markets in Turkey is most visible. Recruitment is rarely the direct result of formal, rational and public procedures but rather the result of existing social and gender relations (Harris and Morris 1986). Recruitment processes not only carry existing social hierarchies and inequalities into workplaces but also generate new forms of clientship and seniority, surveillance and authority between workers. Recruitment also leads to a constant negotiation and configuration of gender relations and hierarchies in Istanbul's garment industry. Moreover, recruitment through 'word of mouth' helps a smooth transition of skills and shifts the control over workers from managerial groups to workers themselves.

Recruitment through 'word of mouth' has resulted in women working with their family members, relatives and friends. This has helped, on the one hand, women's access to the labour market by creating a familiar atmosphere, while on the other hand, it has generated patron-client relationships in which gender and kin relations are imported into the workplace. This has paved the way for the garment industry to have a docile and obedient work force. Moreover, this recruitment strategy has generated hierarchies not only between women and managers or male patrons but also between women whose initiation led a friend or relative to working in the same shop floor. This is most clearly visible in the case of home-based workers, where workers doing piecework for a long time had control over a new pool of people and managed the amount of work they undertook. As White argues, 'the construction of unrepayable debts is a source of power and domination not only within the family but throughout Turkish society... Individuals are usually dominated and dominant depending on their position in the strands of reciprocal relations that have been activated' (1994:101).

Work in the garment industry is organised in different ways in order to overcome women's limited physical mobility. Special transport provided by factories and ateliers and the location of garment firms in the residential neighbourhoods of Istanbul help the garment industry to have easy access to women's labour. Thus, *işçi servisi* (shuttle buses for workers) is an interesting area in highlighting labour relations and the organisation of the garment industry in Istanbul. The factory buses not only generate positive outcomes for employees and employers by making transportation easier, but also serve as an important factor in accessing female labour. The provision of these *servise*(s) serves to protect women from the masculine nature of the public sphere by taking women to and from work door-to-door. Women are prevented from interacting with unrelated men even though they enter into the male world of the public sphere. These measures are used not only to prevent sexual harassment as well as the acquisition of a bad reputation by women on the way to their workplaces, but also to help to construct the subordination of women in the public sphere.

The location of garment businesses helps enterprises to have easy access to female labour and also helps family-owned businesses to exploit their own families' labour. Women spend less time commuting as a result of being employed in workplaces located in their neighbourhoods, obviating the need for public transport. Women appeared happy about working close to their homes as this gave them more time to do their household duties and childcare. The factors shaping women's decisions on where to work in a sense reflect the choices and constraints that women confront during decision making. Women's decisions are mostly the result of their judgment of how they can most easily combine their domestic roles and the responsibilities of paid work. Women's access to information on what kind of work is available is constrained by their immediate surroundings and when women seek work they usually consider finding a job in their immediate vicinity.

These special arrangements to increase women's limited mobility are a way in which private patriarchy (Walby 1990) turns into public patriarchy: privatisation of the public sphere. The continued protection of women in the public sphere is secured by these special arrangements, which carry women's secluded private sphere into the public arena. Thus, the limitations on women's physical mobility and women's confinement to particular places are a culturally specific sexual segregation of urban space and social relations in urban space, where one can find an exclusive insight into gender relations and ideologies in Turkish society.

There are multiple levels at which women participate in garment production in Istanbul. The multiplicity of women's involvement in the garment industry is most visible in their engagement in atelier production. In examining this multiplicity I distinguished two different groups. The first group is composed of close family members and relatives, who are the core workers of garment ateliers. The core group is ready to work as long as their fathers, husbands or uncles run the atelier. Mothers or wives of atelier owners are the invisible heart of this core labour force. Their roles in family businesses are quite diverse and range from direct contribution to production to cooking for workers and cleaning the workplace. Their involvement creates an environment in which the atelier becomes a 'familial' place for women's work. Although these women do not usually get paid for their activities, their contribution to garment production is an overlap between the market-oriented work (productive economy) and the non-market-oriented work of women (reproductive economy) (Elson 1999).

The second group is a more flexible workforce comprised of non-relatives and home-based workers of ateliers. This flexible workforce is usually composed of people who lack the necessary personal relations and contacts that lead to permanent and secure jobs. Therefore, these workers have weaker connections with the workplace than those in the first group and they are the first to be made redundant in times of crisis. Women workers do very repetitive, time-consuming and tedious tasks that require very little skill.

In Istanbul's garment industry, women pieceworkers are usually associated with the neediest women in the community and compose the most casual form of labour force. They are paid low price rates and the total monthly payment is much lower than the minimum wage. The money earned is seen as *pazar parası* (bazaar money for fresh vegetables) (Chapter 7). The women involved in piecework, known to have no economic support from husbands, are divorcees or widows, those whose husbands are not providing any money for them for a variety of reasons, or those who need extra cash for other reasons such as home ownership, and are seen as *fakir* (poor) women who are usually pitied (*yazık*) in their community. The piecework is perceived by atelier owners as a kind of social charity to those women in need even though it is merely a business matter for them. Moreover, this ideology affects the way in which women experience co-operation and reciprocity in the community. That is why these women are helped in their subcontracting work by other women in their neighbourhoods. These women volunteer their labour and maintain the relations of cooperation based on such mutual help, despite the pay for the work being so low, in anticipation of receiving the same kind of help from others, in case they should ever be in a similar situation of need.

8.5 'Weak Winners, Powerful Losers'?

The final question of this book is: what could all these findings on Turkey contribute to the existing body of literature on economic globalisation, women's work and gender relations in the garment industry?

My study had an aim of contributing to the analysis of the globalisation of garment production with a reference to commodity chains in which the garment industry is envisaged to be organised around the market-driven needs of large retailers. 'Buyer-driven chains' formed by large retailers or branded marketers are seen as being the drive behind garment production (Gereffi 1994:99). However, this research clearly illustrates that Istanbul's garment industry is connected to global markets in different ways and not all garment production is for large retailers and European (or Western) markets. Although the industry has been integrated into the global market more than ever, its integration is managed not only via European markets but also through domestic and informal international markets. This perspective helps to conceptualise industrial production not only as an extension of the networking of multinational corporate firms but also as a dynamic entity in which local firms create their own market conditions in response to new opportunities arising through the utilisation of global communication and transportation channels.

Global garment production differentiated by market niches dictates the forms of the labour processes that operate in accordance with the exploitation and utilisation of the local conditions. The local trends governing the industry and its labour requirements in Istanbul has provided a significant example for grounding value chain theories in its geographical specificity and the variety of forms through which the local and global connect to each other. The geographical specificity, but also the global garment industry in Istanbul, provides a good example of what Robertson calls 'glocalisation'. In this regard, globalisation is the realisation of 'independent significance of space and geography under the rubric of globality' (Robertson 1995:27). In this sense, there is no opposition between global and local but rather they are complementary in defining the age and phenomenon of globalisation.

The relationship between women's work and industrial production is complex, varied and in continuous flux as they interact with broader social-economic conjunctures. The complexity is not only observable within a historical perspective across different industries but can be found in one industry. The Turkish garment sector is an interesting example for the exploration of the intersections between supply and demand factors conditioning both the forms of industrial production and the availability of female labour for the industry. Prevailing local cultures and gender relations extensively influence labour processes and the nature of industrial production. In Istanbul, the invisibility or seclusion of women's labour has affected the ways in which the garment industry operates in small sweatshops located in the neighbourhoods in Istanbul, which is the only way to tap into cheap female labour. Thus, any attempt to understand the relationship between women's work and industrialisation needs to take into account those local practices influencing industrial production.

What, then, does the example of women's work tell us further about the prevailing theorisation of women's work in the informal economy? Women's work in the informal economy is established as the expression of their identity rather than as a mere reflection of earning a living. In this regard, women exchange their labour in the informal economy as a token for manifesting their community membership and identity in urban Turkey. Especially, women's work in the family-owned business is strongly tied to their domestic roles as mothers, wives and daughters. Despite the tension created by women's identity formation through paid work, women themselves very often make an extra effort to show that their priority is always given to their domestic identities.

Even as women continue to express their domestic roles as their primary concerns, the reality of their engagement in paid work is powerful. However, its outcome for women is complex. As Kabeer (2000) argues, women are the 'weak winners, powerful losers' of industrial production by expressing the paradox of negative objective conditions and positive subjective evaluations. The weakness of garment workers vis-à-vis powerful employers has made women subject to the exploitative working conditions that prevail in the Turkish garment industry. The capacity of the industry is based on its ability to integrate those who are excluded from the wider labour market without providing any security and working standards. In this condition, women are the powerful losers of global industrial production.

On the other hand, women's work in the garment industry brings them status and power, both at home and in society. While offering a certain degree of independence and increased bargaining power at home, these gains differ for women at different points of their life cycle. Young girls, even though restricted, obtain a chance of moving to better paid jobs, and some of them can gain the freedom to choose their future husbands. For married and unpaid family labour, even though their contribution is 'invisible', the recognition of the invisible labour of women occurs in the form of their socially approved roles as dedicated wives and mothers. Their productive activities might be unrecognised but their dedication is socially rewarded by approving themselves as 'good women' and 'good mothers', not as workers. However, women's involvement in paid work remains tightly limited by patriarchal relations. Being an unpaid family labourer provides only a limited degree of empowerment because both women and their communities consider their participation as 'help' and render it invisible. However, women gain decision-making power at home through the perpetuation of patriarchal relations as mothers and wives, since these relations are accepted as important to both the maintenance of business and strong family relations. While conditions in the workplace such as poor labour standards, long working hours and low pay are the negative aspects of women's work, access to paid work has nevertheless provided these women with something positive in their lives.

The prevalent state of insecurity and informalisation in labour markets, women's extensive participation in those informal activities and women's perspectives on the state of affairs in their daily life pose an important contradiction in prevailing gender ideologies. Even though women's public demands and negotiations are voiced through the utilisation of these traditional roles, they remain within the confines of those roles. Seemingly, women's internalisation of traditional gender roles and identities allows them to move into the public scene and take up paid work without losing social protection and security. Women are able to negotiate effectively with patriarchal structures about what they see as their best advantage and to redefine the terms and conditions for the ground where the next round of negotiations can take place. The strategies adopted by women in Turkey to overcome the constraints of patriarchy lead us to reconsider that these women are not merely passive victims of restructuring policies, the international market, and patriarchy but active players who attempt to utilise the opportunities created by restructuring polices and globalisation of markets. Thus, women's employment in the garment industry has been a form of expression of liberation.

The socioeconomic changes in Turkey coupled with ways in which women are becoming more visible in their own social environment offer new possibilities for women to explore. These social changes may present an excellent opportunity to begin negotiating current gender arrangements and women's position in Turkish society. Only some of the possible avenues of inquiry have been introduced here by my exploratory study amongst a limited number of women workers in Istanbul's garment industry. Further research on women's daily struggles and practices in Turkey is clearly needed.

NOTES

Chapter 2

1 For example, Gereffi (1999) has examined the role of US retailers in shaping clothing production networks and global commodity chains, while Kessler (1999) has examined the increasing power of retailers in US automotive commodity chains. Dolan *et al.* (1999) have looked at UK food retailing in fruit and vegetable commodity chains.

2 Producer-driven commodity chains are those in which large, usually transnational manufacturers play central roles in co-ordinating production networks. These are the characteristics of capital and technology-intensive industries such as the automobile, aircraft, computer, semiconductor and heavy machinery industries (Gereffi 1994:7). What distinguishes the producer-driven production system is the control exercised by the administrative headquarters of the TNCs or other large-scale companies.

3 The second line of trade may be conceptualised as 'extra-global circuits' since the first line is mainly manipulated by what Schmitz and Knorringa (1999) call 'global buyers' and multinational companies.

4 Many case studies have revealed the complexity of emerging patterns of female employment (Elson and Pearson 1981; Fernandez-Kelly 1983; Joekes 1985; Heyzer 1986; Beneria and Roldan 1987; Ong 1987; 1988; Lim 1990; Standing 1989; Stichter and Pappart 1990; Wolf 1992; Safa 1995).

5 Cited in Elson (1996:97).

Chapter 3

1   The interplay of these factors influenced the outcome of the November 2002 National Election. The victory of the Islamic Justice and Development (AK) party is an indication of the fact that urban migrants, with their votes, have protested against the traditional elitist rule of the Turkish Republic by shifting their preferences from central political parties to marginal and conservative political parties. The social alienation of the urban poor has resulted in a majority of the population feeling disenchanted with the state modernisation project. Rapid social transformations have manifested themselves in urbanisation, informalisation and poverty, which are now in fact ready to challenge the overall structure of the Turkish state. This does not mean that these changes will necessarily be towards the formation of an Islamic state in Turkey, but rather a move towards the class rule of urban migrants and "democratic" Islamic government.

2   This form of easy and fast moneymaking is named '*Köşe Dönme*' (turning a corner) in daily spoken Turkish, meaning reaching one's dreams and desires by using any possible means and ways. The introduction of this idiom and its daily use coincided with the implementation of liberal policies of Turgut Özal's government after 1983. Özal's Motherland Party used a similar slogan during its 1987 election campaign. That slogan was 'Turkey leaping into the next century', meaning that Turkey would be a 'modern' country, by whatever means necessary. The popularity and social acceptance of people becoming rich by manipulation of state resources and personal relationships encouraged this form of behaviour to spread into every stratum of society. The roots of informalisation went deep into society and are best expressed by Süleyman Demirel, who became prime minister after the 1992 election. When journalists asked him how civil servants could survive when their salaries were just enough to pay a month's rent, he replied 'My *memur* (civil servants) know how to make ends meet'. The implication of this famous line was to declare the official acceptance of bribing civil servants. Thus, as the state does not pay them enough it is legitimate to accept a bribe for services.

3   This case is not solely valid for Turkey, as 'head of household' and 'household' are central to data collection in censuses and surveys in many countries (Evans 1992).

4   The share of foreign direct investment in GDP was 0.12 per cent in 1987, 0.47 per cent in 1990, and 0.45 per cent in 1995, and had risen to 1.87 per cent in 2001. The share of FDI in GDP remained around

0.5 per cent between 1995 and 2000. This share was 7.2 per cent in Chile, 5.8 per cent in Malaysia, 4.1 per cent in Poland, and 5.4 per cent in Hungary (Arın 2003:581).

Chapter 4

1   Industrial development has increased the share of Anatolian cities in garment production, and their share of total garment exports is set to rise. The increasing export share of Anatolian clothing firms is mainly dependent upon Denizli's production in the textiles and garment sector. In the last two decades Denizli, a medium-sized town in southwest Turkey, has become one of the most important centres for textiles after Istanbul and Bursa. The share of Anatolian firms in total exports rose from 18 per cent to 22 per cent between 1995 and 2000 (Dikmen 2000; Erendil 2000).

2   Although Istanbul has a very important place in garment production, scholarly interest about the development and structure of the garment industry has remained limited to the analysis of macro data provided by TURKSTAT (Duruiz and Yentürk 1992; Diken 2000).

3   By the late 1980s, people started to leave the southeast due to the fighting between the military and the PKK. Forced internal displacement gained pace in the 1990s due to the evacuation of thousands of villages by the military, the PKK's intimidation of villagers who did not support it, and the general feelings of personal and economic insecurity resulting from the conflict. Between 65 to 85 per cent of the Kurdish population in the southeast, that is an estimated 2 to 3 million people, have been forced to leave their villages and towns in the region. Although there are no sound figures, Istanbul might have received up to 1.5 million of the forced Kurdish migrants (Kirişci 1998).

4   At the time of interview, 500,000 Turkish lira was almost 1 US dollar.

5   This concept will be further discussed in Chapter 7.

Chapter 5

1   Erman describes varoş people as those who are political Islamists, nationalist Kurds, radical leftist Alevis, unemployed, street gangs, or the mafia. Within this definition, she compares gecekondu and varoş by saying that 'the varoşlu are defined in terms of both the economic (the poor) and the socio-political dimensions (the rebellious, the outlaw, the misfit)... The varoş is oppositional to the city and is setting itself against the city; it is hostile and antagonistic to the city. The city is besieged by the varoşlu. This is a very different view from that of the gecekondu

as part of an evolutionary process leading towards assimilation as they evolve form the rural end of the rural-urban continuum towards the urban' (Erman 2001: 996). Although Erman's analysis is important to show the media definition of *varoş* it neglects the fact that people living in varoş or gecekondu areas represent the new face of urban life in Istanbul now. Thus, it may be a misleading conceptualisation if varoş is defined by a couple of marginal activities; rather, we shall see it as the latest texture of urban life. Therefore, I will use the term varoş in a broader sense to refer to the new forms of urban life taking place in gecekondu areas. I will also pay attention to the constant conflicts and negotiations among these urban communities as well as with the state.

2   This is a Turkish proverb: *Ev, doğduğun yer değil doyduğun yerdir.*

3   *Gurbet* is a foreign place far from one's homeland.

4   In Turkish, *memleket* means country, but in this context it is homeland of migrants.

5   This confrontation turns out to be the phenomenon of exclusion and otherness based on different religious beliefs and ethnic origins. For example, the exclusion of Alevis generated by official acceptance of the Sunni sect as the form of "legitimate" religious practice is one of the most long-lasting bases of urban conflict (Erder 1997).

6   This classification is based only on the composition of household members. For identification of three types of household, I use nuclear family as the main form and then other forms are the ones which are basically different from the nuclear family.

7   Although there are three and two generational extended families I did not differentiate between those as long as two generations lived under the same roof.

8   *Radikal* daily newspaper published the results of research with regard to how households have changed their structures in response to the economic crisis of February 2001. The most striking conclusion of the research is that families that were internally displaced after 1994 have been dramatically affected by the crisis, as they lost all connections with their villages due to the total evacuation of some villages in southeast Turkey. Thus, they were no longer able to get any food or cash supplements from their villages (*Radikal*, 16th and 21st February 2003). This clearly shows that connections with rural areas are vital for the survival of newly migrated families in cities.

9   In early January 2001, 1 US dollar was 500,000 Turkish lira. This was immediately before the February 2001 economic crisis that led to

the devaluation of the Turkish lira more than double against the US dollar.

10 Government jobs are highly preferable due to their stability, even though people do not get high payment for doing these jobs. There are extra ways of generating extra income for people working in the public sector. Even being a doorman in a public institution is highly valued among low-income people in urban Turkey. For me, the most desirable characteristic of these jobs is their stability since employees stay in the same job until they retire. Thus, stability is always preferred over high payment if it is for a short time. Having these jobs is also an indication of the utilisation of long established strong personal connections, which usually enable people to obtain such jobs.

Chapter 6

1 *Being evinin kadını* (women of their home) is a state of being a housewife with children and a husband who is the head of family with a stable income. In Turkish society, women are most respected and socially accepted when they are women of their home. Especially for migrant and low-income women this position is to be aspired to in every situation, and women's labour market work is constructed to reach this status of being evinin kadını.

2 El-Kholy's study on Egypt's provides meaningful insights into the way women use their trousseau as a kind of bargaining power during their marriage. She also identifies every item of trousseau that women bring when they get married (1998). Hoodfar (1997) also argues similar findings for Egypt.

3 Later in this chapter, an account will be presented of how çeyiz-making, through commercialisation and trade networks created among local women, is transferred from single girls to married women and has become an income-generating activity for poor women in urban areas.

4 Başlık is a certain amount of cash which is negotiated between two families; the total amount of başlık varies dramatically in different regions of Turkey.

Chapter 7

1 The effort to establish a familial environment in the workplace is not only confined to the relationships between men and women in the manufacturing industry. Since the use of kinship-familial idioms gives an immediate identity to a stranger in the Turkish society, it is also a prevailing form of relations between women themselves. For example,

Ozyegin highlights that the relations between domestic workers and their women employees are based on these idioms. Regardless of her age, an employer woman is called *abla* (elder sister), whereas a domestic worker automatically becomes *kardeş* (younger sister) (Ozyegin 2001).

2   In Turkish society, urban life is organised in ways similar to rural areas and based on face-to-face relations. This results in the effective utilisation of relations based on kin and family relations in every aspect of life. This is reflected in the everyday practices of people meeting each other and conducting business. One of the important ways in which people develop relations is related to being stranger and acquainted. People try to find an acquaintance to get even the simplest transactions done. For example, if you want to pay an overdue bill and want to avoid waiting long hours, you go and find someone working in that office who is a friend or related to someone you know. This prevails in both public and private sectors. *Yabancı* (stranger) is a person who is not known to the community and who does not have any acquaintance with the community. Tanıdık (acquaintance) is a person who is familiar, friend or kin. Developing *tanıdıklık* (being acquainted) depends upon personal communications and relations, and *yabancı* (stranger) becomes acquainted through other personal connections. This resembles Rex's conceptualisation of primary communities. According to Rex, 'primary communities' refer to those groups on which individuals depend to keep them out of a state of absolute isolation. 'In primary communities men [sic] reveal more of themselves. ... They feel able to relax and to "let their hair down". ... In stable societies most men [sic] find such a primary community amongst their immediate family and kin. But in a shifting urban environment they seek out some group to which they can commit themselves in an analogous way.' (Rex 1973:15).

3   Several scholars have drawn links between employers' recruitment methods and employees' skill acquisition and likelihood of promotion (Granovetter and Tilly 1988; Barron *et al.* 1985). Employers are likely to put more efforts into actively recruiting employees for jobs where educational qualifications are important and where formal on-the-job training is extensive.

4   During the interview, Sunay was very anxious and shy. She was not as confident as my other informants to volunteer information, especially about her private life. Later, it occurred to me that she acted shy and reserved because she might have thought that I judged her like other people did. It was, however, clear that she was proud of her abilities and

achievements in life. When she was telling me about her achievements of promotion at work and her newly bought flat and her dedication to finishing high school, she showed a strong sense of self-esteem.

5   This implies that she is Kurdish. As Kurdish identity is recently being accepted by the state, being doğulu is usually used in urban areas.

6   Changes in women's bargaining power with the influence of their earning power stress the relevance of rules, norms and practices that govern the relationship between earnings and power in the household. Pahl's research on British households focuses on the actual income and its management as a way of tracking power relationships. She points to the three dimensions of relationship in which access, management and control over income determine the intra-household power distribution. Control over income indicates who makes the policy decisions as to which intra-household resources are to be allocated. Access is the availability of additional resources and management is the transformation of policy decisions into practice (J. Pahl 1989).

7   *Pazar parası* is weekly money allocated from the family budget to buy vegetables and fruits from the market that every neighbourhood has on a specific day of the week, and in which there are usually vegetables, fruit, cheap kitchen utensils and to some degree essential clothes, especially for children. Even in the cases of women who do not have any income-generating activity their husbands give them weekly money to be spent at the market. The shopping helps to prepare the essential meals of the week, such as breakfast, lunch and dinner. However, this money is just enough to feed the family and is not enough to cover other expenses related to daily life. Although family's budgeting strategies differ as to who earns money and how the power relations are allocated within the family, each family has a different meaning attached to the pazar parasi. In some cases it may cover all domestic expenses of the family, from monthly bills to the education expenses of children; in others it may just be an amount to buy vegetables and fruits at the market and not be sufficient to cover the cost of daily bread consumption.

8   This proverb refers to begging and not having a power of control over your daily income.

Chapter 8

1   Recent research, Gecekondu and Socio-Economic Structure of Regions in Istanbul, by Istanbul's Commerce Union announced that women are the key source of total household income (3/4 of total). Men provide

only 25 percent of total income (Radikal 17 March 2004). This is a proof of the main argument of this book that despite receiving little recognition women's work is a very important source of survival for low-income migrant families in Istanbul.

BIBLIOGRAPHY

Acker, J. (1989) 'The Problem with Patriarchy' *Sociology*, 23(2) pp. 235 –240.

Agarwal, B. (1994) *A Field of One's Own: Gender and Land Rights in South Asia*. Cambridge: Cambridge University Press.

Aksoy, A. (1996) *Küreselleşme ve İstanbul'da İstihdam*, (Globalisation and Employment in Istanbul), İstanbul: Friedrich Ebert Vakfı.

Alada, A. B. (1995) 'Belediye Örgütlenmedesinde İlk Basamak: Mahalle' (The First Step for Municipal Organization: Mahalle) *Toplum ve Ekonomi*, 8, pp. 93 –114.

Amin, A. (ed) (1994) *Post-Fordism: A Reader* Oxford: Blackwell.

Anker, R. and C. Hein (eds) (1986) *Sex Inequalities in Urban Employment in the Third World*, Basingstoke: Macmillan.

Anderson, K. and D. Jack (1991) 'Learning to Listen: Interview Techniques and Analysis' in S.B. Gluck and D. Patai (eds), *Women's Words: The Feminist Practice of Oral History*, London: Routledge.

Anker, R. and C. Hein (eds) (1986) *Sex Inequalities in Urban Employment in the Third World*, Basingstoke: Macmillan.

Anker, R., M.E. Khan and R.B. Gupta (1988) *Women's Participation in the Labour Force: A Methods Test in India for Improving its Measurements*, Women Work and Development 16, Geneva: ILO.

Arın, T. (2003) 'Türkiye'de Mali Küreselleşme ve Mali Birikim ile Reel Birikimin Birbirinden Kopması' (Financial Globalisation in Turkey) in A.H. Köse, F. Şenses and E. Yeldan (eds), *Küresel Düzen: Birikim, Devlet ve Sınıflar: Iktisat Üzerine Yazılar I*, (Global System: Accumulation, State and Class), İstanbul: İletisim Yayınları.

Ansal, H. (1995) *Teknolojik Gelişmelerin Sanayide Kadın İstihdamına Etkileri: Türk Dokuma ve Elektronik Sanayilerinde Teknolojik Değişim ve Kadın İstihdamı Araştırması*, (Women's Work in Turkish Textile and Electronic Industries) Unpublished Report Prepared for the Ministry of Women Affair, Ankara.

Appelbaum, R.P., and B. Christerson (1997) 'Cheap Labor Strategies and Export-oriented Industrialization: Some Lessons from the East Asia/Los Angeles Apparel Connection' *The International Journal of Urban and Regional Research* 21(2). pp: 735–739.

Atkinson, J. and N. Meager (1986) *New Forms of Work Organisation: IMS Report 121*, Institute of Manpower Studies, Brighton.

Ayata, S. (1990) *The Labour Market in the Small Industry Town*, İstanbul: Friedrich Ebert Vakfi.

Ayata, S. (1986) 'Economic Growth and Petty Commodity Production in Turkey' *Social Analysis*, No.20 pp. 79–92.

Barrett, M. (1986) *Women's Oppression Today: Problems in Marxist Feminist Analysis*, London: Verso.

Barron, J., J. Bishop and W. Dunkeberg (1985) 'Employer Search: The Interview and Hiring of New Employees', *The Review of Economics and Statistics*, No:67 pp. 45–66.

Beechey, V. (1987) *Unequal Work*, London: Verso.

Bell, D. (1973) *The Coming of Post-Industrial Society: A Venture in Social Forecasting*. New York: Basic Books.

Beneria, L. (2003) *Gender, Development and Globalization: Economics as If All People Mattered*, New York & London: Routledge..

Beneria, L. (2001) 'Shifting the Risk: New Employment Patterns, Informalization, and Women's Work', in *International Journal of Politics, Culture and Society*, 15(1) pp. 27–54.

Beneria, L. and M. Roldan (1987). *The Crossroads of Class and Gender: Industrial Homework, Subcontracting and Household Dynamics in Mexico City*, Chicago: University of Chicago.

Berik, G. (1987) *Women Carpet Weavers in Rural Turkey: Patterns of Employment, Earnings and Status,* Geneva: ILO.

Bolak, H. (1995) 'Aile İçi Kadın Erkek İlişkilerinin Çok Boyutlu Kavramlaştırılmasına Yönelik Öneriler' (Observations on Male–Female Relation in the Household for a Multilateral Conceptualisation), in Ş. Tekeli (ed) *Kadın Bakış Açısından 1980'ler Türkiye'sinde Kadın*, (Women in 1980s Turkey from Women's Perspective) İstanbul: İletişim Yayınları.

Boratav, K., E. Yeldan and A. Köse (2000) 'Globalization, Distribution and Social Policy: Turkey, 1980–1998', *CEPA Working Paper Series I*, Working Paper No: 20, New York: New School University.

Boratav, K., O. Türel and E. Yeldan (1996) 'Dilemmas of Structural Adjustment and Environmental Policies Under Instability: Post-1980 Turkey', *World Development*, 24(2) pp. 373–393.

Borland, K. (1991) 'That is not What I Said: Interpretative Conflict in Oral Narrative Research' in S.B. Gluck and D. Patai (eds), *Women's Words: The Feminist Practice of Oral History* London: Routledge.

Bourdieu, P. (1977) *Outline of a Theory of Practice*, Oxford: Oxford University Press.

Bromley, R. and C. Gerry (1979) *Casual Work and Poverty in Third World Cities*, New York: John Wiley

Brydon, L. and S. Chant (1989) *Women in the Third World: Gender Issues in Rural and Urban Areas*, New Brunswick: Rutgers University Press,

Buğra, A. and C. Keyder (2003) *New Poverty and Changing Welfare Regime of Turkey*, Report Prepared for United Nations Development Programme, Ankara: UNDP.

Bulutay, T. (1995) *Employment, Unemployment and Wages in Turkey*, Ankara: International Labor Office and the State Institute of Statistics.

Buvinic, M., M. Lycette and W.P. McGreevey (eds) (1983) *Women and Poverty in the Third World*, Baltimore: Johns Hopkins University Press.

Cagatay, N. and G. Berik (1994) 'Structural Adjustment, Feminization and Flexibility in Turkish Manufacturing' in P. Sparr (ed), *Mortgaging Women's Lives: Feminist Critiques of Structural Adjustment*, New York: Zed Books.

Cagatay, N. and G. Berik (1991) 'Transition to Export-led Growth in Turkey: Is There a Feminization of Employment?' *Capital and Class, 43*, Spring, pp. 153–177.

Carr, M and M.A. Chen (2002) 'Globalization and the Informal Economy: How Global Trade and Investment Impact on the Working Poor', *Working Paper on the Informal Economy*, Geneva: ILO.

Celasun, M and D. Rodrik (1990) 'Turkish Experience with Debt: Macroeconomic Policy and Performance' in J. Sachs, and S. Collins (eds), *Developing Country Debt and Economic Performance*, Vol:3, Chicago & London: University of Chicago.

Chamberlayne, P. and Rustin, M. (1999) *From Biography to Social Policy: Final Report of the Sostris Project*, Centre for Biography in Social Policy, Department of Sociology, University of East London.

Chant, S. (1995) *Women and Survival in Mexican Cities: Perspectives on Gender, Labour Markets and Low-income Households,* Manchester & New York: Manchester University Press.

Chapkis, W. and C. Enloe (1983) *Of Common Cloth: Women in the Global Textile Industry,* Amsterdam and Washington D.C: Transnational Institute.

Charmes, J. (2000) 'Size, Trends and Productivity of Women's Work in the Informal Sector and in Old and New Forms of Informal Employment. An Outlook of Recent Empirical Evidence', Paper for IAFFE Conference, İstanbul.

Cheru, F. 1989. *The Silent Revolution in Africa. Debt, Development and Democracy,* London and New Jersey: Zed Books.

Cinar, E.M. (1994) 'Unskilled Urban Migrant Women and Disguised Employment: Homeworking Women in Istanbul, Turkey', *World Development,* 22(3) pp. 369–380.

Clean Cloths Campaign (2005) *Workers' Voices: The Situation of Women in the Eastern European and Turkish Garment Industries,* Report.

Cook, I. and P. Crang (1996) 'The World on a Plate: Culinary Culture, Displacement and Geographical Knowledges' *Journal of Material Culture* 1(1) pp. 131–154.

Czaban, L. and J. Henderson (1998) 'Globalization, Institutional Legacies and Industrial Transformation in Eastern Europe' *Economy and Society,* 27(4) pp. 585–613

Delehanty, J. (1999) *A Common Thread: Issues for Women Workers in the Garment Industry,* Women in Informal Employment: Globalizing or Organizing (WIEGO).

Delaney, C. (1991) *The Seed and the Soil: Gender and Cosmology in Turkish Village Society,* Oxford: University of California Press.

Delaney, C (1987) 'Seeds of Honor, Fields of Shame', in D.D. Gilmore (ed), *Honor and Shame and the Unity of the Mediterranean,* Special Publication No:22, Washington: American Anthropology Association.

Denizli Textile and Clothing Exporters' Union (DETKIB), (2001) *Textile and Clothing industry in EU–Turkey Relations,* Report No. 3, Denizli.

De Soto, H. (1989) *The Other Path: The Invisible Revolution in the Third World,* New York: Harper Collins Press Inc.

Dicken, P. (1998) *Global Shift,* 2nd Edition, London: Guilford Press.

Dikmen, A. A. (2000) 'Küresel Üretim Moda Ekonomileri ve Yeni Dünya Hiyerarşisi'(Fashion Industries in Global Production and New World Hierarchies) *Toplum ve Bilim,* No:86 pp. 281–302.

Dolan, C., J. Humphrey. and C. Harris-Pascal (1999) 'Value Chains and Upgrading: The Impact of UK Retailers on the Fresh Fruit and Vegetables Industry in Africa', *IDS Working Paper 96*, Brighton: University of Sussex.

Duben, A. (1982) 'The Significance of Family and Kinship in Urban Turkey' in Ç. Kağıtçıbaşı (ed), *Sex Roles, Family and Community in Turkey*, , Bloomington, Indiana: Indiana University Press.

Duncan, S. (1994) 'Theorising Difference in Patriarchy' *Environment and Planning A*, 26, pp. 1177–94.

Duruiz, L and n. Yentürk (1992) *Facing the Challenge: Turkish Automobile, Steel and Clothing Industries to the Post-fordist Restructuring*, İstanbul: İletişim Yayınları.

Ecevit, Y. (2000) Çalışma Yaşamında Kadın Emeği Kullanımı ve Kadın-Erkek Eşitliği' (Gender Equality and Women's Work) in TÜSAİD, *Kadın-Erkek Eşitliğine Doğru Yürüyüş: Eğitim, Çalışma Yaşamı ve Siyaset*, (A March Towards Gender Equality: Women in Education, Work and Politics) Lebib Yalkin Yayınları, İstanbul.

Ecevit, Y (1991) 'Shop Floor Control: The Ideological Construction of Turkish Women Factory Workers', in N. Redclift and E. Mignione (eds) *Beyond Employment: Household, Gender and Subsistence*, Oxford: Blacwell.

El-Kholy, H. A. (1998) *Defiance and Compliance: Negotiating Gender in Low-Income Cairo*, PhD Thesis, School of Oriental and African Studies, London, UK. (Published in 2002 by Berghahn Books, New York & London)

Elson, D. (1999) 'Labour Markets as Gendered Institutions: Equality, Efficiency and Empowerment Issues', *World Development* 27(3) pp. 611–627.

Elson, D. (1996) 'Appraising Recent Developments in the World Market for Nimble Fingers: Accumulation, Regulation, Organization' in A. Chhachhi and R.Pittin (eds), *Confronting State, Capital and Patriarchy*, New York: St. Martin's Press

Elson, D. and R. Pearson (1981) 'Nimble Fingers Make Cheap Workers' *Feminist Review*, No: 7 (Spring) pp. 87–107.

Epstein, T.S. (1993) 'Female Petty Entrepreneurs and their Multiple Roles' in S. Allen and C.Truman (eds), *Women in Business: Perspectives on Women Entrepreneurs* London & New York: Routledge, London and New York.

Eraydın, A. (1993) 'The New International Relations, Restructuring in the Economy and the Emerging Changes in the Business Behaviour', in C. Rogerson, E. Schamp, and G. Linge (eds), *Business Behaviour, Markets, Finance and Industrial Change*, Berlin: Gruyter.

Eraydın, A and Erendil, A (1998) *Yeni Üretim Süreçleri ve Kadın Emeği: Dış Pazarlara Açılan Konfeksiyon Sanayiinde Yeni Üretim Süreçleri ve Kadın İşgücünün bu Süreçlere Katılım Biçimleri* (New Production Processes in Export-Oriented Garment Industry and Different Ways of Participation of Female Labour to This Process), Ankara: T.C. Başbakanlık Kadının Statüsü ve Sorunları Genel Müdürlüğü.

Eraydın, A. and A. Eredil (1999) 'The Role of Female Labour in Industrial Restructuring: New Production Processes and Labour Market Relations in the Istanbul Clothing Industry', *Gender, Place and Culture*, 6(3) pp. 259–272

Erder, S. (2001) 'Where Do You Hail From? Localism and Networks in Istanbul', in C. Keyder (ed),*Istanbul: Between the Global and the Local*, New York & Oxford Rowman&Littlefield Publishing,.

Erder, S. (1997) *Kentsel Gerilim: Enformel İlişki Ağları Alan Araştırması*, (Urban Antagonism: A Research on Informal Networks) Um:Ag Vakfı Yayınları, Ankara.

Erder, S. (1996) *İstanbul'a Bir Kent Kondu: Ümraniye*, (Ümraniye: A Town in Istanbul), İstanbul: İletişim Yayınları.

Erendil-Türkün, A. (2000) 'Mit ve Gerçeklik olarak Denizli- Üretim ve İşgücünün Değişen Yapısı: Eleştirel Kuram Açısından bir Değerlendirme' (Denizli as a Myth and Reality- Changing Structure of Production and Labor: An Analysis from Critical Theory Perspective) *Toplum ve Bilim*, No:86 pp. 91–117.

Erman, T. (2001) 'The Politics of Squatter (Gecekondu) Studies in Turkey: The Changing Representations of Rural Migrants in the Academic Discourse', *Urban Studies*, 38(7) pp. 983–1002.

Erman, T. (1998) 'The Impact of Migration on Turkish Rural Women: Four Emergent Patterns, *Gender and Society*, 12(2) pp. 146–167.

Erman, T. (1998a) 'Kadınların Bakış Açısından Köyden Kente Göç ve Kentteki Yaşam' (Rural to Urban Migration and Urban Life from Women's Perspectives) in A. B. Hacımirzaoğlu (ed), *75 Yılda Kadınlar ve Erkekler*, (Women and Men in the 75th Year), İstanbul: Tarih Vakfı Yayınları.

Esim, S., E. Ergun, and D. Hattatoglu (2000) *Home-based Work in Turkey: An Overview*, Report.

Eyüboğlu, A., Özar, Ş. ve H. Tufan-Tanrıöver, (1998) 'Kentli Kadınların Çalışma Koşulları ve Çalışma Yaşamını Terk Nedenleri' (Urban Women's Work Conditions and Their Reasons of Leaving Labour Force), *İktisat*, 377.

Fair Wear Foundation (2004) *Background Study on Turkey*, Version 2004–1.

Fantasia, R. (1988) *Cultures of Solidarity: Consciousness, Action and Contemporary American Workers*, Berkeley & London: University of California Press.

Faugier, J and M. Sargeant (1997) 'Sampling Hard to Reach Populations', *Journal of Advanced Nursing* 26, pp. 790–97.

Fernandes-Kelly, M.P. (1983) *For We are Sold, I and my People: Women and Industrialization in Mexico's Frontier*, Albany: SUNY Press.

Freeman, C. (1998) 'Femininity and Flexible Labor: Fashioning Class Through Gender on the Global Assembly Line', *Critique of Anthropology* 18(3) pp. 245–262

Folbre, N. (2001) *The Invisible Heart: Economics and Family Values*, New York: The New Press.

Fraser, N. (1997) *Justice Interruptus: Critical Reflections on the 'Postsocialist' Condition*, London and New York: Routledge.

Frobel, F., J. Heinrichs, and O. Kreye (1980) *The New International Division of Labour*, Cambridge: Cambridge University Press.

Gereffi, G. (1994) 'The Organization of Buyer-Driven Global Commodity Chains: How U.S. Retailers Shape Overseas Production Networks', in G. Gereffi and M. Korseniewicz (eds.), *Commodity Chains and Global Capitalism*, Westport: CT:Praeger.

Gereffi, G. and M. Korseniewicz (eds.) (1994) *Commodity Chains and Global Capitalism*, Westport: CT: Praeger.

Giddens, A. (1990) *The Consequences of Modernity*, Stanford, CA: Stanford University Press.

Glaser, B. G and A. Strauss (1968) *The Discovery of Grounded Theory: Strategies for Qualitative Research,* London: Weidenfeld and Nicolson.

Gluck, S.B. and D. Patai (eds) (1991) *Women's Words: The Feminist Practice of Oral History*, London: Routledge.

Granovetter, M. (1988) 'The Sociological and Economic Approaches to Labor Markets Analysis: A Social Strctural View' in G. Farkas and P. England (eds), *Industries, Firms and Jobs: Sociological and Economic Approaches*, New York & London: Plenum Press.

Granovetter, M. and C. Tilly (1988) 'Inequality and the Labour Market' in N. Smelser (ed), *Handbook of Sociology*, Beverly Hills: Sage Publication.

Grossman, R. (1979) 'Women's Place in the Integrated Circuit' *South East Asian Chronicle*, Vol:66 pp. 2–17.

Güvenen, O. (1999) *Türkiye'nin Orta ve Uzun Dönem Stratejik Hedefleri: Genel Yorumlar*, (Middle and Long-term Starategic Targets of Turkey: General Interpretations), Ankara: State Organization of Planning.

Hammersley, M. and P. Atkins (1995) *Ethnography: Principles in Practice*, 2nd Edition, London & New York: Routledge.

Hanson, S. and G. Pratt (1995) *Gender, Work and Space*, London & New York: Routledge.

Hart, G. (1995) 'Gender and Household Dynamics: Recent Theories and their Implications' in M.G. Quibria (ed) *Critical Issues in Asian Development* Hong Kong: Oxford University Press.

Harvey, D. (1989) *The Condition of Postmodernity: An Enquiry into the Origins of Cultural Change*, Oxford: Blackwell.

Hattatoğlu, D. (2001) 'Ev Eksenli Çalışma Stratejileri' (Home-Based Work Strategies) in A. İlyasoğlu and N. Akgökçe (eds.) *Yerli bir Feminizme Doğru* (Towards a Local Feminism), İstanbul: Sel Yayıncılık.

Heyzer, N. (1986) *Working Women in South-East Asia: Development, Subordination and Emancipation*, Milton Keynes: Open University Press.

Hirst, P and G. Thompson (1999) *Globalization in Question: The International Economy and the Possibilities of Governance*, 2nd Edition, Malden: Polity Press.

Hirts, P. and J. Zeitlin (1991) 'Flexible Specialization versus Post-Fordism: Theory, Evidence and Policy Implications' *Economy and Society* 20(1) pp. 1–56

Hoodfar, H. (1997) *Between Marriage and the Market: Intimate Politics and Survival in Cario,* Berkeley: University of California Press.

Hopkins, T. and I. Wallerstein (1986) 'Commodity Chains in the World economy Prior to 1800' *Review* 10(1) pp. 157–70.

Huges, A. (2000) 'Retailers, Knowledges and Changing Commodity Networks: The Case of the Cut Flower Trade' *Geoforum* Vol.31 pp. 90–115

Humphery, J. (1985) 'Gender, Pay and Skill: Manual Workers Brazilian Industry' in H. Afshar (ed), *Women, Work and Ideology in the Third World*, London: Tavistock.

Humphery, J and H. Schmitz (2000) 'Governance and Upgrading: Linking Cluster and Value Chain Research', *IDS Working Paper*, 120, Institute of Development Studies, Brighton: University of Sussex.

ILO (2002) *Women and Men in the Informal Economy: A Statistical Picture*, Geneva: ILO.

ILO (1996) *World Employment 1996/1997: National Policies in a Global Context*, Geneva: ILO.

Işık, O. and M. M. Pınarcıoğlu (2001) *Nöbetleşe Yoksulluk: Sultanbeyli Örneği*, (Rotating Poverty: The Case of Sultanbeyli) İstanbul: İletişim Yayınları.

Jenkins, R. (1992) 'Industrialization and the Global Economy, in T. Hewitt, H. Johnson and D. Wield (eds) *Industrialization and Development*, Oxford & New York: Oxford University Press.

İlkkaracan, İ. (2000) '*Why are There so few Women in the Urban Labor Markets in Turkey? Findings from an Action-Research Study*" paper presented at the IAFFE Conference, Istanbul, 15–17 August 2000

İlkkaracan, İ. (1998) 'Kentli Kadınlar ve Çalışma Yaşamı' (Urban Women and Work Life) in A. B. Hacımirzaoğlu (Ed), *75 Yılda Kadınlar ve Erkekler*, (Women and Men in the 75th Year), İstanbul: Tarih Vakfı Yayınları.

Iktisat Dergisi (2002) *Ev Eksenli Çalışan Kadınlar Yuvarlak Masa Toplantısı* (Round Table Discussion of Home-Based Women Workers), No: 430 pp. 3–17.

Jelin, E. (1988) 'Women and the Urban Labour Market', in R. Anker, M. Buvinic and N.H. Youssef (eds), *Women's Roles and Populations Trends in the Third World*, London: Routledge.

Joekes, Susan (1995) *Trade-Related Employment for Women in Industry and Services in Developing Countries*, Geneva: UNRISD.

Joekes, S. (1987) *Women in the World Economy*, Oxford: Oxford University Press.

Joekes, S. (1985) 'Working for a Lipstick? Male and Female Labour in the Clothing in Morroco,' in H. Afshar (ed) *Women, Work and Ideology in the Third World*, London: Tavistok.

Lazreg, M. (1999) 'Rural to Urban Migrant Women's Participation in the Labour Force in Turkey: A Qualitative Analysis', *Poverty Reduction Economic Management*, Washington D.C: World Bank.

Lordoğlu, K. (1990) *Eve İş Verme Sistemi İçinde Kadın İşgücü Üzerine Bir Alan Araştırması*, (A Fieldwork on Women's Labour in the Home-Based Subcontracting System), İstanbul: Friedrich Ebert Vakfı.

Kabeer, N. (2000) *The Power to Choose: Bangladeshi Women and Labour Market Decisions in London and Dhaka*, London & New York: Verso.

Kabeer, N. (1994) *Reversed Realities*. London: Verso

Kalaycioglu, S. and H. Rittersberger (1998) 'İş İlişkilerine Kadınca Bir Bakış: Ev Hizmetinde Çalışan Kadınlar' (Workplace Relations from Women's Perspective: Women in Domestic Services) in A.B. Hacımirzaoğlu (ed), *75 Yılda Kadınlar ve Erkekler* (Women and Men in the 75th Year), İstanbul: Türkiye Tarih Vakfı.

Kalleberg, A.L. and I. Berg (1988) 'Work Structures and Markets: An Analytic Framework' in G. Farkas and P. England (eds), *Industries, Firms and Jobs: Sociological and Economic Approaches*, New York & London: Plenum Press.

Kandiyoti, D. (1998) 'Gender, Power and Contestation: Rethinking Bargaining with Patriarch' in C. Jacson and R. Pearson (eds), *Feminist Visions of Development: Gender Analysis and Policy*. London and New York: Routledge

Kandiyoti, D. (1997) 'Gendering the Modern: On Missing Dimensions in the Study of Turkish Modernity', in S. Bozdoğan and R. Kasaba (eds), *Rethinking Modernity and National Identity in Turkey*, Seattle: University of Washington Press.

Kandiyoti, D. (1996) (ed) *Gendering the Middle East: Emerging Perspective*, London & New York: I.B. Tauris.

Kandiyoti, D. (1989) 'Women and Turkish State: Political Actors or Symbolic Pawns?' in N. Yuval-Davis and F. Anthias (eds) *Women-Nation State*. New York: St.Martin's, Press.

Kandiyoti, D. (1988) 'Bargaining with Patriarchy' *Gender and Society*, 2(3) pp. 274–290.

Kandiyoti, D. (1985) "Continuity and Change in the Family: A Comparative Approach" in *Family in Turkish Society*, T. Erder (ed), Turkish Social Science Association, Ankara.

Kaytaz, M. (1994) 'Subcontracting Practice in the Turkish Textile and Metal Working Industries', in F. Şenses (ed), *Recent Industrialization Experience of Turkey in a Global Context*, Westport, Greenwood Press.

Keleş, R. and M.N. Danielson (1985) *The Politics of Rapid Urbanization: Government and Growth in Modern Turkey*, New York: Holmes and Meier.

Kessler, J. (1999) 'The North America Free Trade Agreement, Emerging Apparel Production Network and Industrial Upgrading: The Southern California/Mexico Connection', *Review of International Political Economy*, 64(4) pp. 565–608.

Keyder, C. (2001) 'The Setting' in C. Keyder (ed), *Istanbul: Between the Global and the Local*, New York & London: Rowman & Littlefield Publishers.

Kirişçi, Kemal (1998) *Turkey: Internally Displaced People: A Global Survey*. London: Earthscan Publications..

Kıray, M. (1999) *Toplumsal Yapı: Toplumsal Değişim*, (Social Structure and Social Change), İstanbul: Bağlam Yayınları.

Kıray, M. (1985) 'Metropolitan City and the Changing Family' in T. Erder (ed), *Family in Turkish Society*, Ankara: Turkish Social Science Association.

Lash, S. and J. Urry (eds) (1987) *End of Organized Capitalism*, Cambridge: Polity Press in association with Basil Blackwell.

Lazreg, M. (1999) *Making the Transition Work for Women in Europe and Central Asia*. Washington: World Bank

Lee, R.M. (1993) *Doing Research on Sensitive Topic*, London: Sage Publications.

Lerner, G. (1986) *The Creation of Patriarchy*, New York: Oxford University Press.

Lim, L. (1990) 'Women's Work in Export Factories: The Politics of a Cause' in I. Tinker (ed.), *Persistent Inequalities* Oxford: Oxford University Press.

Lim, L. (1983) 'Capitalism, Imperialism and Patriarchy: The Dilemma of Third World Women Workers in Multinational Factories' in J. Nash and M.P. Fernandez-Kelly (eds), *Women, Men and the International Division of Labour*, Albany: SUNY Press.

Lummis, T. (1987) *Listening to History: The Authenticity of Oral Evidence*, London: Hutchinson Education.

MacGaffey, J. 1991. *The Real Economy of Zaire. The Contribution of Smuggling and Other Unofficial Activities to National Wealth*, Philadelphia: University of Pennsylvania Press.

Marchand, H.M. and A.S. Runyan (2000) 'Introduction: Feminist Sightings of Global Restructuring: Conceptualisation and Reconceptualisations in H.M. Marchand and A.S. Runyan (eds) *Gender and Global Restructuring: Sightings, Sites and Resistances*, London & New York: Routledge.

Marchand, H.M. and J. Parpart (eds) (1994) *Feminism/Postmodernism/Development*, London and New York: Routledge.

Massey, D. (1984) *Spatial Division of Labour: Social Structures and the Geography of Production*, New York: Methuen.

Meyer, D. R. (1986) 'System of Cities Dynamism in Newly Industrializing Nations', *Studies in Comparative International Development*, No:21 pp. 3–22.

Mies, M. (1982) *The Lace Makers of Nasapur: Indian Housewives Produce for the World Market*, London: Zed Publication.

Mingione, E. (1981) *Social Conflict and the City*, New York: St. Martin's Press.

Mitter, S. (1994) 'On Organising Women in Casualised Work: A Global View', in S. Rowbotham and S. Mitter (eds.), *Dignity and Daily Bread: New Forms of Economic Organising Among Poor Women in the Third World and the First*, London & New York: Routledge.

Mitter, S. (1986) 'Industrial Restructuring and Manufacturing Homework: Immigrant Women in the UK Clothing Industry', *Capital and Class*, vol:27 (Winter Issues), pp. 37–80.

Monghadam, V.M. (1996) 'Development Strategies, State Policies and the Status of Women: A Comparative Assessment of Iran, Turkey and Tunisia' in V.M. Monghadam (ed) *Patriarchy and Development*, Oxford: Clarendon.

Mohanty, C. T. (1997) 'Women Workers and Capitalist Scripts: Ideologies of Domination, Common Interests, and the Politics of Solidarity' in A. J. Alexander and C. T. Mohanty (eds) *Feminist Genealogies, Colonial Legacies, Democratic Futures*, London: Routledge.

Mohanty, C. T. (1988) 'Under Western Eyes: Feminist Scholarship and Colonial Discourse' *Feminist Review*, No:30 p.65–88.

Moore, H. (1994) *A Passion for Difference*, Cambridge: Polity Pres.

Moore, H. (1988) *Feminism and Anthropology*, Cambridge: Polity Press.

Moser, C. (1993) *Gender Planning in Development Theory: Practice and Training*, London & New York: Routledge.

Moser, C. and P. Sollis (1991) 'A Methodological Framework for Analysing the Social Costs of Adjustment at the Micro-Level: The Case of Guayaquil, Ecuador', *IDS Bulletin* 22(1) pp. 23–30.

Mukohya, V. (1991) 'Import and Export in the Second Economy in North Kivu' in J. MacGaffey (ed) *The Real Economy of Zaire. The Contribution of Smuggling and Other Unofficial Activities to National Wealth* Philadelphia: University of Pennsylvania Press.

Müftüoğlu, B. G. (2000) 'İstanbul Gedikpaşa'da Ayakkabı Üretiminin Değişen Yapısı ve Farklılaşan İşgücü' (Changing Structure of Shoe Production and Labour in Istanbul, Gedikpasa), *Toplum ve Bilim*, No:86 pp. 118–138.

Nash, J. and M.P. Fernandez-Kelly (eds) (1983) *Women, Men and the International Division of Labour*, Albany: SUNY Press.

Nelson, N. (1988) 'How Women and Men Get By: The Sexual Division of Labour in the Informal Sector of a Nairobi Squatter Settlement' in J. Gogler (ed), *The Urbanization of the Third World*. Oxford: Oxford University Press.

Nicholson, L. (1994) 'Interpreting Gender' *Signs*, 20(1) pp. 79–105.

Nugent, P. (1996) 'Arbitrary Lines and the People's Minds: A Dissenting View on Colonial Boundaries in West Africa' in P. Nugent and A.I. Asiwaju (eds) *African Boundaries Barriers, Conduits, Opportunities* London: Pinter.

Oldersma, J. and K. Davis (1991) 'Introduction' in K. Davis, M. Leijenaar and J. Oldersma (eds), *The Gender of Power*, London: Sage Publications.

Olson, E.A. (1982) 'Duofocal Family Structure and an Alternative Model of Husband–Wife Relationship' in Ç. Kağıtçıbaşı (ed), *Sex Roles, Family and Community in Turkey*, Bloomington, Indiana: Indiana University Press.

Ong, A. (1991) 'The Gender and Labour Politics of Postmodernity' *Annual Review of Anthropology* Vol: 20 pp. 279–30

Ong, A. (1988) 'Colonialism and Modernity: Feminist Re-presentation of Women in Non-Western Societies' *Inscriptions*, 3 (4) pp. 79–93.

Ong, A. (1987) *Spirits of Resistance and Capitalist Discipline: Factory Women in Malaysia*, Albany: SUNY Press.

Ortaylı, I. (1984) 'Osmanlı Toplumunda Aile' (Family in Ottoman Society) in L. Erder (ed), *Türkiye'de Ailenin Değişimi: Toplumbilimsel İncelemeler* (Research on Changing Family Structure), Ankara: Sosyal Bilimler Derneği Yayını.

Ozyegin, G. (2001) *Untidy Gender: Domestic Services in Turkey*, Philadelphia: Temple University Press.

Özar, S. (2000) *Kadın İstihdamı için Yeni Perspektifler ve Kadın İşgücüne Muhtelif Talep*, (New Perspectives for Female Employment and Demand) Ankara: T.C. Basbakanlik, Kadın Statüsü ve Sorunlarını Genel Müdürlüğü.

Özar, S. (1996) 'Kentsel Kayıtdışı Kesimde İstihdam Sorununa Yaklaşımlar ve Bir Ön Saha Çalışması' (A Pilot Study of Urban Informal Sector and Perspectives for Employment), *METU Studies in Development*, 23(4) pp. 509–534.

Özbay, F. (1998) 'Türkiye'de Aile ve Hane Yapısı: Dün, Bugün, Yarın' (Family Structure in Turkey: Past, Today and Future) in A. B. Hacımirzaoğlu (ed), *75 Yılda Kadınlar ve Erkekler*, Istanbul: Tarih Vakfı Yayınları..

Özbay, F. (1990) 'Kadınların Eviçi Uğraşlarındaki Değişme' (Changes in Women's Domestic Activities), in Ş. Tekeli (ed), *Kadın Bakış Açısından 1980'ler Türkiye'sinde Kadın,* (From Women's Perspective: Women in the 1980s Turkey) İstanbul: İletişim Yayınları.

Pahl, J. (1989) Money and Marriage, London: Macmillan.

Pahl, R. E. (1984) *Divisions of Labor*, Oxford: Blackwell Publishers.

Palpacuer F. (2002) 'Subcontracting Networks in the New York Garment Industry: Changing Characteristics in a Global Era', in G. Gereffi, D. Spener and J. Bair (eds.) *Free Trade and Uneven Development: The North American Apparel Industry after NAFTA*, Philadelphia: Temple University Press.

Palpacuer F. and A. Parisotto (1998), 'Global production and local jobs: issues for discussion', *Global Production and Local Jobs: New Perspectives on Enterprise networks, employment and local development policy*, Institut International d'Etudes Sociales, Geneva: BIT.

Pearson, R. (1998) "Nimble Fingers' Revisited: Reflection on Women and Third World Industrialisation in the Late Century' in R. Pearson and C. Jackson (eds), *Feminist Visions of Development: Gender Analysis and Policy*, New York: Routledge,

Pearson, R. (1992) 'Gender Issues in Industrialization' in T. Hewitt et.al. (eds), *Industrialization and Development*, Oxford: Oxford University Press.

Piore, M.J. (1990) 'Work, Labour and Action: Work Experience in a System of Flexible Production' in F. Pyke, G. Becattini, W. Sengenberger (eds), *Industrial Districts and Inter-firm Co-operation in Italy*, Geneva: International Institute for Labour Studies.

Piore, M. and C. Sabel (1984) *The Second Industrial Divide*, New York: Basic Books.

Portes, A. and R. Schauffler (1993) 'Competing Perspectives on the Latin American Informal Sector', *Population and Development Review* 19(1) pp. 33–60.

Portes, A. and M. Castells (eds) (1989) *The Informal Economy: Studies in Advanced and Less Developed Countries*, Baltimore: The Johns Hopkins University Press

Portes, A. and S. Sassen-Koob (1987) 'Making it Underground: Comparative Material on the Informal Sector in Western Market Economies' *American Journal of Sociology* 93(1) pp. 30–61

Radikal (Daily News Paper) *Gelir Kadindan* (Women are the Main Provider), 17 March 2004

Radikal (Daily News Paper) *Kriz Haneleri Vurdu* (The Crisis Hits Households) Special Report, 16/21 February2003.

Rakowski, C. A. (1994) 'Convergence and Divergence in the Informal Sector Debate: A Focus on Latin America, 1984–92' *World Development* 22(4) pp. 501–516

Rasuly-Paleczek, G. (1996) 'Some Remarks on the Study of Household Composition and Intra-Family Relations in Rural and Urban Turkey' in G. Rasuly-Paleczek (ed), *Turkish Family in Transition*, Frankfurt am Main: Peter Lang.

Redclift, N. and E. Mingione (eds) (1985) *Beyond Employment: Household, Gender and Subsistence*, Oxford: Blackwell.

Rex, J. (1973) *Race, Colonialism and the City*, London: Routledge & Kegan Paul.

Rodgers, G. (ed) (1989) *Urban Poverty and the Labour Market: Access to Jobs and Incomes in Asian and Latin American Cities*, Geneva: ILO.

Safa, H. (1995) *The Myth of Male Breadwinner: Women and Industrialization in the Caribbean*, Boulder: Westview Press.

Safa, H. (1981) 'Runaway Shops ad Female Employment: The Search for Cheap Labour' *Signs: Journal of Women in Culture and Society*, Vol:7 pp. 418–433

Salaff, J. W. (1981) *Working Daughters of Hong Kong: Filial Piety and Intrafamilial Power*, Cambridge and New York: Cambridge University Pres.

Sassen, S. (1997) "Informalization in Advanced Market Economies', *Issues in Development Discussion Paper: 20*, Geneva: ILO.

Sassen, S. (2001) *The Global City: New York, London, Tokyo*. 2nd Edition, Princeton: Princeton University Press.

Sayer, A. and R. Walker (1992) *The New Social Economy: Reworking the Division of Labour*, Cambridge MA: Blackwell.

Schmitz, H. and P. Knorringa (1999) 'Learning From Global Buyers', *IDS Working Paper 100*, Institute of Development Studies, Brighton: University of Sussex

Scott, A.M. (1995) 'Informal Sector or Female Sector? Gender Bias in Urban Labour Market Models' in D. Elson (ed), *Male Bias in the Development Process*, 2nd Edition. Manchester: Manchester University Press.

Scott, A.M. (1990) 'Patterns of Patriarchy in the Peruvian Working Class', in S. Stichter and J. Parpart (eds), *Women, Employment and the Family in the International Division of Labour*, London: Macmillan..

Scott, A.M. (1986) 'Women and Industrialization: Examining the 'Female Marginalization' Thesis', *Journal of Development Studies*, 22(4) pp. 649–680.

Sharma, U. (1986) *Women's Work, Class, and the Urban Household: A Study of Shimla, North India*. London: Tavistock.

Sen, A. K. (1990) 'Gender and Cooperative Conflict', in I. Tinker (ed), *Persistent Inequalities,* Oxford: Oxford University Press.

Sik, E. and Wallace, C. (1999) 'The Development of Open-air Markets in East-Central Europe', *International Journal of Urban and Regional Research*, 23(4) pp. 697–713.

Singerman, D. (1995) *Avenues of Participation: Family, Politics, and Networks in Urban Quarters of Cairo*. Princeton: Princeton University Press.

Sönmez, M. (1996) *İstanbul'un İki Yüzü: 1980'den 2000'e Değişim*, (Two Faces of Istanbul: Transformations from 1980s to 2000) Anklara: Arkadaş Yayınları.

Standing, G. (1999) 'Global Feminization Through Flexible Labor: A Theme Revisited', *World Development* 27(3), pp. 583–602

Standing, G. (1999a) *Global Labour Flexibility: Seeking Distributive Justice*, London: Macmillan Press.

Standing, G. (1989) 'Global Feminization Through Flexible Labour', *World Development* 17(7) pp. 1077–1095.

State Planning Organisation (SPO) (2001) *The Report on Income Distribution and Poverty*, (DPT. 2599 - ÖİK. 610) ISBN 975-19-2803-6.

Stichter, S. (1990) 'Women, Employment and the Family: Current Debates' in S. Sticher and J. Papart (eds), *Women, Employment and the Family in the International Division of Labour*, Basingstoke: Macmillan.

Stichter, S. and J.L. Parpart (eds) (1990) *Women, Employment and the Family in the International Division of Labour*, Basingstoke: Macmillan.

Storper, M. and R. Walker (1983) 'The Theory of Labour and the Theory of Location', *International Journal of Urban and Regional Research*, Vol:15, pp. 142–68.

Şenyapılı, T. (1981) *Gecekondu: Çevre İşçilerinin Mekanı*, (The Gecekondu: The Place of Periphery Workers) Ankara: METU Yayınları.

Taylor, M. and N. Thrift (eds) (1982) The Geography of Multinationals: Studies in the Spatial Development and Economic Consequences of Multinational Corporations, London: Croom Helm.

Taymaz, E. (1997) *Small and Medium Sized Industry in Turkey*, Ankara: State Institute of Statistics.

Tekeli, Ş. (1990) 'The Meaning and Limits of Feminist Ideology in Turkey' in F. Özbay (ed), *Women, Family and Social Change in Turkey*, Bangkok: UNESCO.

Tienta, M. and K. Booth (1991) 'Gender, Migration, and Social Change', *International Sociology*, Vol: 6 pp. 51–72.

Timur, S. (1972) *Türkiye'de Aile Yapısı*. (Family Structure in Turkey), Ankara: Hacettepe Üniversitesi.

Tunalı, I. (1997) 'Education and Work: Experiences of 6–14 Year Old Children in Turkey' in T. Bulutay (ed), *Education and Labour Market in Turkey*, Ankara, State Institute of Statistics.

TURKSTAT (2005) *Turkey's Statistical Yearbook*, Ankara: Turkish Statistical Institute.

TÜSİAD (2000) *Kadın-Erkek Eşitliğine Doğru Yürüyüş: Eğitim, Çalışma Yaşamı ve Siyaset*, (A March toward Gender Equality: Women in Education, Work and Politics) İstanbul: Lebib Yalkin Yayınları.

TÜSIAD (1999) *Türkiye'nin Fırsat Penceresi: Demografik Dönüşüm ve İzdüşümleri*, (Turkey's Opportunity Window: Demographic Transformations and Influence) İstanbul: Lebib Yalkın Yayınları.

Walby, S. (1997) *Gender Transformations*, London and New York: Routledge.

Walby, S. (1990) *Theorizing Patriarchy*, Oxford and Cambridge: Basil Blackwell.

Walby, S. (1989) 'Theorizing Patriarchy' *Sociology*, 23(2) pp. 213–234.

Waters, M. (1989) 'Patriarchy and Viriarchy: An Exploration and Reconstruction of Concepts of Masculine Domination' *Sociology*, 23(2) pp. 193–211.

White, J.B. (1994) *Money Makes us Relatives: Women's Labor in Urban Turkey*, Austin: University of Texas Press.

Wolf, D. (1997) 'Daughters, Decisions and Dominations: An Empirical and Conceptual Critique of Household Strategies' in N. Visvanathan et.al.(ed), *The Women, Gender and Development: Reader*, London & New Jersey: Zed Books.

Wolf, D. (ed) (1996) *Feminist Dilemmas in Fieldwork*, Boulder: Westview Press.

Wolf, D. (1992) *Factory Daughters: Gender, Household Dynamics, and Rural Industrialization in Java*, Berkeley: University of California Press.

World Bank (2006) *Turkey: Labour Market Study, Summary*, Document of World Bank, Ankara.

World Bank (2000) *Turkey: Economic Reforms, Living Standards and Social Welfare Study*, Country Report: 20029-TU, Washington.

World Bank (1993) *Turkey: Women in Development*, A World Bank Country Study, Washington D.C.

Yeldan, E. (2001) *Küreselleşme Sürecinde Türkiye Ekonomisi: Bölüşüm, Birikim ve Büyüme*, (Turkish Economy in the Era of Globalization: Distribution, Accumulation and Growth), İstanbul: İletişim Yayınları.

Yeldan, E. (1995) 'Surplus Creation and Extraction under Structural Adjustment: Turkey 1980–1992', *Review of Radical Political Economics*, 27(2) pp. 38–72.

Yentürk, N. (1997) *Türk İmalat Sanayiinde Ücretler, İsthidam ve Birikim* (Wages, Employment and Accumulation in Turkish Manufacturing Sector), İstanbul: Friederich Ebert Vakfı.

Yuval-Davis, N. (1997) *Gender and Nation*, London: Sage.

Yükseker, D. (2003) *Laleli-Moskova Mekiği: Kayitdışı Ticaret ve Cinsiyet İlişkileri* (Laleli and Moscow: Unrecorded Trade and Gender Relations) İstanbul: İletişim Yayınları.

GLOSSARY OF TERMS

Abi: Older brother
Abla: Elder sister
Aile Resisi: Head of household
Atölye: Atelier
Bacı: Sister
Başlık: Bride price
Çeyiz: Trousseau
Doğu: East
Doğulu: People from east (Kurdish)
Dükkan: Shop
Dünya evi: the house of the world- marriage
Ekmek Parası: Bread money
Elalem: Starngers
Elişi: Handicraft
Ev Kadını: Housewife
Ev Kızı: House-girl
Evinin Kadını: Women of their home
Fabrika: Factory
Fakir Kadın: Poor women
Gecekondu: Squatter Settlement
Gelin almak: a girl taken as bride
Gelin: Bride
Gurbet: A foreign place far from one's homeland
Hafif kadın: "easy" woman
Haylaz: Lazy/idle person

Hemşehri: People from the same place of origin
Hemşehrilik: State of being *hemşehri*
İlçe: Constituency
İmam Hatipler: Religious schools
İş: Work, engagement, employment
İşçi Servisi: Special bus for workers
Istanbullu: Istanbulites
İzin: Permission
Kadın günleri: Women's afternoon tea meetings
Kapalıçarşı: Big Bazaar in Istanbul
Kardeş: Younger sister or brother
Kilim: Lightly waved rug
Konfeksiyon: Ready-to-wear
Köşe Dönme: Turning a corner
Küçük İşletme: Small-scale firm
Kuma: Second wife (usually without official marriage certificate)
Mahalle: Neighbourhood
Mahalleli: Neighbourhood resident
Makinacı: Sewing machine operator
Memleket: Country
Memur: Civil servant
Müdür: Manager
Muhtar: Elected head of neighbourhood
Namuslu: Honour
Ortacı: All purpose helper, unskilled garment worker
Pazar Parası: Weekly allowance
Piyasa: Market/ Business
Saçaklanma: Spread towards outskirts
Sigortalı: Worker with social security
Tanıdık: Acquaintance
Tanıdıklık: being acquainted
Ustabaşı: Foreman
Usta-Çırak: master and apprentice
Vakıf: Religious charitable endowment
Varoş: Pre-urban settlements
Varoşlu: People living in pre-urban settlements
Yabancı: Stranger
Yazık: Pitied
Yumak: Yarn
Yumuşak başlı: Obedient

INDEX

www.ingramcontent.com/pod-product-compliance
Lightning Source LLC
Chambersburg PA
CBHW050432280326
41932CB00013BA/2080